Wrestling with God and Men

Wrestling with God and Men

Homosexuality in the Jewish Tradition

Steven Greenberg

THE UNIVERSITY OF WISCONSIN PRESS

The University of Wisconsin Press
1930 Monroe Street
Madison, Wisconsin 53711

www.wisc.edu/wisconsinpress/

3 Henrietta Street
London WC2E 8LU, England

5   7   6   4

Printed in the United States of America

Library of Congress Cataloging-in-Publication Data
Greenberg, Steven.
Wrestling with God and men: homosexuality in the Jewish tradition /
Steven Greenberg.
p.   cm.
Includes bibliographical references and index.
ISBN 0-299-19090-0 (cloth: alk. paper)
1. Homosexuality, Male—Religious aspects—Judaism.
2. Orthodox Judaism.   3. Homosexuality in the Bible.
I. Title.
BM729.H65G74   2004
296.3′66—dc22   2003020568

ISBN 0-299-19094-3 (pbk.: alk. paper)

Contents

Acknowledgments

This book is the product of eight years of work during which I traveled quite a distance. I am indebted to many people who prepared me for this journey, to others who encouraged and supported me on the way, and most importantly to the friends and colleagues who contributed directly to the words on the page.

Many teachers have set me on my path. Sara Pfaff taught me to love the written word. Rabbi Joseph Vilensky, of blessed memory, introduced me to a spiritual world that would have otherwise remained sealed, and Rabbi Moshe Besdin, of blessed memory, a master educator, taught me how to teach.

Rabbi Dr. Aharon Lichtenstein of Yeshivat Har Etzion taught me to read human experience with a religious eye and conversely to read religious texts with a human eye. His moral and intellectual rigor and his passionate faith inspired me as a young man and still nourish me today. I also thank my teacher and friend, Rabbi Yitz Greenberg, whose vision of a God made vulnerable by covenantal love and of a human being dignified by that very love has become my own.

I might never have trusted my own words had I not been given the opportunity to write a "coming out" piece, as it were, while still in the closet. I owe special thanks to Michael Lerner and *Tikkun* magazine, who agreed to publish "Gayness and God" under the cover of a pseudonym. Following the publication of the article I began a learning diary, but I was much too busy to plumb deeply into the questions that were brewing in my head. Here my thanks must go to the Mandel Institute's Jerusalem Fellows Program for providing me with two years of freedom to begin to think my way through the issues and the texts. Their commitment to educational leadership demanded that each fellow be given a significant block of time to work on an individual project. Thanks to their support, I was able to study with two scholars who quickly became dear friends,

Professors Jacob Milgrom and Daniel Boyarin. My many conversations with them have deeply enriched these pages.

For nearly twenty years I have worked at the National Jewish Center for Learning and Leadership (CLAL). Few educators are blessed with a community of colleagues and friends as intellectually acute and as diverse as the CLAL faculty and staff. So, to my past and present CLAL comrades, Irwin Kula, Brad Hirshfield, Daniel Brenner, David Nelson, David Elcott, Vanessa Ochs, Bene Lappe, Rachel Sabbath, Regina Stein, Robert Rabinowitz, David Kraemer, Tzvi Blanchard, and Michael Gottsegen, thank you! Deep appreciation as well goes to Donna Rosenthal and CLAL's lay leadership, whose encouragement and support over the years I truly value. To my CLAL students—you have sharpened my thinking with your questions and enriched me with your insights.

The imprint of friends is everywhere in this book. Shai Held, Pinchas Klein, Elisha Anscelovitz, Tova Halbertal, Tanya Zion, Richard Juran, Joyce Klein, Moti Bar-Or, Fred Hyman, Bob Goldfarb, Daniel Reichwald, Simon Kaminetsky, Noam Zion, Nigel Savage, Jill Hammer, Louis Berlin, and Gary Schaer have all accompanied me on this journey and have served as trusted confidants, readers, and sounding boards. Ruth Bregman, CLAL's technical editor extraordinaire, cleaned up the manuscript so that I could deliver it to the press without embarrassment. But of everyone who has read through the manuscript and commented on the book, I owe the most profound gratitude to two friends, scholars of great erudition and humanity, Elliot Dorff and Art Green. With enormous attention to detail and concern for the path of my argument, they have, in different ways, improved the book immeasurably.

While this book was being written in Jerusalem and later in New York City, I was swept into a film project that had a profound impact not only on my writing but also on my life. Sandi Simcha DuBowski's documentary, *Trembling before G-d,* follows six people as they struggle to make sense of their passion for traditional Jewish life and their gayness. I agreed in 1999 to appear in the documentary, and in 2001 joined Sandi in an outreach project, traveling to hundreds of screenings and dialogues across the globe, from São Paulo to Seattle. The ideas in this book have been deepened by the many people we met on our journeys, souls whose healing began in a theatre. My thanks to Sandi go well beyond his indirect contributions to the book. *Trembling* breaks one's heart and evokes a great desire for the very wrestling with God and men that I have attempted to carry forward in these pages.

To Jerry Levinson and Hagai El-Ad of the Jerusalem Open House—When we met I was a closeted Orthodox rabbi studying in Jerusalem, and you were dreaming about a gay and lesbian community center. Your courage and persistence taught me that religious values live in action. You took a motley crew of volunteers and shaped a safe haven for all the gay and lesbian people of the holy city. It was you, Jerry, who challenged me to publicly come out of the closet, to put aside fear and begin the work of reconciliation. For these concrete translations of faith and conviction, I thank you.

After I returned to New York City, I was working full time at CLAL, so my writing time had to be squeezed out of weekends and evenings. Early in the project Rita and Stanley Kaplan generously provided me with the funds to dedicate a number of months to research and writing. Toward the middle of the project I was again in need of a solid block of undisturbed time. Again a friend came to my aid. Al Baum organized support for this purpose in the Bay Area. Thanks go Jay Cohen, Larry Colton, Simon Glinsky, Bob Gutterman, Arnie Jackson, Walter Leiss, Jeff Lewy, Dagny Maidman, Steve Polsky, Emily Rosenberg, and Arthur Slepian. At the very end of the project there was again a need for uninterrupted time to do the final editing and to knit the whole work together. Special thanks go to Marty Spagat, who appeared out of nowhere and generously funded this undertaking. Harold Grinspoon provided a much needed respite in the midst of this work, and lastly, Rachel Cowan and the Nathan Cummings Foundation leveraged my efforts and cared for my well being at the same time. I am immeasurably grateful to you all.

To Raphael Kadushin of the University of Wisconsin Press, who pushed for the book; to Erin Holman, who guided it through the process; and to Barbara Wojhoski for her careful copyediting, much thanks.

To Mom and Dad, my siblings, and the whole Greenberg-Toder family—while I have surely taken the road less traveled, your love

Acknowledgments

and acceptance have eased my way. Lastly, my thanks go to my partner, Steven Goldstein, who has surely suffered the most for this project. You are my *ezer k'negdo,* my helpmeet opposite me. Your plain good sense uncluttered many passages; your instinct for subtlety has added grace to the book. But above all your love has deepened my heart and calmed my spirit. I could not have done this without you. I love you.

Author's Note

In order to make the text accessible to a wide array of readers, I have departed from some of the more scholarly Hebrew transliteration forms and have mixed common usages with traditional Orthodox forms.

1. While I usually transliterate the letter *he* with an *h*, in cases where this practice conflicted with common usage, I have left it out.

2. *Het* is transliterated as *h* and *khaf* as *kh* except in cases where this practice would conflict with a more commonly used transliteration. For example, *Mordechai* is not spelled *Mordekhai,* even though it contains a *khaf.*

3. I have chosen Hebraic forms of names rather than Anglicized versions only where I surmised that Orthodox readers familiar with the authors would find the Anglicized forms highly stilted. Just as Yitzhak Rabin would not be referred to as Isaac Rabin, so too Rav Moshe Feinstein is not commonly known as Rabbi Moses Feinstein. In instances where the Anglicized name is as commonly used as the Hebraicized, I generally chose it over the Hebraicized form. In short, I attempted to chose forms that would be familiar to readers steeped in the tradition yet recognizable to those who are not. This approach has the benefit of making the book accessible to readers of different backgrounds, with, I hope, minimal inconsistency. For those who are not acquainted with either the Hebraicized or the Anglicized forms, the following list of given names that appear frequently in the book should be helpful.

HEBRAIC	ANGLICIZED
Aharon	Aaron
Avraham	Abraham
Eliyahu	Elijah
Moshe	Moses
Shmuel	Samuel
Shimon	Simeon

HEBRAIC	ANGLICIZED
Shlomo	Solomon
Yakov	Jacob
Yehiel	Jehiel
Yehoiada	Jehoiada
Yehudah	Judah
Yirmiyah	Jeremiah
Yishmael	Ishmael
Yitzhak	Isaac
Yoash	Joash
Yohanan	Johanan

Wrestling with God and Men

Introduction

Two verses in the Torah (Lev. 18:22 and 20:13) have been understood for millennia to prohibit same-sex sexual relations between men. Since Orthodox Jews believe that the Torah is the word of God, the Levitical prohibition against sex between men has the full weight of divine authority. On the basis of ancient rabbinic teaching, same-sex male relations were not only prohibited but deemed particularly abhorrent and dangerous. The security of the family, the community, and even the cosmos might be threatened if men had sex with men. Sex between women was also deemed a violation of the tradition, albeit in a much less threatening way. The absence of any specific biblical verse prohibiting lesbian sexual relations resulted in a significantly less problematic legal status. At the very least, however, sexual relations between women were deemed indecent, and under certain conditions women who had such relations were subject to public flogging. Men who engaged in sexual intercourse with each other were, if only on the books, worthy of the death penalty.

While contemporary Orthodox rabbis differ in their stridency, most have judged the recent openness toward gay and lesbian people as a sign of social decline and decadence. They insist that while the world may change, the law does not. Young gay people seeking help from rabbis have been given an array of advice and reproof. Some have been told to fast and roll in the snow (or bathe in ice if snow isn't available), to recite certain psalms, or to eat figs. Others are told to seek God's help in prayer and to fight the inclination by spending more time studying Torah. Many, until recently, were encouraged to

marry, with the promise that it would all work out. The more understanding rabbis over the past twenty years adopted a pathological
view of homosexuality and advised gay people to enter therapy
designed to change their sexual orientation. When therapy, fasts, or
figs failed, absolute celibacy was demanded. When people responded
that they were unable to totally repress their sexuality, they were
often told to "dress in black and go violate the law in another city,"
meaning "Do what you will, but dress in black as a sign of sadness
and mourning and go to a place where you are not known so that
your sinful depravity will not become a public scandal!"[1]

All this should have been irrelevant to me. I was not raised in an
Orthodox home or community and should not have cared a whit
about Orthodoxy or about its normative stance on homosexuality.
As a child I was taught that the purpose of science was to sift
through religion to clean out its primitive notions and superstitions.
First and foremost among these notions was the Orthodox claim of
divine authorship of the Torah. I was given the sense in my childhood that for all its nostalgic quaintness, Orthodoxy was a backward
form of Judaism not suited to contemporary life.

If Orthodoxy was ridiculed by the adults of my young world,
gayness was utterly nonexistent. Same-sex attraction or homosexuality as an idea, let alone as a reality, was absent from my childhood.
Never do I remember hearing the words *gay* or *homosexual* spoken
by family or friends. The very possibility of sexual desire or sexual
activity between men or between women was inconceivable. Knowing how these two words, *gay* and *Orthodox,* condensed into realities
and entered first separately and then together into my life will
perhaps help the reader place my various subjectivities. I have attempted to write this book in a fair and balanced way, although I
am not a disinterested party. I am, of course, quite implicated on
both the Jewish and the gay score. It is only fair, then, that as a
starting point I begin by sharing the experiences that have framed
my perspective. This is how I became a gay Orthodox rabbi.

Orthodox Attractions

My encounter with Orthodoxy began when a gentleman rabbi from
Manchester, England, alighted in Columbus, Ohio. Rabbi Joseph

Vilensky brought with him a proper English elegance along with a very strict Orthodox rabbinic education. The afternoon we met was totally serendipitous. I was invited to his house for lunch, and by the end of the meal I had been invited to study with him weekly, "over tea and oranges."

I thoroughly enjoyed the study each week, and eventually I brought a few of my friends into the circle. After two months we added an evening of Talmud study with the rabbi and were amazed to discover in the raucous cross-historical debates of the sages a mirror for our own search for meaning. The rabbi not only introduced us to Jewish learning; he adopted us into his community. We were invited to meals on Shabbat and holidays. We were welcomed into the synagogue with open arms and learned to share the joys and sorrows of a caring community. In a matter of a few months we had all become extended members of the rabbi's family and cherished members of his community. Rabbi Vilensky had not persuaded us to adopt traditional observance by argument or debate. He had simply welcomed us into a community of minds and a community of hearts that was too rich to ever leave.

My mother was not pleased when I announced that I had decided to keep kosher, knowing that she was powerless to resist. What Jewish mother would let her teenage son starve, the definition of starvation being his inability to eat her stuffed cabbage and chicken soup? The kitchen was made kosher within a week. My Sabbath observance restrictions annoyed the family. They wondered if I had been body-snatched by the soul of some Polish great-grandparent.

Adolescent Discovery

While the origins of my religious identity are remembered in detail, the origins of my gayness are not. By the time I was ten, I had a sense that I was different from others. At the age of eleven I had begun to feel threatened by groups of boys. When I was twelve, I remember being mesmerized by the handsome teenage son of distant cousins at family seders. I felt a secret excitement when my father would take me with him to the Jewish Center Men's Club. Young adult men walking around naked were both scary and thrilling.

Later, in my early teens, I vaguely recall my head once turning sharply in the high school locker room toward an athletic boy two grades older than I. At the time I noticed my body's involuntary movement, but I could not name it. I had no idea what it meant to be homosexual. *Faggot* and *homo* were words reserved for the boys hounded for being passive and unathletic. None of this said anything about sexual attraction. There were no categories for this experience, no way to explain the jerking around of my head, the warm sensation on my face, or the flutter in my chest.

A few years later the arrival of the hormonal hurricane left me completely dumbfounded. Just when my body should have fulfilled social expectations, it went completely mute. I still had no conscious response to boys, but despite the great expectations I also had no physical response to girls. By this time I was already religiously observant, and my saving grace was *negiah,* the religious prohibition to embrace, kiss, or even touch girls until marriage. The premarital sexual restraint of the tradition was a perfect mask, not only to the world but also to myself. While it gave me religious cover for my active self-exclusion from the world of teenage romance and sexual exploration, even more importantly it allowed me not to know what I knew.

When my buddies were running off on Friday afternoon after school to play ball, I was going for a pre-Shabbat ritual bath in the local mikvah with Rabbi Vilensky. I would attend parties on Friday night without breaking Sabbath rules, drink beer, and laugh at the sexual exploits of my peers. I did not share with my friends the mix of jealousy, fear, and moral superiority that the topic of "fooling around" with girls raised in me.

After high school I escaped Ohio and landed in New York City at Yeshiva University and later in Israel at Yeshivat Har Etzion. My years in yeshiva, in New York and then in Israel, were spectacular. I was welcomed into a monastic world of sorts, where hundreds of twenty-something men studied and debated in pairs for twelve hours a day. The emotional and intellectual intensity of these young men sequestered away from women was likely fueled by a good deal of sublimated sexual energy. For me the male camaraderie and physical affection, the spiritual passion and intellectual head butting was wonderfully nourishing for many years. But over time, as my sexual repression wore thinner every year, male closeness itself became a strange frustration, and the consciousness of desire bubbling up from inside me became undeniable.

On one desperate occasion, beset with an increased awareness of my attraction to a fellow yeshiva student, I visited a sage, Rav Yosef Shalom Eliashuv, who lives in one of the most secluded ultra-Orthodox communities in Jerusalem. He was in poor health but still taking visitors, who daily waited in an anteroom for hours for the privilege of speaking with him for a few minutes. Speaking in Hebrew, I told him what, at the time, I felt was the truth. "Master, I am attracted to both men and women. What shall I do?" He responded, "My dear one, my friend, you have twice the power of love. Use it carefully." I was stunned. I sat in silence for a moment, waiting for more. "Is that all?" I asked. He smiled and said, "That is all. There is nothing more to say."

Rav Eliashuv's words calmed me, permitted me to temporarily forget the awful tensions that would eventually overtake me. His trust and support buoyed me above my fears. Of course, I was not asking for permission to act on my feelings, nor was he offering any. I needed to understand what my sexual desire for men meant. From his words I understood that strong desire was not to be feared, that it was evidence of a great potential for loving. In an amazing turnaround I began to feel that this piece of my soul might actually make me a better rabbi. As a bisexual I could have a wider and richer emotional life—and perhaps a deeper spiritual life than is common—and still marry and have a family.

I came back to New York City in 1978 to finish college, start rabbinical school, and get married. At the age of twenty-two half of my friends were engaged or married, and I was eager to join their ranks. I dated women regularly during this period, but I had no clue what specifically I was supposed to feel. Since I was becoming an Orthodox rabbi, none of the women I dated actually expected me to engage in any sexual behavior. During this period I "fell in love" three times, each time coming to the awful conclusion that, while I loved the woman, she was not attractive enough for me. What else might explain my total absence of sexual interest?

In one of my pathetic attempts at inducing passion I brought a woman to the most romantic spot on Roosevelt Island, where in

1984 I was a congregational rabbi. The lighthouse on the northern end of the island was quiet and secluded. The sound and smell of the river's swirling at its tip was the perfect setting for what I had planned to be the violation of the tradition with a first kiss. That kiss never happened.

The next week I was a wreck. The humiliating failure to feel any desire for a woman I cared so much for left me confused and deeply depressed. A new friend invited me out to dinner and the topic of homosexuality came up. He asked me point blank if I had ever felt desire for a man. Somehow he had figured me out. I surprised myself and nodded my head. Yes, I had. The conversation swirled in my mind as I returned to Roosevelt Island on the tramway over the river. I looked up to the other side of the tramway's cabin and saw a very handsome young man looking at me. At that moment I let myself feel what I had never consciously felt before. A great weight came crashing down on me. I nearly swooned and would have fallen had I not been holding on tightly to the tramway grip above my head. I turned away from the young man to catch my breath.

Later that week I found myself in Greenwich Village, at a celebration marking the end of a project I had helped put together. When the meal ended, I found myself alone in the Village. Spurred on by the bravery of a half bottle of wine, I pulled my yarmulke off my head, bought a baseball cap to put in its place, and took my first steps toward Christopher Street. Within a month the released feelings had taken their course, and in 1985 I began my first gay relationship with the new friend who had evoked my "coming out."

But lifelong dreams are not so easily extinguished. The sexual discoveries, as amazing as they were, offered no credible life trajectory. Despite the dramatic realization I still could not give up on the hope of marriage and family. So, for the next five years, while in the thick of my first relationship with a man, I furiously dated women in a desperate attempt to marry.

At one point a lovely and very religious woman hinted to me that if I would ask, she would say yes. Overnight I decided to close my eyes and jump. I grabbed a bottle of expensive wine and in the middle of Central Park in a horse-drawn carriage, under a moonlit April sky, I proposed to a woman whom I barely knew. We excitedly called our families and friends, drank another toast to our future life together, and chastely said goodnight. The next morning I was on the plane to Los Angeles for a speaking engagement. By the time I landed, I was in utter panic to the complete confusion of my brothers, who were waiting there to celebrate with me. Within a month the whole thing crumbled under the weight of the truth that I simply did not want to marry her.

The idiocy of hope is sometimes beyond exaggeration. Even after this humiliating episode I was still determined to get married. I kept dating and found myself twice again in serious relationships, each time unable to make it stick. On the last occasion I decided to be honest with the young woman about my struggle. While the openness helped to build a much deeper trust and intimacy than I had ever before achieved, the absence of a fundamental mutual desire was too difficult for either of us to bear. Only after many years of persistent denial, knocking my shins again and again into the hard truth and then coming back for more, was I able to fully acknowledge that I am gay.

For many gay Orthodox Jews it is this realization that ends, once and for all, their identification with Orthodoxy. Being an Orthodox rabbi made such an option quite difficult for me. I was not interested in being a liberal rabbi. I had become Orthodox in my teens for reasons that, despite my particular conflict, still felt valid. I loved the life of observance that I had shaped within the community for over twenty years. I treasured my work as teacher of Torah. For whatever mix of cowardice, arrogance, stubbornness, or faith, I simply could not bear to give it up. However, if I was not going to leave the Orthodox world that I had come to love, I would need to explain the sense of my choice to be both Orthodox and gay. Was such a juxtaposition even possible?

I began to put pen to paper in the summer of 1992, with no idea where it would take me. The writing began like a confession: "I am an Orthodox rabbi, and I am gay." When I finished the piece, I had no idea what to do with it. A friend read it and convinced me to submit it to *Tikkun* magazine. I was both terrified and overjoyed when the magazine accepted the article for publication. "Gayness and God" appeared in fall 1993 under the pseudonym Rabbi Yaakov Levado, meaning "Jacob alone."[2]

The name, plucked out of the biblical account of Jacob's return to Canaan, expressed both my loneliness and my struggle. In the story Jacob is returning from Ur to face his brother, Esau. He crosses back over the Yabbok River and there, finding himself alone, encounters a man who wrestles with him until the morning light. "And Jacob was left by himself [Yaakov levado], and there a man wrestled with him until the break of day" (Gen. 32:23–25). I wrote that for many years I was Yaakov Levado—Jacob alone, wrestling with terrifying sexual desires for men, wracked with guilt, and angry at God. Toward the end of the article I tried to explain why it was important for me not to reveal my true identity. I feared that the cost of honesty and realness would be isolation and marginalization. Coming out would compress my life into a narrow and grossly overdetermined identity. I bristled at the thought of being known widely as the "gay Orthodox rabbi."

During the first few months following the publication of the article, I received a number of letters forwarded to me through the magazine. I heard from many gay and lesbian Jews, most of whom had left Orthodoxy years before, and from an interesting group of straight Jews as well. The letters were my first taste of support and acceptance, and through them my world began to open up. I had finally found a voice for my experience by venturing, under cloak, outside the closet.

Coming Out

With the publication of the *Tikkun* article I had become an address for gay and lesbian Orthodox people seeking support. In responding to the letters my world expanded. In opening up to other gay people, I felt the beginnings of a community and a growing sense of responsibility to it. I knew that I would have to carry the introductory sentiments of the article into a more sustained argument for the inclusion of gay and lesbian Jews in the Orthodox community.

I had been working for eleven years as an educator of Jewish communal leaders at the National Jewish Center for Learning and

Leadership (CLAL). I was living during these years in Riverdale, a very straight upper-middle-class Bronx suburb filled with young Orthodox couples and families. I clearly needed a change. That opportunity miraculously presented itself in 1996, when I received a two-year fellowship for professional development from the Mandel Institute in Jerusalem. I packed up my apartment and left New York City in a matter of weeks.

I decided soon after I settled myself in Jerusalem that if I was going to meet interesting gay men, I had to invent something to draw them out of the woodwork. So, along with a friend, I decided to start a gay men's study group, which we named Moah Gavra (meaning "male mind"). This rather eclectic group—a once-religious doctor from Tel Aviv, a Hasidic teenager, a few secular academics, a number of Modern Orthodox young men, and two married men—came together monthly. Moah Gavra became an incredible gift. The spirited give-and-take with others over the thorny talmudic texts on the topic of homosexuality was thrilling. Texts that had seemed at first to shut down possibilities, on further inquiry actually opened them up. Even the difficult texts began to point us in fruitful directions. The study confirmed to me that there was more than enough material to justify a serious rethinking of the issues at hand.

In the beginning of my first year in Jerusalem I was approached by a group of young gay activists in the city seeking to build a gay community center. They had heard of Moah Gavra and wondered if I might consider coming to their planning meetings. Within a month I was an integral part of the organizing team, beginning to translate my growing self-acceptance into action. Six months later we had galvanized a community, developed a clear set of goals, and had everything we needed for Jerusalem's first gay and lesbian community center except money. In the summer between my years of study, I flew back to New York to seek initial funding and returned with enough money to rent a sizable space in Jerusalem. We scoured the city for a place to call home and were repeatedly turned down. By the time I was packing my bags to return to New York City in the summer of 1998, we had found a landlord willing to rent us a shell of a space in the center of town with no walls and in some places no floors. If we could pay a year's rent in advance, the landlord would have the place ready for occupancy by the spring of 1999.

Back in New York City I decided that whatever the outcome, I could no longer remain in the closet with integrity. I timed my self-outing two weeks before the Open House was scheduled to open its doors, and an article appeared in the Israeli daily newspaper *Maariv* on Friday, March 5, 1999. It was titled "In the name of partnership."

Orthodox Response

A week later, *The Forward,* a North American Jewish weekly, picked up the Israeli story and published an article that described me as the world's first openly gay Orthodox rabbi. I had expected a barrage of verbal and written attacks. To my surprise nothing of the sort happened. Friends were wonderfully supportive, and a number of my colleagues called to offer their praise and encouragement. They said things like, "Gutsy move, Steve! Congratulations, but, ah—don't quote me on it." Those of my rabbinic colleagues who did not approve did not call to tell me so.

In fact, my coming out was largely ignored by the organized Orthodox community. The worst written statement came from a rabbinic scholar at Yeshiva University who was asked to respond to my announcement. He replied that a gay Orthodox rabbi is an absurdity as inconceivable as an Orthodox rabbi who eats cheeseburgers on Yom Kippur.[3] There is no such thing as a gay Orthodox rabbi.

I was asked by *The Forward* to respond to that rabbi's comment. I wrote that while commitment to halakhic norms is central to the definition of Orthodoxy, the rabbi's comparison was absurd. Human sexuality is not a gastronomic whim, and lifelong intimacy is not a cheeseburger. Nobody jumps off a bridge because he or she is deprived of cheeseburgers. No one sinks into clinical depression or submits to electroshock therapy for the sake of a ham sandwich. The gross misunderstanding of human sexual expression as mere bodily gratification is all the more shocking in this case because the rabbi who made the comparison between sexuality and cheeseburgers is not only a scholar in the rabbinical school but a physician as well.

However, this rabbi's position is hardly uncommon in the Orthodox community. The choice to accept oneself as gay is seen by many, if not by most, as a full-fledged rejection of the Torah. A gay Orthodox Jew (and how much more so a gay Orthodox rabbi) is a confounding oxymoron or, worse, a dangerous perversion of the truth. The question is a fair one: What sort of "Orthodoxy" am I speaking of? Is a rabbi Orthodox merely because he once received Orthodox ordination, or are there other, more substantive criteria?

Orthodoxy and Deviance

No definition of Orthodoxy would make any sense without a firm commitment to the halakhic system. The Halakhah, the layered authoritative legal literature that implements the Torah's commandments and so governs Jewish life, is central to any definition of Orthodoxy. So, given that the Halakhah, as presently articulated, would reject the legitimacy of same-sex love and commitment, in what sense am I Orthodox? What is the meaning of deviance from the system? Is it possible to believe that, in light of new realities, the standard halakhic ruling on homosexual relations is in error and still be a loyal advocate of the system?[4]

I think so. I am committed to the halakhic system, both in theory and in practice. However, I believe that the proper Halakhah, the one that treats this phenomenon responsibly, honestly, and intelligently, is not the present one. In fact, I believe that avoiding the issue of sexuality and gender at this moment of history will prove disastrous. It will, in the words of Yeshayahu Leibowitz, the celebrated Israeli Orthodox thinker, "endanger the very continuation of Torah and mitzvah Judaism in our world."[5]

Leibowitz wrote these words in 1982 in reference to the Orthodox resistance to listen and to respond to the deep moral claims of feminism. Few Orthodox scholars or leaders took him seriously then. Today, more than two decades later, the Jewish Orthodox Feminist Alliance gathers thousands for study and reflection on this very issue. Yesterday's line in the sand has, for at least some in the movement, become a clarion call to a deeper commitment to the image of God in us all.

No doubt only history will say if such a bold course of action will bear fruit. The ultimate aim, of course, is not to be Orthodox per se. I have chosen to remain inside the Orthodox community because for all its difficulty with contemporary social issues, it is the Jewish community that for me possesses the richest religious resources. It is the community that most unambiguously accepts the Torah as God's word. It is consequently the community most trusting of the Torah, most dedicated to its study and transmission, and most passionate in the service of heaven that it enjoins. Its weaknesses are no secret. It is a community far too dominated by fear and insecurity, overly suspicious of contemporary culture, largely closed to the subjectivity of women and so to the fullness of the image of God, and socially more conformist than I would like. I simply prefer this set of strengths and weaknesses over the others. I also must admit that it helps to be a man in this choice.

Lesbians have good reason to doubt the possibility of a viable Orthodox lesbian option. Not surprisingly, far fewer lesbians than gay men have come out of the closet and remained Orthodox. The reasons for this distinction are multiple. Foremost is the fact that many Orthodox women marry young and only discover their lesbian identity once married and burdened with the care of many children. There are many lesbians trapped in loveless marriages, who for the sake of their children live quiet lives of desperation. In such cases women remain Orthodox and hidden to all but their closest allies, if they are fortunate enough to have any. Women who have less at stake, who have never married or have divorced, often choose to leave Orthodoxy for the simple reason that there are few avenues of membership in the Orthodox community for "unattached" women. While things are slowly beginning to change in some Modern Orthodox communities, a woman is still largely socialized into the community as a daughter, a wife, or a mother. Single straight women tend to suffer this sense of displacement as well. In synagogues dominated by young singles, single women are somewhat more involved and valued. The most promising communities where single women are full-fledged members are the two Orthodox synagogues, in New York and Jerusalem, where women are able to read from the Torah and lead portions of the prayer service.[6] Throughout this book I have noted ways that the demotion of women has led to demotion of gay men. In my estimation we cannot address the question of homophobia without also addressing the question of misogyny.

Increasingly Modern Orthodox Jews want to belong to a community that actively includes the subjective voice of women in celebration and, even more importantly, in the deliberation of halakhic norms. It is just this sort of process that, in time, will challenge Orthodox leadership to engage the question of sexuality in new and thoughtful ways. Just as with women, gay people's presence in Orthodox environments, as faithful committed members, will move the system in its own time and its own way.

This is my hope. However, the reality today for gay Orthodox Jews is very far from this grand vision of inclusion. Most still suffer in the closet, paralyzed by the fear of rejection and emotionally stunted by years of internalized self-hatred. Today in most Orthodox Jewish communities homosexuality is thought of as a liberal ideology to be resisted, a dangerous character flaw requiring correction, or a disease requiring a cure. When it marches in the public square, homosexuality is reviled as an ideology of pleasure for its own sake, a social agenda that elevates sexual freedom above all else. In the rabbi's study one-on-one encounters tend to be somewhat calmer and more understanding. Often rabbis feel stuck, not knowing how to care for people and at the same time protect and defend the tradition as they understand it.

Even while the individual homosexual is pitied, the phenomenon of homosexuality is often perceived as a social menace threatening the family and the community. To manage the conflict Orthodox rabbis have largely adopted the position of so many Christian religious leaders, of "loving the sinner and hating the sin." Given that spiritual effort, moral will, or therapy cannot heal a person of the scourge of homosexual desire, the Orthodox rabbinate, sometimes with painful recognition, sometimes not, demands lifelong celibacy.

Homosexual love and partnership is perceived not only as a functional threat to family and community but also as a profound threat to the divinity, truth, and goodness of the Torah. The very notion of a person who is essentially and unchangeably gay is terribly challenging. How could the Torah command the impossible? There is a great temptation for rabbis to believe that sexual orientation is largely chosen or, at very least, susceptible to therapy. Gay people who approach rabbis are routinely told that change is possible and that homosexual desire is a test. Rabbis tell us that God has given us a spiritual challenge to struggle with same-sex desire and defeat it with abstinence. Some even promise that if we are truly penitent and work hard to overcome our desires, we will be able to change our sexual orientation altogether. Since character is ordinarily shaped by the restraint of personal desire for the sake of loftier goals, the choice, we are told, is ours. Choose Orthodoxy and resist gay sexual expression, or be gay and leave the community.

This book is a departure from these Orthodox responses to same-sex desire and love. Instead of defeating either our religious life or our sexuality, I intend to clarify how both identities, gay and Orthodox, can engage each other in conversation in new and productive ways. Religions, and especially ancient faiths like Judaism, have had many encounters with changing social realities to which they eventually responded. Jewish history is full of such engagements.

Change and Halakhah

In the Orthodox community people are taught to think that the law does not change. However, anyone who has studied Talmud or Jewish history knows that while principles tend to remain firm, rulings often change. This is hardly a revolutionary understanding of Halakhah. When social conditions shift, when reality dawns on us in new ways, then the same principles will often balance out in different ways, producing different rulings. We experience these halakhic "reapplications" as the proper commitment to the Torah's original purposes.

The historical record marks an ongoing negotiation between texts and changing social, economic, and political realities. Attitudes and legal rulings concerning sacrificial service, slavery, marriage, divorce, interest taking, inheritance law, corporal punishment, legal procedure, mourning customs, and relations with gentiles, to name just a few, have changed in various ways over the past two thousand years and more of Jewish life.[7] These changes generally occurred slowly and without grand revolutionary ideologies to support them. They were pragmatic responses to new situations. The tidal wave of modernity beginning in the 1800s so overwhelmed the system's traditional mechanisms of legal responsiveness that a bulwark against change was erected in order to preserve the character of traditional Jewish life.

The Birth of Orthodox Judaism

By the beginning of the nineteenth century the ghetto walls in communities in central and western Europe were falling. For the first time Jews could imagine being citizens in their countries of domicile. National citizenship essentially ended whatever legal authority local rabbis once exercised over their communities. Along with the new social freedoms came new intellectual, cultural, and professional opportunities. The spirit of the age tended to valorize change at the expense of tradition. Thousands of Jews, tempted by the first taste of the larger world, abandoned Jewish life. In response to the growing alienation the Jewish community produced three of the four current denominational movements, Reform, Conservative, and Orthodox Judaism.

Reform Judaism began as a grassroots response to the growing disaffections brought about by the emancipation and the Enlightenment. At the turn of the nineteenth century groups of lay reformers eager to make the synagogue more aesthetically pleasing abbreviated the liturgy, added choral singing with organ accompaniment, and supplemented the Hebrew prayers with prayers in the vernacular. Initially the incremental leniencies and accommodations were pragmatic rather than ideological. A generation of university-trained rabbis linked the new religious sensibility to the great intellectual challenges of the age, and a movement was born. The Reform movement was so successful in America that in 1880, of the two hundred synagogues in America, all but twelve were Reform.

At the famous 1885 Pittsburgh conference the kosher dietary laws, Sabbath regulations, and a host of customs and rituals that had been part of Jewish life and worship for nearly two thousand years were deemed inconsistent with the "views and habits of modern civilization" and so jettisoned.[8] In response to this radical departure from tradition, a group of rabbis split off and created the Jewish Theological Seminary, a rabbinical school dedicated to what was to become the more moderate movement, Conservative Judaism.

In response to the mass defection of Jews from classical religious observance and belief, traditionalists created a movement of their own, which they called Orthodoxy. The term *Orthodox* (meaning "the right doctrine") was actually a derogatory word used by nineteenth-century progressive Jews to describe the traditionalists that they believed they were superceding. While rejected at first, the term was so pervasive that in 1886 it was adopted by Rabbi Samson Raphael Hirsch when he established the first alliance of traditional congregations in Europe, the Free Union for the Interests of Orthodox Judaism.

A generation of great Orthodox thinkers emerged; some attempted to integrate social emancipation with Jewish life, while others propelled a turn inward toward deeper faith, halakhic stringency, and separatism in order to defend the remnant of the faithful. The language of progress and change had been used so successfully by the Reform movement that some Orthodox religious leaders actually invented the idea of a changeless tradition. In the words of Rabbi Moshe Sofer, "all that is new is prohibited by the Torah."[9]

Which Orthodoxy?

The word *Orthodox* can be a very confusing one. While there is much agreement on basic religious observance and belief, there is no centralized authority governing either. The customs, sensibilities, and world-view of different communities that call themselves Orthodox are widely divergent.

Orthodox Judaism is the least organized and most diverse of contemporary denominational movements. There is no central body governing synagogue life and no universally accepted source for contemporary halakhic rulings. Orthodox Jews do tend to agree on a number of fundamentals such as the divine origin of the Torah (the five books of Moses), the duty to study the Torah (both written text and oral tradition), and to faithfully observe Jewish law (Halakhah).

Among the more defining Orthodox practices are the honoring of the Sabbath and holidays by refraining from all forms of creative work, the kosher dietary laws, the sexual purity laws that restrict intercourse between husband and wife during and a while after menstruation, and for men, prayer three times daily and the study of

Torah.[10] While these pillars of faith and action provide a frame for denominational unity, individuals and communities differ widely on many issues. Within Orthodox circles there is a range of approaches to theology, mysticism, secular learning, leadership models, educational philosophies, Zionism, interaction with non-Jews and with non-Orthodox Jews, accommodation to contemporary culture, and women's roles. Much of this internal variance hinges, on the simple question of the meaning of modernity and how classical Judaism ought to engage with it.

The form of Orthodox Judaism that has most vigorously engaged the modern world has been called neo-Orthodoxy or Modern Orthodoxy. The dean of Modern Orthodoxy in America was the great heir of Lithuanian talmudic scholars, Rabbi Joseph Dov Soloveitchik. Rabbi Soloveitchik was a preeminent Talmud scholar and a doctor of philosophy from the University of Berlin. During his fifty-year tenure as the head of Yeshiva University's rabbinical school, he trained over two thousand American Orthodox rabbis and educators. Significantly, while other Orthodox rabbinical seminaries tend to discourage liberal arts university training, Yeshiva requires a minimum of a B.A. for entry into its rabbinic program and provides opportunities for graduate study as well.

Modern Orthodox Jews are likely to be college educated and actively involved in American culture and society. Modern Orthodox rabbis tend to be more sympathetic to certain contemporary critiques of the tradition, and some have begun to consider changes, for example, the possible expansions of the law toward a fuller inclusion of women.[11]

Ultra-Orthodox Jews have typically resisted all secularizing trends. Jews in these communities have largely rejected university education and its values. There are a handful of large ultra-Orthodox seminaries and dozens of smaller yeshivot (talmudic academies) that produce rabbis. Men tend to spend their early adult years in the study of Talmud and are ushered into marriages by their early to mid-twenties. From their teens women are groomed for marriage, mothering, and managing a home. Intellectual achievement for men is played out in the yeshiva study hall or later in business rather than in academia or the professions. For many ultra-Orthodox Jews, even the possession of a TV or going to see a movie is seen as a capitulation to the secular world.

In light of this internal debate within Orthodoxy, I am best described as a Modern Orthodox rabbi. I believe deeply in the divinity of the Torah. Its letters are an extended name of God. The ink on the parchment of a Torah scroll is described by Jewish mystics as black fire on white fire, every letter bearing significance and meaning. But while every word is revelatory, Jewish tradition never believed that those words embodied a single divine intent. We are taught that there are seventy faces to the Torah, that every soul present at Sinai heard the revelation differently, that two contradictory legal rulings based on mutually exclusive readings of Scripture can both be "the words of the living God."[12] When there was disagreement over what words meant or how laws ought to be formulated or implemented, the rabbis of the Talmud trusted that the holy writ, the learned conversations of the wise, and the rule of the majority of scholars would carry the Jewish community as close to God's truth as any human community might get.

I intend to demonstrate that within the tradition there is ample room to respond creatively to the challenging issues of every age, homosexuality included. It is my view that halakhic thinking on this issue has been influenced more by Western prejudices that religious leaders presume. The Torah is meaningful for all times because it does not lapse into the past. "Today it was given, if you hearken to his voice!" (Ps. 95:7). It is alive and meaningful for all times, given that it does not suffer forever under the constrained limits of the moral imagination of any one age. In a sense the very divinity of the Torah depends on our covenantal commitment to its ability to engage meaningfully with constantly changing circumstances and expanding human knowledge.

The Problem of Bias

I have been criticized by members of the Orthodox community for voicing a halakhic opinion on a matter that is so personally significant for me. Some have put the matter bluntly, that my reasoning will be inevitably flawed because of my bias. It is true that I am not a disinterested party on the matter of homosexuality. But why should an acknowledged personal stake of this sort be a problem? Biases can be problems when they are hidden, but revealed biases can often help to tease out of a text a possibility others would not have seen. Moreover, if bias disqualifies, then why not disqualify people for whom homosexuality is emotionally disturbing? Would we wish to exclude the opinion of someone who admits that he is disgusted by the idea of men loving men or women loving women? Rather than seek a bias-free process, I prefer one that admits the multiple subjectivities that we all bring to issues.

While the risks of mere subjectivism are never fully avoidable for anyone, philosopher Emanuel Levinas has suggested a few rabbinic principles that can help to minimize the risk. First, he suggests that one must go through the tradition of commentators on the text that precedes one's own commentary. This sort of passage through the tradition molds a person's subjectivity. "A renewal worthy of the name cannot circumvent the reference to what is called the Oral Law."[13] Second, trustworthy readings demand exertion, painstaking attention, and care to language and context. "One must rub the text to arrive at the life it conceals."[14] Third, the interpreter must not read in a vacuum, as if in a private universe, but engaged and open to the life of the city, to the present tense, to life shared with others.[15] This last criterion is one that demands the most from contemporary Orthodoxy. It requires a fearless openness to other human beings, a curiosity about their lives, and a willingness to receive them on their own terms.

However, this formal effort, no matter how compelling, will not be enough. Were the case for gay inclusion to be made, well grounded in Jewish legal texts and employing precedent in methodologically sound ways, it would still be unable to convince rabbinic authorities to overturn the prohibition against same-sex relations. Real-world solutions to human problems require much more than a change of mind. They are made possible by the rising tide of new moral awareness, by gradual changes of the heart that push against the comforts of habit and stasis.

The fight to win the vote for women in America took seventy years. This great change in social consciousness was not brought about from above by legal argumentation and enactment. It was a grassroots movement that began with the slow dawning of a new and deeper sense of human solidarity. Only by great social labor are outsiders enfranchised. The constitutional reworking, the legal expression of change, is often one of the last steps on the journey toward realizing a just society.

Why Remain Orthodox?

So, given that the Orthodox community will be taking its time, likely over many years, why would a self-accepting gay person want to stay Orthodox? Why remain part of a community that, for the foreseeable future, will be so blatantly rejecting? Why would a gay person choose to remain Orthodox?

For some the reason is surely comfort and familiarity. Especially for those who have grown up in Orthodox communities and have close ties to their families, leaving the Orthodox world entails an enormous loss. Orthodox life is hypersocial. The intensity and extent of relationships is born of large families, communal proximity (everyone lives within walking distance to be able to attend synagogue by foot on the Sabbath), and a daunting schedule of holiday meals and life-cycle celebrations that routinely bring together extended families, and their friends. For many who grow up in this world of overlapping human ties, it is virtually inconceivable to imagine a life outside its embrace.

Others claim that their loyalty to Orthodoxy is a matter of conviction, a love of God and Torah that cannot be separated out of identity. The suggestion that such folks change their religious orientation (to make life easier for them) is as disquieting and self-defeating to them as the suggestion that they deny or repress their sexual orientation.

Surely some remain Orthodox to protect parents and extended family from the shame of having a child or sibling who has "left the path." In more ultra-Orthodox communities people often lack the basic life skills necessary to function effectively in the outside world. Orthodox lesbians are especially vulnerable. Typically young women are ushered into early marriage and childbearing before they are able to understand their feelings. Locked into the daily grind of child rearing with no marketable skills, these women feel utterly trapped, isolated, and hopeless.

For those, such as myself, who did not grow up Orthodox but embraced Orthodoxy later in life, the issues can be very different. Returnees to faith and religious observance *(baale teshuva)* have much less to contend with in regard to coming out. The specter of familial rejection and religious devastation is usually much less harrowing for us. Most importantly *baale teshuva* do not associate religious observance with conforming to parental expectations. Often the opposite is the case.

For many such returnees traditional religion was the epitome of nonconformity, a countercultural revolution against the stultifying banalities of American life. Choosing a religious tradition, coming to trust its moral, spiritual, and intellectual sensibilities, adopting a religious community rather than being born into it can serve (if somewhat paradoxically) as a source of trust in oneself. Orthodox need not mean conformist.

The Jewish tradition has rich resources for countercultural critiques of regimes of certainty, even when the regime was of its own making. Nonconformist prophets denounced the kings and priests of ancient Israel, the mystics disparaged the philosophers (and vice versa) in the medieval period, and the Hasidic masters in the nineteenth century criticized the great scholars of eastern Europe for being soulless. In our long history we have been nourished by great social architects and impassioned dissidents.

While Orthodoxy for many is indeed a defensive bulwark against uncertainty, a way to simplify a complex world, I am profoundly grateful to my teachers who taught me to embrace the tradition as a great cross-historical conversation, a spiritual and moral ground from which to contend with life's myriad possibilities, a disciplined and balanced way to live a great life in the midst of inevitable uncertainty. There is great hope in a tradition that loves good questions even more than good answers, a tradition that teaches that God listens to the deliberation of the sages in order to know what the Halakhah is.

God

It is important to add that faith in God has paradoxical powers for gay and lesbian people. God can surely be the source of self-condemnation and torment, but for many religious gay and lesbian people God is also the ground of hope. Over time many of us have come to feel through our suffering, prayer, and reflection that—no matter what God's rabbis or priests may tell us—God does not reject us.

This conviction that God is on our side comes mostly from the pains of the struggle against ourselves. Having tried for years to become as those who love us (and everyone else as well) would wish us to be, and having failed repeatedly to feel or be different than what we are, we come to see our gayness, not as a moral failing, but as a hardwired element of our selves.

At first this blighted self can be worse off, suffering not merely from a failure of moral will but from an unchangeable nature. The experience of an essential gay self can also turn the problem on its head. If gayness is indeed hardwired in us, then surely we were created this way. It would make no sense for God to make people unchangeably gay and then punish them for being so. Could our gayness somehow be God's will?

Orthodox Jews and Jews generally tend to be wary of those who claim to have a direct line to heaven. "God said to me" is a preamble that can lead to the most appalling abuses of religion.[16] Claims to a direct relationship with God, unhinged from the normative frames of the law, can legitimate almost anything.[17] Still, people of faith often find a reservoir of hope in just this sort of personal relationship with God.

For years I prayed to God to take the scourge of perversity away from me. At times I felt that God was my tormentor. Sometimes, despairing, I would go to the roof of my apartment building in the Bronx, put on my tefillin, and sit numb and silent staring at the Hudson below, unable to pray.[18] Years later, when I began my first gay relationship, prayer returned to me. No longer numb, I was overwhelmed with feeling. I swung back and forth between celebration and guilt, sometimes reverting back to old penitential tears and at other times rejoicing with God in the discovery of myself. Some mornings, having lain in the arms of my lover all night, I could not bear to put on my tefillin in the morning. At other times I took enormous pleasure in my morning davening (prayer), celebrating my very aliveness, having been half dead for so many years. It was for me a very slowly dawning awareness that, in spite of the verses in Leviticus, the God who had made me according to his will did not reject me. This sense that God is the ground of hope was never clearer to me than when I met Izhar.

Izhar and Daniel the Tailor

Izhar was a forty-year-old Israeli, a slight and gentle man with warm eyes and light brown hair. He had heard of the Jerusalem study group and wanted to speak with me. Raised in an antireligious home, Izhar had later searched for meaning and spirit. His quest had carried him to India, where, among a generation of post-army Israeli hippies, he discovered Buddhism. But while he found profound wisdom and new levels of being in Eastern religion, he did not find God. Later, upon his return to Tel Aviv and in the midst of his coming out of the closet, he began to read the Hebrew Bible and was overwhelmed to discover how powerfully the book spoke to him. He felt, in reading the Torah for the first time, that he had finally kept an appointment long delayed and in the meeting had encountered God in a very personal way.

Coming out for Izhar had started him on a spiritual path leading through the Torah to an ongoing awareness of the overflowing of divine compassion. He spoke of God as a lovesick youth would speak of his beloved. His eyes sparkled as he cautiously gave expression to his feelings that were as closeted as once were his desires for male companionship. Talking so animatedly about God with no kipah on his head, Izhar seemed like a figure out the Bible itself, one of the *bnei haneviim,* the young men of Saul and David's time who were touched by the spirit.[19]

We arranged to meet at a cafe in a trendy area south of the center of Jerusalem. He spoke about his love of God and about his need for acceptance by God despite the verses in the Torah condemning homosexuality. He asked me how I lived with God in the context of my life. I told him that I had no unequivocal way to reinterpret Leviticus, but that I was helped by a modest tailor named Daniel.

Daniel the Tailor is a little-known character of the rabbinic period. While he has no rabbinic title and is an audacious critic of the rabbis, they quote him. Daniel interrupts the rabbis' study of the melancholic Book of Ecclesiastes (Kohelet) and challenges them with a bold interpretation.

Kohelet dispenses with the saccharine fantasies of the Book of Psalms and admits that, in reality, the oppressed are most often left without a redeemer, indeed, even without a comforter. Interpreting these verses in an unusual manner, Daniel the Tailor offers a broadside attack on rabbinic power. Daniel claims that sometimes the tears of the oppressed are caused by the rabbis themselves who have misread or wrongly applied scriptural verses and then, acting with the authority of the Torah, become oppressors. In such cases, where there is no comforter, God says, "It is upon me to comfort them."[20] In the absence of any human understanding or compassion, God is called upon to mend the broken hearts.

I shared the midrash of Daniel the Tailor with Izhar and suggested to him that perhaps the verses in Leviticus have been read in oppressive ways that do not please God. "Imagine that God wishes to comfort you," I said, "like a parent who reassures a tearful child taunted by the neighborhood bullies. He is saying to you. 'Izhar, listen to me. You're all right. The law and society will get fixed in time, but, you . . . I love you as you are. You're fine. You're just fine.'" As I repeated the words, tears welled up in Izhar's eyes.

Why Write a Book?

When I tell Orthodox folks that I have written a book on this subject, I am often greeted with disbelief. Given that Orthodox Judaism is grounded in Jewish law and the law against male sexual relations has been interpreted in basically the same way for at least two thousand years, what is there to say? What could be found in the corpus of religious Jewish thought that might make any significant difference? The law is the law, no?

If the history of an uncontested ancient law is not to be denied, neither is the reality of human experience. Here is but one of the dozens of remarkably similar letters that I have received from troubled young Orthodox men and women.

Dear Rabbi,

For the past six years of my life, I have been terribly depressed. I think the only thing that has kept me from doing anything drastic (and I am sure that you know what I mean) is my love for my family and the fear of putting them through any tragedy. I should begin with a bit of history. I'm a Yeshiva [University] graduate and after that I spent some time studying at an Israeli yeshiva.

The heart of the matter is that I would love to "love a woman," but this is my deep dark secret that goes as far back as I can remember. Even from my childhood, I knew I wasn't like all the other guys. My earliest memory of having a crush on someone was on a guy friend of mine in the third grade. For many, many years, I never dealt with the issue, because I always felt somehow it might go away. It wasn't like I could tell my parents. I just figured that it was a phase I was going through.

Well, things don't really work that way. This is a serious issue, and whether it is genetic or socially acquired makes no difference to me. I hate it and myself for feeling this way and am beginning to lose the battle because I am at a critical decision-making period in my life. I DON'T WANT TO BE ALONE ANYMORE!

For a period of time, I was seeing a religious psychiatrist. At first it seemed to give me some hope, but turned out to be useless. I also met with a doctor from the organization NARTH [National Association for the Research and Therapy of Homosexuals]. This turned out to be nothing but mental torture.

I have been fixed up many times and gone through the motions of dating. . . . I dread every time we set a date, because I have to put on this big charade of being interested. How could I ever marry under these conditions? I would be absolutely miserable, not to mention how unfair that would be to her and any children we might have.

Going the other way is not an option either. I know some gay coworkers, and I see that it's such an empty and narcissistic lifestyle where all value is placed on youthfulness. But in spite of all this, I have a very strong sexual attraction to other guys.

This has caused [me] a tremendous amount of anxiety and depression. Outside of work, I rarely leave home anymore. . . . I feel so trapped. I can't be around other people for very long. I see them with their spouses or family, and I want to get out of there so fast and just run like a crazy man down the street. It has become overwhelming, and I'm so confused and feel that I'm running out of options.

Thanks,

Shlomo[21]

For the sake of this young man and many men and women very much like him, the first goal of this book is to demonstrate that, contrary to the assumptions of many liberal and traditional Jews, an argument *can* be made in defense of gay relationships from within the canon of traditional Jewish textual resources. What this young man needs is not the permission to have sex with men. That is hardly enough. What he needs is a way to envision a life of love, intimacy, and commitment with a man in the context of a religiously alive Orthodox community. The task of writing on this topic is to mark a path that is responsible to these human realities and deeply committed to God and Torah.

Testimonies

Since the movement of attitude, at least initially, depends so much on empathetic hearing, the most important work will be our "coming out" and the telling of our stories. In the Orthodox community this is especially true. Not until the issue is fully situated in its human context, when family ties, longstanding friendships, and affections are on the line, will any text-based argument for inclusion be even minimally effective.

The most significant documentation to date of the experience of gay and lesbian Orthodox Jews is the film *Trembling before G-d,* a documentary by Sandi Simcha DuBowski. It is a moving and responsible piece of work that depicts the intersections of faith and gayness in the lives of a handful of men and women. It also offers a range of interview segments with Orthodox rabbis (including me) on the topic.[22]

The film takes us on a journey into the lives of seven people as they tell us their stories and share their ongoing struggles. We meet David, a Modern Orthodox Jew who returns to the rabbi who twenty years earlier encouraged him to fight his homosexuality. Devorah shares her torment in knowing that she cannot offer her husband what he needs. We meet Israel, an angry man whose love of Yiddishkeit was poisoned by his family's utter rejection of his life. Malkah and Leah, a lesbian couple who met and fell in love in Yeshiva high school, introduce us to their deeply religious household, and Marc and Michelle carry us into their lost worlds.

The power of DuBowski's work lies in the very humanity of all his subjects, the rabbis included, as they struggle toward different forms of personal and religious integrity. The great achievement (and for some a great frustration) of this documentary is that while it faces the religious quandary of its subjects, it does not attempt to "solve" their halakhic dilemma. Leviticus is neither sidelined nor interpreted out of existence. Had any specific resolution been considered, the Orthodox community would have rejected the film out of hand. In order to open up dialogue DuBowski stops short of resolutions, eliciting rather than providing the next steps.[23]

Gay and lesbian Jews who view the film are understandably impatient for the solution, the conclusive way to make sense of homosexual orientation and Torah. For many of these seekers, liberal Jewish communities have become a desperately needed haven. Non-Orthodox rabbis have been thinking and writing about Judaism and homosexuality for quite a while. Arthur Waskow, Hershel Matt, Elliot Dorf, Rebecca Alpert, Joel Roth, Jacob Milgrom, and Brad Artson have provided an array of engaging responses. I owe these writers a debt of gratitude for challenging me to seek my own set of answers to the questions that we share. Rather than repeat and contend systematically with what has been written, I have chosen instead to offer a different take on the issue, one that emerges from an Orthodox (if uncommonly Orthodox) perspective.

First and foremost, offering an Orthodox argument for gay inclusion is crucial for gay and lesbian Orthodox Jews. We desperately want a way to stand before our maker and to counter those who have read us out. We long for a reading of Scripture that replaces the depiction of perversity with mere difference and sinful desire with the simple human longing for loving. Whether or not Orthodox religious leaders are convinced by the arguments in this book, the individual gay person deserves the opportunity to make sense of his or her life before God.

There are others who need a plausible, religiously coherent, text-based argument for gay inclusion. Straight Orthodox people who have affection for the gay people in their lives are troubled. The distress of their gay children, siblings, or friends and the damaging power of religious texts and rabbinic attitudes pose a deep challenge to their religious world. They may welcome a reading of Scripture and tradition that preserves the sacred divinity of the text and still avoids the hurt.

The Reform and Reconstructionist Jewish communities have formally taken on gay liberation as a part of their religious mission. Despite this, many of the rank-and-file in liberal communities are resistant to the full integration of gay and lesbian couples into their synagogues. Conservative Jews have been characteristically ambivalent on the issue. While many of the most creative writers on the issue are Conservative rabbis, the two Conservative rabbinical schools will still not ordain an openly gay candidate.[24] The assumption of an unchangeable Orthodox certainty on the matter has supported the continuing emotional resistance to gay inclusion on the part of many members of liberal communities.

All sorts of people who have otherwise rejected traditional religious life have exploited the assumed biblical condemnation of homosexuality, dressing up their ignorance and prejudice as a sign of virtue, common decency, if not religious piety. Distinguishing the Bible from the destructive uses that it can be put to is critical if we are to challenge the political assumptions that have portrayed gay people as threats to family and society.

Lastly, the Hebrew Bible is a founding resource of Western culture and law. Christians consider it sacred Scripture. While Christendom has rejected much of the Levitical law, dietary regulations among the most famous, it has insisted on keeping nearly all of the Levitical sexual prohibitions.[25] Consequently, a sensible way to read Leviticus that does not castigate homosexual people will, I hope, be useful to many straight and gay non-Jews as well.

In a sense this book is a defense of the Torah, an apologia of sorts. For most gay Jews and many others as well, gayness is not up for reconsideration. It exists. It will not go away because the Torah is deemed to prohibit it. Many people attracted to the spiritual élan of traditional Jewish life have found communal attitudes toward women and gay people simply intolerable. Increasingly, I encounter young people eager to adopt Orthodox observance but put off by these issues. For many Jews homosexuality is not on the line; Judaism is. The challenge of gay inclusion tests any tradition's capacity to engage with diversity, to encounter the world responsibly as it is rather than as it is wished to be.

Religions have often been stymied and corrupted by their claim to the possession of a Truth above life. The world is desperately in need of religious traditions that work their truths through life, rather than above it, inside its complexities, and not blindly mouthing simplicities on the sides. Access to an unmediated, superhuman Truth, a perspective that transcends the limitations of human subjectivity, is not available to flesh and blood. As God explains to Moses, "No human can see me and live" (Exod. 33:20). The truth is worked out best through the earthy realities of life, in an open conversation. "How does one know what the truth is when there are so many varied and contradictory experiences and interpretations?" asks Rabbi Eleazar. His answer: Acquire for yourself an ear like a funnel and a perceptive heart to understand all the contradictory voices.[26]

Koshering a Reptile

Let me remind those who are not immediately sympathetic to the gay Orthodox struggle that a true scholar of the Torah, according to the Talmud itself, must have enormous intellectual imagination and fluidity. Rabbi Yehudah said in the name of Rav: We appoint to the Sanhedrin only someone who knows how to purify a reptile (almost the epitome of biblically impure animals) according to the Torah.[27] Rabbi Yohanan said: Anyone who does not know to prove a reptile pure and then to prove it impure a hundred times cannot open in the defense of the accused.[28]

The profound halakhic questions of our moment surely demand a generous sense of the possible. Rabbis will need to be as fearless as were their forebears to imagine the opposite of their suppositions. When an accused is before the court, when the consequences are dire for a maligned defendant, then only the most versatile of minds should be trusted to speak.

Such a process would, by definition, be open to differing views. That is the nature of the court. People have a right to disagree on a matter as difficult and complex as human sexuality. Thousands of years of precedent should not be taken lightly, but neither should the living presence of hundreds of thousands of people whose sexual orientation does not fit traditional boxes. What is required is a dialogic halakhic enterprise, one that does not decide the fate of the other by talking only to itself. For such an enterprise to work, we will all need to be curious about one another, to wonder what it is like to inhabit a different skin, to have a different biography. Torah study is most alive when people bring their differences to the table and when we all listen very well. The thrill of learning is just this: that you never quite know in advance what's going to happen when you encounter the sacred text through someone else's eyes.

A Short Introduction to Classical Jewish Texts and Halakhic Authority

Before we venture further into the vast sea of rabbinic literature, it may help the reader to have a thumbnail historical frame for our explorations. From the perspective of Jewish law the Torah (the five books of Moses: Genesis, Exodus, Leviticus, Numbers, and Deuteronomy) is the foundation of authority. Ancient understandings of the sacred text transmitted over generations were greatly expanded upon by the dynamic creativity of the rabbis of antiquity. Beginning roughly around the end of the Hasmonean Dynasty in 60 B.C.E. and continuing until the fifth century C.E., an immense literature was generated in Judea and then in Babylonia.

The Mishnah is the compendium of collected traditions, organized by a Galilean rabbi, Rabbi Yehudah HaNasi, in the year 200 C.E. The Mishnah is sometimes univocal but quite often records multiple opinions. When R. Yehudah HaNasi edited the Mishnah, he included conflicting voices but still left out many opinions. Material that was not included in the Mishnah was referred to as *beraita,* or "outside teaching," and was deemed of only somewhat less authoritative significance. When the Mishnah was in turn interpreted, debated, expanded, and implemented in a commentary referred to as the Gemara (literally, "learning"), the *beraita* material was often recovered in order to clarify the terse language of the Mishnah and, not rarely, to challenge the Mishnah's conclusions. The Tosefta, a collection of *beraitot,* was compiled and edited in the fourth century as a supplement to the Mishnah.

The rabbis of the Talmud also used precedent, logic, practical reason, literary context, formal legal principles, repetition, and common practice among other devices to get at the active meaning of the Torah for their moment. The raucous debates over the Mishnah, taking place over three centuries, were remembered, recited, and edited into two different works. The Jerusalem (or Palestinian) Talmud, redacted in the early part of the fifth century, and its more extensive counterpart, the Babylonian Talmud, in the middle of the sixth century.

It is difficult to characterize a literature as wide-ranging and as varied in modes and topical interests as the Talmud. Essentially the Talmud is an edited work of conversational writing. In it one finds legal maxims, hermeneutic arguments, long philological inquiries, legal battles, questions and answers, and fabulous legends. In many of the debates on normative practice, no final position is clarified. Talmudic writing has been described as a Bakhtinian carnival, full of juxtapositions of the proper and the grotesque, the legal and the fantastic, the redemptive and the morose. The rabbis of the Talmud seem to be only vaguely interested in solving problems in final ways. The Talmud instead draws its excitement from delving through layer after layer of problems, stretching its inquiry over generations of scholars through prior rulings, hypothetical illustrations, and odd cases, raising possibilities, and then knocking them down. The editors of the Talmud expose the paradoxes that human dilemmas raise and seem to enjoy a fecundity of ideas for its own sake.

Even before the Talmud was finally redacted, there were rabbinic commentaries that followed the biblical text line-by-line and addressed the legal implications of each verse. The interpretive method of the rabbis was termed midrash, from the Hebrew word *darash,* meaning "search." The Torah was seen as a dynamic resource, a fountain capable of gushing forth waters if just beneath the surface. The wise student needed to dig, to scratch the surface of text, to coax forth her secrets. A running legal midrash on the Torah, the

Midrash-Halakhah, was redacted in the third and fourth centuries. Genesis, being essentially narrative, has no Midrash-Halakhah; however, the other four books each possess a unique legal-interpretive commentary. (On Exodus the Midrash-Halakhah is titled the *Mekhilta;* on Leviticus, the *Sifra;* on Numbers and Deuteronomy, the *Sifrei.*) Nonlegal midrashic material, Midrash Aggadah, was likewise collected into edited works. All five books of the Torah as well as a number of later biblical books have major works of Midrash Aggadah, most of which were edited in the ninth century C.E. These collections of homilies and sermons, legends and word plays were the most popular genre of rabbinic literature. The wide appeal of Midrash Aggadah led to the generation of many different collections, the latest of which was composed in the thirteenth century.

By the Middle Ages great commentaries had grown up around the raucous talmudic debates, particular on the more popular Babylonian Talmud. The medieval commentators, referred to as the *rishonim* on the Talmud, produced an enormous religious and legal literature that is the foundation of the Halakhah. Rashi (Rabbi Shlomo ben Isaac), the Tosafot (Rashi's grandsons and others), the Ritba (Rabbi Yom Tov ben Abraham Ishbili), the Rashba (Rabbi Shlomo ben Abraham Adret), the Meiri (Rabbi Menahem ben Solomon Meiri), the Ramban (Rabbi Moshe ben Nahman), and the Rambam (Rabbi Moshe ben Maimon, also referred to as Maimonides), among many others, sharpened the talmudic debates, explored their logical underpinnings, integrated the rabbinic literature into a single legal corpus, and made halakhic determinations.

Despite the attempt of the *rishonim* to give final determination to many talmudic debates, the fundamental openness of these sacred texts and the many voices of the *rishonim* explaining them could not be contained. There was pragmatic need for a clearer cross-communal process of halakhic decision making. At the turn of the eleventh century Rabbi Isaac of Fez (referred to as Alfasi) wrote an abridged Talmud that essentially omits a good deal of the discussion and presents the concrete legal conclusions.

A century later Rabbi Moshe ben Maimon (referred to in English as Maimonides and in Hebrew by the acronym RaMBaM) wrote his monumental code of law, the *Mishneh Torah,* or "second Torah." Maimonides claimed that his fourteen-book masterpiece of Halakhah was all that any student would need to determine the law. While the Rambam's work brilliantly organized the vast talmudic material in a useable fashion, many European traditions still had not been included. A sixteenth-century work of enormous erudition that combined the efforts of two great halakhic scholars from the competing Sephardic (Spanish and Occidental) and Ashkenazic (Germanic-Central European) communities emerged to fill this gap. The *Shulhan Arukh,* written by Rabbi Joseph Caro with the added notes of Rabbi Moshe Isserles, came to be widely accepted among both Ashkenazic Jews and Sephardic Jews. However, even the success of the *Shulhan Arukh* could not absolutely quash the fundamental halakhic independence of local rabbis, and all sorts of differences persisted.

To minimize confusion, individuals were obliged to pose their halakhic questions to the rabbi of their community and to abide by his rulings, but with the expanding freedoms of movement, conscience, and affiliation of the twentieth century, this structure of authority has largely disappeared. As Americans felt free to choose their religious affiliations, Orthodox Jews have felt free to choose their religious leadership and so their halakhic authorities.

Consequently, to the dismay of some in the community, there is considerable variance between Orthodox Jews of different kinds. A male Orthodox Jew can be wearing a black kaftan and a fur hat or a tank top and a knitted yarmulke. Sensibilities regarding the presence of women at Orthodox prayer services also differ widely. The barrier (mehitzah) that separates women from men in Orthodox synagogues can be a four-foot lace curtain, a balcony where women sit separately from the men on the ground level, or an adjoining room where women hear the male voices dimly through a hole in the wall. While services are led exclusively by males, controversial Orthodox services have recently begun in which women have taken on some of the public roles, leading portions of the service and reading from the Torah.[29]

The breadth of Orthodoxy is perhaps no more pronounced than in Israel, where the political issues have complicated the picture further by producing the ultra-Orthodox anti-Zionist, Neturei Karta;

Hasidic non-Zionist hawks, Lubavitch; the Israeli Religious Zionist Settlers Movement, Gush Emunim; and the Religious Peace Movement, Netivot Shalom. The diversity of Orthodoxy is actually its greatest asset in that many individuals are able to find what suits them best inside its rather wide (if contentious) boundaries.

Outline

The book is divided into four parts: Sacred Texts, Evidence, Rationales, and Conversations. The first part, Sacred Texts, deals with the biblical material that introduces us to gender and sexuality in the world. The creation of Adam and Eve, their sinful disobedience, punishment, and exile from Eden are all cornerstones of Western civilization. These stories have created a template of gender and sexuality for all those societies under the sway of the Hebrew Bible. For some communities these texts have served as a foundation for the indictment of homosexuality as a violation of the Creator's explicit intent. In chapter 1, "The Birth of Gender and Desire," we begin the task of reconciling same-sex union with Jewish tradition by returning to the beginning.

Chapter 2, "The Sons of God, Ham, and the Sodomites," focuses on three sexual encounters that follow the creation story in the Book of Genesis. The first two are fragments of narratives that, when read with rabbinic commentary, obliquely touch on homosexual relations; the third text is the more famous story of Sodom. The biblical analysis continues in chapter 3, "Leviticus," with the verses in the Book of Leviticus that specifically prohibit and punish male intercourse. While many have claimed that the verse is an unambiguous condemnation of homosexuality, careful attention to language and syntax will demonstrate otherwise.

The verses in Leviticus that address homosexual relations focus exclusively on sex between men. Sexual relations between women are not mentioned once in the entire Torah. Despite this absence the rabbis of the first century argued that "women who rub" had imported a lewdness from pagan society. Chapter 4, "Lesbian Omissions," addresses the halakhic details of the omitted prohibition, which the rabbis nonetheless felt they needed to supplement, if only on the level of rabbinic enactment.

The second part of the book, "Evidence," turns from the five books of Moses to the poetry and prose, legend and law that in direct and indirect ways address same-sex desire. While Leviticus prohibited sexual relations between men, the literary and historical record is a good deal more interesting. Chapter 5, "Princely Love," and chapter 6, "Rabbinic Heroes," address two stories, one biblical (David and Jonathan), the other rabbinic (Rabbi Yohanan and Resh Lakish), associated with male homosexual themes. Unfortunately, lesbian evidence is virtually nonexistent. Since women have drawn considerable strength from the biblical story of Ruth and Naomi, mention is made of this material at the end of chapter 5. While I will contend that these biblical and talmudic narratives do not insinuate full-fledged "gay" love affairs in the modern sense, they all convey the tensions and complexities of love that members of the same sex can feel for each other.

Chapter 7, "The Queer Middle Ages," continues the search for evidence of same-sex love and desire and finds remarkable examples of it in poems and prose of medieval Spanish and French scholars. After the Talmud was completed, an ongoing give-and-take around important issues of Jewish law and practice was recorded in what became the vast Responsa literature. Jewish legal scholars for a thousand years have written their answers to questions posed to them. Chapter 8, "The Legal Literature," explores various responsa that deal with homosexuality. While the prohibition is not challenged, these writers seem to have had none of the modern horror associated with contemporary homosexuality. The cases paint an interesting and very different picture of the social meaning of homosexual relations from the one that we might expect.

Moving from the historical record to the present, chapter 9, "Rav Moshe and the Problem of Why," explores one of the few contemporary responsa written directly on the issue of homosexuality. Rabbi Moshe Feinstein, or Rav Moshe, as his adherents warmly referred to him, was the leading halakhic authority of American Jewry for over forty years. His view that homosexual desire could be motivated only by rebellion against God is presented as a caution and as a foil against which the rest of the book unfolds.

The third part of the book, "Rationales," returns to the fundamental prohibition in Leviticus but now begins to ask the obvious question. Given that Leviticus prohibits homosexual intercourse, one might wonder why. What is particularly problematic, immoral, or offensive about male-male intercourse in the first place? And why is the Torah so concerned about gay male sexual relations and not about lesbian relations?

Four rationales gleaned from the traditional textual resources are offered, each with differing grasps of the problem of male homosexual relations and each inviting very different analyses and policy implications. Chapter 10, "The Rationale of Reproduction," suggests that male intercourse is prohibited because it is a sexual expression that, by definition, cannot produce a child. Chapter 11, "The Rationale of Social Disruption," concerns itself less with sex and more with marriage. This rationale claims that the law prevents husbands from abandoning their wives for sexual adventure with men. Chapter 12, "The Rationale of Category Confusion," presents male intercourse as gender confusion. It claims that the categories of maleness and femaleness are undermined by same-sex intercourse. Chapter 13, "The Rationale of Humiliation and Violence," calls for a full rereading of the verses in Leviticus and suggests what troubles the text is not sex between men per se, but sex that by its nature humiliates and demeans another.

The last section of the book, "Conversations," takes us out of broad textual interpretation and into a practical methodology for rabbis and their gay congregants to begin talking about policy despite their sharply differing subjective experiences. Chapter 14, "Admitting Difference," models such a pragmatic negotiation. Because most Orthodox authorities will not accept any bold rereadings of Leviticus at present (if ever), the chapter elucidates a more narrowly defined jurisprudential way of compassionately addressing the gay Orthodox question. A number of frames for considering homosexuality will be entertained along with a gay hearing of them as two very different subjective worlds are brought together. Chapter 15, "Welcoming Synagogues," offers a framework for congregations to navigate between tradition and responsiveness. The chapter ends with a bid for a religious culture that can tolerate ambiguity.

Sacred Texts

The Birth of Gender and Desire

The Hebrew Bible is among the world's most lasting, comprehensive, and popular master narratives. It is important to begin with the Hebrew Bible not only because the Torah is the revelatory foundation of Judaism, but also because Western culture has been profoundly shaped by it. The Genesis creation stories in particular have constructed a *terra cognita* in which to live.[1] Our very sense of knowledge about the world presumes a coherence and unity that emerge from Genesis.

Genesis not only renders our cosmos intelligible; it shapes our self-knowledge as well. Our essential humanness is described as a reflection of the divine. In the first account of creation in chapter 1 we are in the image and likeness of God; in the second account in chapter 2 we are part dust of the earth and part divine breath of life.

Among the most enduring social, political, and psychological legacies of the Genesis stories are their grounding of sex and gender. We crave to unearth the mysteries of our being. "Know from where you have come and to where you are going," say the sages. The rabbis of antiquity were fond of giving very concrete expressions to great questions. "Where am I from?—A smelly drop. And to where am I going?—To decay and worms."[2]

As gritty as this answer is, it is right on the money. All creation stories start here with the smelly mysteries of sex, life, and death. Human existence, being and unbeing, ecstasy and pain, union and separation are all tied to the great difference of all differences, the

41

male-female divide and the mystery of sexual union that is the foundation of ongoing life. The fundamental human question about the origin and meaning of human life leads one directly to gender and sex. This is where our story begins.

> And God created humankind in his image,[3] in the image of God made he it, male and female made he them. (Gen. 1:27)

> God made the rib he had taken from Adam into a woman and brought her to Adam and he said: This time, she is it! Bone of my bones, flesh of my flesh! She shall be called woman *(ishah)* for from man *(ish)* was she taken. Therefore shall a man leave his father and his mother and cleave to his wife, and they become one flesh. (Gen. 2:24)

The stories in the first two chapters seem to relate two very different accounts of creation. Male and female are created in chapter 1 simultaneously and in chapter 2 sequentially. Like dreams they did not need to share a single time line. In the first story male and female are created as a pair and commanded to reproduce. In the second story, Adam's history is represented as male destiny: from loneliness to partnership, from desire to satisfaction with women. Men search for their helper-counterpart; women are found.

For classical Judaism and Christianity these verses are a blueprint. From them it is concluded that heterosexuality is the fundamental and original intention of the Creator. Even where these stories are no longer thought of as divine word, their traces still run deep. Once a master story is embedded in a culture, those living in the culture, even those who have actively rejected its authority, cannot help but share in its constant repetition. Master narratives, even contested ones, are deeper than conscious thought.

For thousands of years in the societies affected by the Hebrew Bible, chapters 1–3 of Genesis, the seven-day creation story and the story of Adam and Eve in the garden of Eden, have produced a natural world in celebration of heterosexuality and in utter rejection of homosexuality. Genesis seems uniquely responsible for the inventing of a "straight" cosmos, the consequence of which was the marking of same-sex loving not merely as irregular or different, but as unnatural and contrary to divine intention.[4]

Samuel Dresner, the late professor of rabbinics at the Jewish Theological Seminary, made the claim quite clearly that "homosexuality is a violation of the order of creation." The Bible forbids homosexuality because it affirms heterosexuality as the way in which humans were made and intended to behave. His proof, not surprisingly, was the first chapters of Genesis, the stories of creation.

To argue for the goodness of homosexual partnership, one must first address the deeply rooted convictions about life, gender, and sex that Genesis has bequeathed us. Homosexuals are either horrible corruptions of God's intention or variations of God's creative genius. It would appear that to many believing Jews and Christians we are the former.

Surprising as it may seem, some rabbis of the first and second centuries had a very different understanding of these stories. For them the separation of the human into two opposing and mutually attracting sexes in the creation stories is not God's original intent. As we will see, the biblical creation epic, according to these sages, does not assume human sexuality at all but invents it as a solution to a problem. A closer reading of the Scripture will reveal a much more interesting picture of Eden than the one we have traditionally received.

In the Beginning God . . .

The starting point of the Genesis story is God. Before creation God fills existence. There is nothing else, no place for another. God's oneness is without division or separation. One is always all-powerful without needing any power over something to be so. One is stable and sure, unchanging and whole. One is before creation. The seed of creation is the idea of more than one. At the moment of creation the magisterial oneness of God, according to Jewish mystics, concentrated itself to leave room for an other. Creation begins with the possibility of two.

Two is a rickety thing, a temptation, a suspicious thing, an ecstatic, thrilling, dangerous thing. Two always have a history. The pain and pleasure of difference, the tragedy and glory of the lines that separate things are the subtext of the first chapters of Genesis. Separation between things inaugurates creation. Light and dark, day and night, the waters below and above, the dry land and the seas are all separated. It is by these separations that creation unfolds. Much like the infant separates first physically and then psychically from its mother, little by little the world comes to be by separations amid the chaos.

This birthing of the world was not without resistance. As the waters above and below separated, they suffered to be split. Rabbi Berechiah said: The upper and lower waters separated from each other in weeping.[5] The waters long to be as they were, undifferentiated in the Godhead. Creation sunders them apart. It appears that matter is not indifferent to its condition. All things want union. And so creation struggles against a resistance. Like a newborn the waters above and below come into the world kicking and screaming, salting the seas with their tears.

Lights and Monsters

Twos pose another problem. Separation is a birth pang that passes, but once there are two, how are they to relate? On the third day of creation two great lights are created, and on the fourth day two great sea monsters are created. Of all the creations in the first chapter of Genesis, only the great lights and the great sea monsters are called great *(gedolim)*. What is more, in Hebrew both the word for lights *(meorot)* and the word for sea monsters *(taninim)* are missing a letter in their plural endings. The missing letters are not crucial for the meaning of the words, but the irregularity suggests that something is wrong. In each case the sages explain that the pair of lights, sun and moon, and the pair of sea monsters, male and female, were unstable in some way related to their being two. These twin creations became so highly problematic that God had to alter the original plan. For now we will turn our attention to the great lights.

> And God made the two great lights, the greater light to rule the day and the lesser light to rule the night, and the stars. (Gen. 1:16)

On the third day God made the two great lights. However, after introducing the sun and the moon both as great, the text adds that actually one light was great and the other was lesser. The contradiction between the verses generated a legend that is recorded in the Talmud.

"And God made the two great lights," but later it says: "the great light and the lesser light"! The moon said before the Holy One: Master of the world, is it possible for two kings to share [literally, "to use"] one crown? God said to her: Go and diminish yourself! She said before God: Because I asked a good question, I should diminish myself? God said: Go and rule both in day and in night. She said: What advantage is that? A candle in the daylight is useless. God said: Go and let Israel count their days and years by you. She said: They use the daylight [of the sun] to count seasonal cycles as well. . . . Seeing that she was not appeased, the Holy One said: Bring a (sacrificial) atonement for me that I diminished the moon! This is what Rabbi Shimon ben Lakish said: What is different about the ram of the new moon that it is offered "for God" (And one ram of the flock for a sin offering for God. . . . Numbers 28:14). Said the Holy One: This ram shall be an atonement for me that I diminished the moon.[6]

The problem of two great rulers sharing a single crown is a problem that God does not anticipate. The moon raises the problem, and the Creator solves it with a fixed hierarchy. The moon complains that she got the raw end of the deal just for asking a tough question, one that ostensibly might have been thought out in advance by the Creator. Failing to appease her, God accepts the duty to offer a sin offering on the occasion of every new moon, a monthly atonement for the lesser status he forced on her.

For asking a question to which God has no answer, the moon is diminished. If the problem of two equals managing to share power requires a resolution, then why didn't God simply begin with a hierarchy in place? Or to put it another way, why were the sun and the moon both created equal to begin with? If hierarchy is inevitable, then why not start with it? Was there a way to avoid the sin that is now in need of atonement? Perhaps the Holy One too quickly turned the moon's question into an answer. Only after an extended conversation with the moon in which she does not accept any of the consolation prizes offered her is God led to the awareness that a wrong has been committed. If so, then why does God not right the wrong and restore the moon to her original size? What is the meaning of offering a sacrifice without the return of the stolen property? For the time being we have encountered a creation much less perfect and finished than we might have expected. God appears to be an artist, learning by trial and error.

Among the lessons that God learns, so to speak, is that twos seem to require power arrangements to make them safe.[7] Otherwise they might just destroy each other. Two are stable only when the rules of power are made clear from the outset. One might ask why the Creator needed to make two lights in the first place. Why not just one? It seems that the whole point of creation involves struggling with the problems of two. The waters weep, the moon is unfairly diminished, and the story carries forward toward the one and two of humanity.

Creation of One by One

The human being is presented in the first story of creation as the end achievement of a grand evolution of matter toward God. From the start of creation there is a movement of inert material to the magnetized essence of divine life. Pulled along by divine will, matter takes on increasingly complex life forms and in so doing becomes more and more like God. From random atoms to molecules, from molecules to life cycles, from primitive life forms to warm-blooded mammals, and from beasts to sentient beings, all creation aspires to become like God. The stage of creation that most fully embodies God is the one that most expresses life and movement, individuation and relationship, mind and feeling, self-consciousness, freedom and love.[8]

Since God is one, the human, made in the image and likeness of God, is created alone in the world. Single. Among the sages of antiquity there were those who thought that creation of the human could not possibly begin with a pair.[9] The singularity of human consciousness speaks of a primordial being alone with God in the universe. While a straightforward reading of the stories seems to suggest that in chapter 1 a pair is created and in the second chapter a male human and then a female human are created in succession, the rabbis read both stories together as a single overlapping story of one becoming two. From what we have seen so far, this should not come as a surprise. The path from one to two is central to the very purpose of creation.

The Mirror

And God made *adam* in his image
In the image of God made he him
Male and female made he them.

In Hebrew *adama* is earth. The best translation of *adam* is "earth-ling."[10] In the beginning of this verse the earthling is singular (his image, him), while at the end the earthling is split into genders and is plural (male-female/them). Jumping off from this self-contradictory text, the rabbis explain how one became two.[11]

> Rabbi Yirmiyah ben Eleazar said: When the Holy One created the first *adam,* he made it androgynous. That's what it means when it says "male and female he created them."[12]

The human created in the image of God was not male at all. The original human according to Rabbi Yirmiyah was a hermaphrodite. The interpretation sounds outlandish at first hearing. Adam has been depicted in hundreds, if not thousands, of artistic portrayals as the primordial male. However bizarre the thought of an androgynous *adam,* the verses, read carefully, actually invite this interpretation.

> (a) And God made *adam*/(b) in his image
> (b) In the image of God/(a) made he him
> (b) Male and female/(a) made he them.

The first and second phrases repeat the same idea in reverse order, that *God made the human / in God's image.* The third phrase alters the pattern by replacing God's image with another idea: *God made the human / male and female.* In this phrase *male and female* is in the po-sition of *the image of God* in the two earlier statements. From the par-allelism of this short poem it appears that God's image = male-and-female. While the Hebrew language has no neuter pronoun and so usually gendered God male, this biblical triplet reveals a deeper understanding of God and consequently how we together, male and female, are in God's image. Indeed, the supposed "maleness" of God would pose a number of problems. If God is male and unlike pagan gods has no consort, then indeed God's first creation in "his image" would by necessity be a male *adam*. This reading dangerously portrays women as not quite like God and as an afterthought, a concession to a male need. The model also generates a good deal of ambivalence in regard to male sexuality, because men are patterned after a sexless God. The rabbi's construction of God as beyond gender solves both problems.[13] Each human gender is part of a larger unity in the Divine that includes both.

However, the rabbis go further in their exploration of the androgynous *adam* and by inference God's androgyny. Directly following Rabbi Yirmiyah's statement that Adam was a hermaphrodite is the statement of Rabbi Shmuel bar Nahman.

> Rabbi Shmuel bar Nahman said: When the Holy One created the first *adam*, he created it two faced and then (later) sawed it (in two) creating for it two backs, a back here and a back there. They asked him: But what of the verse "and he took one of his ribs *(tzela)*?" He answered them, [it really means that] "he took one of the flanks *(tzela)*." The word *[tzela]* is also used to describe the flank or side of the tabernacle in Exodus 26.[14]

This two-faced Adam is similar to Rabbi Yirmiyah's androgynous Adam, but the difference between the two portrayals is very interesting. It would appear that there are two theories, two different formulations of the double-gendered *adam*. According to R. Yirmiyah, the *adam* was a wholly integrated androgynous creature with a single face. This creature was male and female only inasmuch as it contained the totality of human capacities, a human with all the powers and natures and so sexually undifferentiated. According to R. Shmuel, the *adam* was a creature with two faces, one on each side. This *adam* is not fully integrated. It is a being with two perspectives, two faces gazing in opposite directions and perhaps with two proto-gender identities already in dynamic tension.

R. Yirmiyah and R. Shmuel are having a theological debate, albeit indirectly. For R. Yirmiyah God is the totality of all integrated into one. Adam before the invention of the male-female split is not differentiated at all. There is no inner tension in this *adam*. It is a whole and peaceful being as is God. For R. Shmuel God's oneness is dynamic. It is a unity negotiated between contrary or opposing parts, back to back. In the Godhead there are elements in tension, and God's unity is fullest when, as the Jewish mystics would say, the masculine aspect in the Godhead is united with the feminine. R. Shmuel's *adam* may have one body and even one mind, but its two faces already express an original psychic split along gendered lines. This human, even before the invention of the sexed body, experiences conflict between its two sensibilities.

This surprising midrashic reading of the creation of the first *adam* raises a very interesting point. No matter which view of the earthling we adopt, that of R. Yirmiyah or that of R. Shmuel, the creation of two separate beings, male and female, was not the first plan of creation. God's plan was explicitly to create one human.

However one works it out, at least according to our two sages, heterosexuality as we know it was not the original plan for humanity. That Scripture commands the male and the female in chapter 1 to be fruitful and multiply does not seem to have worried either sage. "There is no early or later Scripture."[15] As in dream interpretation, sequencing is not fixed. According to rabbinic tradition Scripture is not always interested in giving a historically linear portrayal of things.

It is, of course, true that in chapter 2 of Genesis, the traditional Adam and Eve appear as the celebrated couple that we have always known. Eventually the single androgynous earthling will be split; the two will join in desire and love and become one flesh. The question is why. If a single human was God's first intent, why was the plan changed? It seems that the flaw in the creation was just this, *adam*'s singularity.

Loneliness and the Imperfection of Creation

Creation has finished its grand symphony on the final notes of our earthling. Creation pleases God. Every phase of the creation process is judged to be good, and on the last day of creation, when the earthling is finished, the whole cosmos is deemed "very good." And now, with everything seemingly in place, God informs the *adam* of one rule that must be obeyed on pain of death.

> "Of every tree of the garden you are free to eat; but as for the tree of knowledge of good and evil, you must not eat of it, for as soon as you eat of it, you shall die."

49

The moment the threat of death is uttered, even as a possibility, everything changes. Following God's announcement, "You shall die," the *adam* says nothing. God responds, but to what? Did God see something in the *adam*'s face, posture, or spirit?

> The Lord God said, "It is not good for *adam* to be alone; I will make a fitting helpmate for him." (Gen. 2:17–18)

After every successful creative effort in the first chapter of the story, "God saw, and behold it was good *(tov)*." At the very moment of fulfillment, as the tree of knowledge of good and evil is planted and protected and Eden is complete, God discovers a flaw in the plan. Something is unexpectedly "not good" *(lo tov)*.[16] The first fly in the ointment of creation is human loneliness. Again the unpredictable consequences of creation are a surprise. The human created in the image of God is catapulted from playing in the garden to contemplating mortality. A single rule about a forbidden fruit has given birth at once to freedom, sin, and death. Suddenly Eden is a very lonely place.

Until now creation was to satisfy God. Until now only God could judge the outcome of things as good or not good. Now, the *adam* must be satisfied. It is assumed that the *adam* will know the fulfillment of desire, the end of aloneness when it comes, and will be able to judge what is "good" when it is discovered.

Animal Partners

If *adam*'s aloneness is a problem, then the creation of a fitting helper should solve the problem. Given this, the story should proceed directly to the creation of Eve. Oddly, what happens next in the story is not the creation of Eve but the creation of the animals and beasts. God forms the creatures and then introduces them to Adam. Is this an attempt at solving *adam*'s aloneness?

> The Lord God said, "It is not good for the *adam* creature to be alone. I will make a fitting helper for him." And the Lord God formed out of the earth all the wild beasts and all the birds of the sky, and brought them to the *adam* creature to see what s/he would call them. (Gen. 2:18–19)

50

How do the animals fit into *adam's* quest for intimacy and love? The sages were bothered not only by this question but also by Adam's later claim when he discovers Eve, "this time" to have found the perfect help mate. Why this time? Were there other times? In the end human emotional and physical intimacy and companionship are so important for the success of the creation that the sages of the Talmud are willing to imagine an outrageous interpretation of the parade of animals. This teaches, they claim, that the *adam* had intercourse with all the animals and beasts and was not satisfied (literally "his mind was not cooled") till he had intercourse with Eve.[17]

What an incredible portrayal of God as matchmaker providing the *adam* with every conceivable partner available to assuage his loneliness, and not one of them cools the creature's desire. Key to this interpretation is that what the *adam* craves is not a platonic friendship but a sexual companion as well.[18] If we are to take this statement in the Talmud seriously, then the *adam's* sexual needs were not something God determined in advance and imposed on him or even predicted correctly for him. God encourages the *adam* to *discover* what he needs by trial and error. We are not surprised to discover that this audacious and playful fantasy of the *adam's* sexual exploits with the animals does not satisfy the need. We know that the story will end with heterosexual union. However, a shift has taken place between God's imposing power and the *adam's* freedom. God cannot impose the solution to the *adam's* aloneness by divine fiat. Only the *adam* will know what comforts the pain of alienation, and toward this end God offers the *adam* the animals to see what union the *adam* might deem *tov*, good. Until the problem of human intimacy and companionship is resolved, the world is not a good place. The very power to proclaim creation good has, in this instance, been ceded to the *adam*.

One Becoming Two Becoming One

Having tried to create *de novo* a partner for the *adam* and having failed, God decides on a radical idea—surgery. The *adam* must be separated into two beings. For Rabbi Yirmiyah the operation is a total reconstruction of the earthling into two new creatures, man and woman. Dividing the whole human into two sexes is to shape two totally new beings out of the material of one. For Rabbi Shmuel bar Nahman the operation is more like separating Siamese twins so that they might face each other. Two sensibilities in tension will now finally have two bodies to play them out differently, to walk away from each other, and to fully face each other in love.

For R. Yirmiyah the invention of this primary difference in the bodies and psyches of humans called sex is a solution to the problem of aloneness and death. Until the reconstructive surgery nothing of the common distinctions between the male and the female in either body or mind existed. Sex difference is thus the result of God's trip back to the drawing board in order to solve the problem of human loneliness. Heterosexual love and union, while one of the most impressive bulwarks of humanity against loneliness and alienation, is not original to God's intention for the world.

For R. Shmuel bar Nahman sexual difference is original, at least in potential, not only in the original human but in God as well. The two-faced creature is always engaged in the struggle between its internal desires. Surgery then comes to externalize what was once only an internal conflict. Gender distinction and perhaps even the seeds of the future gender hierarchy are already present in this *adam* creature.

Male and Female

After the operation, the *adam* creature awakes as Adam and Eve.
And Adam said, "This time it is bone of my bone and flesh of my flesh. She shall be called *ishah* (woman) because from *ish* (man) was she taken. Therefore shall a man leave his mother and his father and cleave to his woman and they shall be as one flesh. (Gen. 2:23–25)

Unlike the sun and the moon created as independent entities, the human begins as one and becomes two. The tensions of twos earlier in the creation story begin here as Adam's presumption. Two cannot share a single crown, and he has taken charge for the time being.

He gives her a name. She is called Eve (Havah), meaning "life." We have been told in Genesis 2:7 that God formed the human from the dust of the earth and the breath of life. Earth *(adama)* and life *(hayim)* are the two ingredients in the creation of the human. The two names, Adam and Havah, are these two elements, which they both possess.

However, the male has already taken the role of speaking, possessing, of claiming a past, and in doing so appears to have silenced Havah.

There is a good deal of confusion in regard to the way the names work. The *adam* before the split is an earth-creature, as we have suggested according to the sages, an androgynous being. Following the split the male appears to retain an original connection with the prototype *adam* in a way that the female does not. Only he is called Adam. He speaks; she does not. She is "his" ("bone of my bone, flesh of my flesh"), not he hers. At the moment of their separation/creation we might have expected an original equality. Perhaps when God splits the original *adam* creature into two, he already expects trouble, the trouble of equals sharing a crown. Before the sin that will fracture everything, there is already a problematic hierarchy between the male and the female.

As the story progresses, Havah will act decisively and take charge in her own way. It is she who engages the serpent, who entertains the existential, aesthetic, philosophical, and legal questions about the one prohibited tree in the garden. The snake does not tempt her as much as he questions her about what she really knows. Independence from God is interesting to her and its risky powers and pleasures alluring. It is she who needs to test the limits, to know truly where she stands in relation to things. Like the moon that is bold enough to ask how power works between two who share a single crown, she, too, dares to expose the true power relations between God and human.

After the sin in the garden, innocence lost, the two sense their nakedness, clothe themselves, and hide from God. The sweet tending of the garden will become back-breaking work, the earth freely giving of its fruit will yield to thorn and thistle, friendly relations between the animals and humans will become vicious, and the joyous union of one flesh will now be given over to passion, domination, and pain. The diminishment of the moon now parallels the subjugation of the woman. The couple is banished from the garden to a world of incongruities.

With this reading of Genesis the sages have not provided a positive mythic foundation for homosexual love, but what their reading offers is immensely important for us. First, this reading affirms that heterosexuality is not original. If anything was original, it was the androgynous *adam,* the first effort of creation. This first androgynous *adam* was perhaps too whole, too much like God. Having no distance to overcome, the creature perhaps began to long for longing, for a wholeness not to possess but to realize. The prohibition to eat of the tree of the knowledge of good and evil introduced Adam to the very possibility of lack. The threat of death gave birth to the desire for union, for a love that cannot be conquered by death.

Second, there is no romance in two. Romantic love can comfort, but it cannot redeem. The pain of loneliness is not fixed with the healing of heterosexual union. For Adam and Eve, the experience of being one flesh does not defend them against the mutual recriminations. At first they hide from God in solidarity, but very quickly they feel the need to hide from each other. Maybe upon their exile from Eden clinging to each other for support they were able to share their grief and grow toward love. With a great deal of effort, the earth can be made to bear fruit, children can be born, a life of partnership can be negotiated, and love can be sustained, but nothing in this picture is whole or certain.

Last, this reading offers a trajectory for those of us eager to see the world healed when it comes to gender. The subjugation of females to males, punishment for the sin in the garden, is seen by the sages as a fracture in the plan, a distortion of God's original intent. It must not be denied that in the larger corpus of the rabbinic tradition the rabbis most often enforced the power hierarchy between the genders. In various ways, women were silenced and controlled, infantilized and disempowered, as they were cared for, idealized, and protected. However, the cracks in the fortress are visible, and the same sages point them out to us, reminding us that this is not the world as it ought to be. Since the gender hierarchy is a broken condition, try as they may, they cannot fully contain the desire to fix it. For all the limitations of their efforts, the sages often increased the powers of women beyond what was normative in the cultures around them. Later generations of rabbis found ways to provide even greater independence for women than did their predecessors. While the rabbinic record hardly conforms to contemporary egalitarian standards, one finds the desire to see the hierarchy healed and the moon restored.

Restoring the Moon: Kiddush Levanah

The sages understand the moon's diminishment as a sin committed against the moon for which God asks to atone. The midrash is an invitation by the rabbis to project toward a world of restored harmony and equality. A mystical liturgy of sanctifying the new moon was introduced into Jewish custom by Rabbi Isaac Luria in the sixteenth century. If God brings a sacrificial atonement for the diminishment of the moon, then there must be some desire on high to truly repent of the violence done to her. The laws of repentance require it. We learn that there is no forgiveness for sins between parties until the offended party has been appeased. A sacrifice alone cannot right a wrong done. Pregnant in the midrash of the first century is Luria's prayer for the moon's restoration.

Kiddush Levanah, the sanctification of the moon, is generally recited during the second week of the lunar cycle. Commonly the prayer is said at the conclusion of the Sabbath falling during this period. On this Saturday evening following the end of the prayer service, the congregation files outdoors and underneath a visible moon chants Kiddush Levanah. The sources of the first paragraph are biblical and rabbinic, but the messianic prayer that follows is pure Jewish mysticism.

> They taught in the school of Rabbi Ishmael: Were Israel able to greet their Father in heaven only once a month, it would be enough. Abbaye says: For this reason it should be said standing.[19] "Who is she, coming up from the desert, leaning on her lover?"(Song of Songs 8:5)
>
> May it be your will, O Lord, my God and the God of my fathers to fill in the darkness of the moon that she not be diminished at all. And let the light of the moon be as the light of the sun, and as the light of the seven days of creation, just as she was before she was diminished, as it is said: "the two great lights." And may we be a fulfillment of the verse: "And they shall seek out the Lord their God and David their king" (Hosea 3:5). Amen.[20]

Jewish feminists have used this imagery to restore and to build on women's traditions and rituals associated with the new moon. Many cultures associate the moon's monthly cycles with femininity. The tradition of the moon's diminution and its future restoration in the

55

world to come is explicitly understood by Rashi, the most famous of medieval Jewish exegetes, as a veiled reference to women. He says that in the world to come women will be renewed like the new moon.[21] It may be that the moon is a veiled reference to the feminine in the world or perhaps, as mystics might say, to the feminine face of God, the Shekhinah. This prayer chanted before a waxing moon imagines an increasing feminine light that will someday be restored to her full equality with the masculine light. Based on the sages' suggestion that God atones for diminishing the moon, Rabbi Isaac Luria assumes that if the diminishing of the moon (and the subjugation of Eve) for asking questions about power is a sin for which God atones monthly, then perhaps this is not the way things ought to be or will be. The disharmonies of the creation story are a work plan, a set of duties, the last act of which will include God's joyous restoration of the moon.

Quoted in the prayer, the Song of Songs is the evidence that the world of hierarchy and disharmony after the exile from Eden is not the world God wishes to enforce on us, but a world we are called on to transform back into Edenic bliss.

Song of Songs

The Song of Songs is the one book in the biblical canon that provides a nearly perfect portrayal of the garden of delights beyond the disharmonies of Genesis. According to tradition the song was written by King Solomon himself in the vigor of his youth. Both the male and the female lover is erotically idealized in the poem. It is quite amazing that the tradition posits that a man, the wisest of all men, Solomon, wrote these verses.

> Like an apple tree among the trees of the forest
> so is my beloved among the youths.
> I delight to sit in his shade
> and his fruit is sweet to my mouth,
> He brought me into the banquet room
> and his banner of love was over me.
>
> (2:3–4)
>
> My beloved is bright and ruddy,
> preeminent among ten thousand.

His head is like finest gold,
his locks are curled
and black as a raven.
His eyes are like doves
by the watercourses,
bathed in milk,
set by a brimming pool.
His cheeks are like beds of spices,
banks of perfume.
His lips are like lilies,
they drip with flowing myrrh.
His hands are rods of gold
studded with beryl,
his belly like a tablet of ivory
adorned with sapphires.
His legs are like marble pillars
set in sockets of fine gold.
He is majestic as Lebanon,
stately as the cedars.
His mouth is delicious
and all of him is delightful.

(5:10–16)

The sensuous poetry of the song is without parallel in the Hebrew Bible. While the verses quoted here are a rapture to a beautiful man, parallel verses just as stunning are found throughout the poem in praise of the female lover. The song flows smoothly through different voices: a narrator's voice, a woman's voice, the voice of a humble shepherdess in the fields, and a man's voice, that of an aristocrat in the court of King Solomon. While the poem is a celebration of heterosexual love, the reader is invited to take on both desires, to shift back and forth between the gazes of the lovers, swooning for a handsome man and then for a beautiful woman.

Phyllis Trible, in her illuminating book *God and the Rhetoric of Sexuality*, suggests that the Song of Songs is much more than a paean to romantic love. She shows how the book picks up where the Eden narrative ends, attempting to heal the very separations and conflicts that have exiled us from Paradise. While the song does not return us to the original garden, another garden of Eros is claimed in which all the disharmony, pain, and dislocation in the creation story give way to an even richer harmony, pleasure, and union.

When male and female first became one flesh in the Garden of Eden, their sexual union is briefly reported in Genesis 2:24. In the song the same union is enjoyed luxuriously as the lovers praise the pleasures of sexual intercourse. "My garden" becomes "his garden" in which he now pastures, gathering lilies. Possessive adjectives do not separate here. The female body of the lover is both hers and his, a garden of their shared delights. All the senses are engaged in this celebration. The senses that tempt Eve into disobedience in Genesis now saturate the poetry of love. Taste, smell, touch, sound, sight, and hearing all permeate this garden of delights.

Plants and animals, both part of the Edenic sin, are now on the poet's palate of joy. Trees of all sorts, flowers, and spices all adorn our lovers. On the pastures and hills grow lotuses and lilies, palms and cedars, mandrakes and fig trees, pomegranates and frankincense trees. There is no tree of prohibition. Friends are invited to eat and drink in the midst of unspoiled and unbounded beauty and harmony. The animal world adds motion and grace to our lovers. They are compared to gazelles, stags, goats, doves, and fawns. The couple traverses a landscape where lions, leopards, and foxes live but do not threaten. There is no treacherous serpent, no enmity between human civilization and the creeping creatures. The animal world shares in the celebration of Eros.

There is no distinction between work and play in the song. Daily bread is won without great toil. Even though forced to labor in the orchard, the woman associates her work with play. Motherhood is associated with punishing labor pangs in Genesis and with love and pleasure in the song. Erotic love separates families in Genesis and binds them together in the song. In Eden we are told a man must leave his parents' home in order to cleave to a woman; in the garden the woman is at the center of the action, bringing her lover into her mother's home, where they will make love in the chamber where she was conceived. The concerns are not tribal but relational. In the song the woman is never called wife. She is the beautiful Shulamit, the lover. The poem celebrates a world of harmony, a circle of love and relationship, nature and pleasure that heals Genesis of its wounds of separation and conflict.

The Song of Songs is indeed a remarkable book to find in Hebrew Scriptures. The sages of the second century hotly debated its merits for inclusion in the scriptural canon. The rabbinic paramour par excellence, Rabbi Akiva, came to its rescue. He said that all of the Torah is holy, but the Song of Songs is the Holy of Holies. The standard explanation is that the Song of Songs is one long, beautiful metaphor of the love between Israel and God. God is cast as the handsome male lover, and the lovely Shulamit is Israel. The whole poem is chanted by pious men on Friday afternoons before welcoming the Sabbath. This means that ordinary male Jews prepare for the coming of the Sabbath by singing a dramatic love song, casting themselves as a graceful and passionate young woman longing for her love and God as the dew-drenched young man, knocking on her door.

The Sabbath is twenty-five hours of messianic time, a virtual taste of Eden. Thus it makes perfect sense to think of the book as God's deepest desire, a Holy of Holies where life is healed of its damaging fractures. What better way to invite in the Sabbath bride than to sing of an Edenic kingdom where all the disharmonies of the world are resolved—where the earth yields her fruit freely, where work and play are one, where the two sexes, like the moon and the sun, are both equal and great, and where Eros is marked not by power or control, but by playful delight.

2

The Sons of God, Ham, and the Sodomites

Despite the fractures in creation and the problems of hierarchy, sex itself in the creation story appears as a great joy, a loving union. Adam and Eve in intercourse become one flesh in pleasure and fulfillment. At the moment of sexual union, in their joy and pleasure, they are as close to the original androgynous being, the perfect image of God, as they can become.

In contrast to sexual intercourse as the epitome of connection, we are introduced a few chapters later to sexual intercourse as the height of self-aggrandizement, power, and violence. The most famous of these texts in Genesis is the Sodom story. However, two earlier stories read obliquely by the rabbis speak to the issue of male homosexual relations. The first appears just before the flood story in Genesis 6:1–3 and the second just after the story of the flood in Genesis 9:20–22. These verses contain no explicit mention of homosexuality, but the rabbinic midrashic tradition commonly interpolates into the text to fill in narrative gaps and to harmonize conflicts. In Scripture vacancies are invitations to imagine.

The Sons of God

There is a bizarre record in the Book of Genesis of divine beings marrying human daughters that appears out of sync with the Hebrew Bible. Bible scholars have associated this strange story with the many similar pagan myths in Hurrian, Phoenician, and Greek sources. There are a number of traditional Jewish readings of this text, but the comments of Rabbi Shlomo ben Isaac, the most famous of medieval Jewish Bible exegetes, known by the acronym Rashi, will guide our reading.

> When men began to increase on earth and daughters were born to them the sons of God *(b'nei ha'elohim)* saw the daughters of men *(b'not ha'adam)* and how beautiful they were and they took women for themselves from among all they chose. (Gen. 6:1–3)

The language of *b'nei ha'elohim* poses a good deal of difficulty for Bible commentators. *Elohim* is the word for God in Genesis. Some interpretations associated the *b'nei ha'elohim* with fallen angels who allegedly came to earth and procreated with human women. But Rashi offers a very different portrayal of the sons of God and their dalliance with the daughters of men. Rashi suggests that the *b'nei ha'elohim* were not angels but the "sons of the princes and judges." When the young brides of the common men were adorned for their wedding day, the lords would steal then from their homes and "have intercourse with them first."[1]

Rashi seems to have read these biblical verses in light of a familiar European custom. Droit du seigneur was the right of noblemen to have sex with commoner brides on the eve of their weddings. The *b'nei ha'elohim* for Rashi were the young lords of the manor, arrogant and possessive, whose entitlement led them to take whatever they wanted. According to this custom every bride belonged first to the noble of the manor; by depriving couples of their first intimate union, the noble showed every husband the pitiful limits of his protective power. The only protective power was that of the lord. This custom was so common in Hungary that for a period of time the rabbis of Hungary required brides to shave off all their hair days before the wedding, so that they would be repellant to the nobles, who would otherwise ravish them.

Rashi interprets the last phrase of the verse, "from among all they chose," as a descent into depravity. Whetted with the power to get anything they desired, they eventually gave complete reign to their sexual conquests, seeking not only unfettered sexual union with unmarried brides, but with married women, men, and animals as well. While sexual union in the creation story appears as a great joy, here we discover that it can easily become entangled with power and violence.

Ham

Following the receding of the waters of the flood, the earth was desolate. Noah, a tiller of the soil, planted a vineyard.

> He drank of the wine and became drunk, and he uncovered himself within his tent. Ham, the father of Canaan, saw his father's nakedness and told his brothers outside. But Shem and Japheth took a cloth, placed against both their backs, and, walking backward, they covered their father's nakedness; their faces were turned the other way, so that they did not see their father's nakedness. When Noah awoke from his wine and learned what his youngest son had done to him, he said: "Cursed be Canaan; the lowest of slaves shall he be to his brothers." (Gen. 9:20–25)

From these verses we know only that Ham saw Noah drunk and naked and that his brothers, when they learned of the situation, entered backward into the tent and covered their father's nakedness. Ham's crime is so vague that commentators have no choice but to interpolate. According to Nahmanides, the medieval Spanish commentator, the story is about honor and shame between fathers and sons. Ham's accidental glimpse into his father's tent is not the crime. Ham's crime is taking pleasure in the sight of the father's drunken nakedness. He found the whole episode terribly funny. He ran to bring his older brothers to the tent so they, too, could gawk at their pathetic father. Noah was publicly embarrassed by Ham, derided and made sport of by a son duty bound to honor him. Shem and Japheth avoided looking at their father in this condition, and to protect him from the eyes of others, they covered him.

The text still does not make much sense. Why would nakedness in one's tent be so shaming anyway? Were Noah not drunk, would his naked body have drawn such attention, shame, excitement, horror? Even more confusing is Noah's curse. Why would enslavement be an appropriate punishment, and why is Canaan, Ham's son, cursed and not Ham? Something is missing. Here is what the sages add to the narrative.

> "And Ham saw": Rav and Shmuel (disagreed). One said he castrated him and the other said he raped him. The one who claims that he castrated him explains in this way: that Ham thus prevented

Noah from having a fourth son, which is why Ham's fourth son, Canaan, is cursed. The other claims by a comparison of expressions that he raped him. Here it is written, "And Ham, the father of Canaan, saw the nakedness of his father" and there (Gen. 34:2) "And Shechem, son of Hamor the Hivite, chief of the country, saw her (Dina) and took her and lay with her by force."[2]

The wild imagination of the rabbis here is shocking. Rashi quotes these two horrifying suggestions of rape and castration in his interpretation. Students of Rashi know that he does not employ this sort of legendary material in his commentary unless he finds that it solves problems intrinsic to the understanding of the text. Rashi cannot accept that Ham happened to see his father drunk and naked, that he found the sight amusing and told his brothers. Something central to the language of the narrative prevents Rashi from taking the text at face value.

When Noah awakened and described Ham's rather passive "seeing" of his nakedness as what his young son "did" to him, we are led to feel that something happened in the tent that has been covered up. It is for this reason that Rashi finds the midrash helpful. This "seeing" was more than meets the eye. It was the kind of seeing that is about violence and possession, about control and domination.

As the viceroy of Egypt, Joseph accused his brothers, who did not recognize him yet, of espionage, the kind of seeing that reveals the enemy's weaknesses, the sort of piercing stare that precedes attack. "And Joseph remembered the dreams he dreamt and said to them, 'You are spies! You have come to see the nakedness of the land!'" (Gen. 42:9). To see nakedness is to prepare to appropriate, to take by force, to enforce one's power.

Ham saw his father in a position of weakness, and this seeing became an opportunity to seize control by unmanning his father one way or another. How castration works is obvious. Castration is one way to deprive a man of all male privilege and power. Male rape is another way. Given a certain publicity, male rape conveys brutally and graphically who is in charge. Penetrative anal intercourse empowers the penetrator and humiliates the penetrated. This distinction between active and passive partners was a common cultural feature in the ancient world.

This reading of the midrash also solves one of the puzzles that confounded the biblical commentators. Why was Canaan punished for Ham's crime and why with servitude? Ham wished to seize the power of the father for himself. In replacing the father, he would be lord over his brothers. Instead, the horrific Oedipal crime brought in its wake the opposite. His children would serve the children of his brothers. While Canaan was particularly fit for cursing because of subsequent Israelite history, the rabbis associate all the children of Ham with the curse of Noah.[3]

Sodom

The story of Sodom and Gomorrah is surely the best known of the biblical texts used to condemn homosexuality. Preachers for over a millennium have employed it with dramatic effect to prohibit and to punish sex between men. The word *sodomy*, invented by an English churchman to describe male intercourse, helped to transform male sexual relations into an unparalleled evil. For generations men who were accused of sodomy were humiliated, persecuted, tortured, and put to gruesome death in imitation of the violent divine destruction of Sodom. American Puritans warned their flock of the doom that lay before them as a community if they would not stamp out the sodomites among them before it was too late. Why else would God order the most violent and spectacular punishment since the flood? Fire and brimstone falling from the sky are an inversion of hell. This blazing sulfuric furnace was thought to be the just and fair deserts for the debased men of Sodom and all who act like them. Today the men who carry placards reading "God hates fags" know this must be so by reading their Bible.

The details of the story in chapter 19 of Genesis are well known. God already knew that the cry from Sodom was great. He sent angels to investigate the gravity of the situation. Lot ushered the angelic guests into his house, knowing the dangers. After dinner the townsfolk clamored at the door for him to send out the guests "that they might know them." Lot offered his daughters to no avail. The replacement of the guests by virgin daughters is, no doubt, a horrific suggestion to contemporary sensibilities. Later we will explore a story in the Book of Judges that parallels this account in Genesis.

There it is made very clear what happens when a woman is actually substituted for the male visitor at the request of just such a crowd. Here, however, the mob wanted only the angelic male guests.

Despite the common perception that the sin of Sodom was rampant sexual vice, Jewish literature has largely rejected this reading. The prophet Ezekiel located the sin of Sodom in its inhospitality, its cruelty and perversion of justice, and not in its homosexuality. He described Sodom as arrogant and insensitive to human need. She and her daughters had plenty of bread and untroubled tranquility, yet she did not support the poor and the needy (Ezek. 16:49).

Among the early rabbinic commentators, the common reading of the sin of Sodom was its cruelty, arrogance, and disdain for the poor. The sages of the Babylonian Talmud also associated Sodom with the sins of pride, envy, cruelty to orphans, theft, murder, and perversion of justice.[4] While the event that sealed the fate of the Sodomites was their demand for Lot to bring out his guests so that the mob might "know" them, this still was seen not so much as sexual excess as hatred of the stranger and exploitation of the weak.[5] Midrashic writers lavishly portrayed Sodom and the surrounding cities as arrogant and self-satisfied, destroyed for the sins of greed and indifference to the poor.[6]

Rabbinic legends about Sodom describe an area of unusual natural resources, precious stones, silver, and gold. Every path in Sodom, say the sages, was lined with seven rows of fruit trees. Jealous of their great wealth and suspicious of outsiders' desires to share in it, the city's inhabitants agreed to overturn the ancient law of hospitality to wayfarers. The legislation later included the prohibition to give charity to anyone. One legend claims that when a beggar would wander into Sodom, the people would mark their names on their coins and give him a dinar. However, no one would sell him bread. When he perished of hunger, everyone would come and claim his coin. A maiden once secretly carried bread concealed in her water pitcher to a poor person in the street. After three days passed and the man didn't die, the maiden was discovered. They covered the girl with honey and put her atop the city walls. The bees came and ate her. Hers was the cry that came up to God, the cry that inaugurated the angelic visit and its consequences.[7]

Another famous rabbinic tale mirrors the Greek myth of Procrustes. Both the Jewish and the Greek story are about beds that invert the ethic of hospitality. The people of Sodom had a bed upon which weary guests might rest. However, when the wayfarer would lie down, they made sure that he fit the bed perfectly. A short man was stretched to fit it, and a tall man was cut to size.[8] Eliezer, Abraham's loyal servant, was once invited to lie on it, but he declined, claiming that since his mother died, he had pledged not to have a pleasant night's sleep on a comfortable bed.

In the Greek myth Procrustes (meaning "he who stretches") kept a house by the side of the road for passing strangers. He offered them a warm meal and a bed that always fit whoever lay on it. Once a guest was lying on it, Procrustes would likewise cut off the legs that were too long or stretch those too short. Theseus, the hero of the Greek tale, turns the tables on Procrustes and fatally adjusts him to his own bed.

The people of Sodom were not only protective of their wealth and punishing of acts of charity, they were also desperate to force everyone to fit a single measure. They had a well-to-do gated community that made sure no beggars disturbed their luxury and peace. They had zoned out poverty. But what made Sodom the "right" kind of neighborhood was that no difference was tolerated. "Our kind" of folk were welcomed and protected, and the rest were excluded or eliminated. It can hardly be incidental that the locus of this one-size-fits-all violence was a bed. How enormously potent is the portrayal of the evil of Sodom as a bed turned guillotine/rack. The place of sleep, comfort, and sexual pleasure in Sodom had been transformed into a place of threat and malice, a device of torture for strangers.

Eliezer saved himself from being amputated or stretched by mourning his mother. Mourning the dead is a particularly selfless expression of relationship and love. The people of Sodom treated all who were not inside the walls as already dead, and Eliezer treated the dead as still alive. Sodom was a place where compassion was punished brutally, as the story of the young maiden suggests. Eliezer was saved from Sodom's evil not by his sword or cunning, as was Theseus in the Greek myth, but by his own loving beyond all boundaries or benefit—by a loving that, like a mother's love, had no reasons.

The brutality of the Sodom story is redoubled in a similar narrative from the Book of Judges, only this time without the saving intervention of angels. Chapter 19 recounts that a Levite traveled to Bethlehem to win back his concubine, who had deserted him. At her father's house he tarried. Finally, he refused to stay any longer, and toward evening he left with his concubine. They reached Jebus (Jerusalem), but since that town was populated by non-Israelites, they continued to Gibeah. No one in Gibeah took them in until an old man met them and offered them lodging with him. Just as in Sodom, the men of the town gathered at the old man's house, pounded on the door, and demanded that he bring the visitor out that they might know him. However, this time there were no angels on hand to save the day. As the crowd began to threaten the old man, the Levite pushed his concubine out the door to them. The multitude assembled at the door "raped and abused her all night long until the morning" (Judg. 19:25).

There is no doubt here that the men gathered at the door were a violent crowd intending a sexual crime. According to historians and anthropologists, human societies at many times and in many regions have subjected strangers, newcomers, and trespassers to homosexual anal violation as away of reminding them of their subordinate status.[9] These scenes of group rape are about the fusion of sex and power as a single marker of hierarchy. What appeases the men in Gibeah is the option to humiliate the visitor by gang-raping his wife. Read as a commentary on the Sodom story, the Gibeah story demonstrates the intent of the mob at the door. When there are no saving angels, the fusion of sex and power leads not only to rape but also to murder.

The early church fathers, like the rabbis of their time, focused their attention on the sins of inhospitality, gluttony, or sloth rather than on homosexuality.[10] Origen, for example, writes: "Hear this, you who close your homes to guests! Hear this, you who shun the traveler as an enemy! Lot who lived among the Sodomites . . . escaped the fire on account of one thing only. He opened his home to guests. The angels entered the hospitable household; the flames entered only those homes closed to guests."[11]

There are a handful of texts that associate Sodom with general sexual immorality, and two that do so with specific reference to homosexuality, though even in these texts the theme of violence seems paramount. In Hellenistic apocryphal books, such as the *Epistle of Jude*, one finds references to a general sexual license in Sodom. Influenced as well by his Roman cultural surroundings, Josephus Flavius describes the angels visiting Lot as young men of extraordinary beauty, so much so, that the men of Sodom took up lodging with Lot in order "to enjoy these beautiful boys by force and violence."[12]

In the Tosefta, a third-century collection of rabbinic material, Sodom is made guilty of all three cardinal sins, murder, idolatry, and sexual immorality.[13] While this source might suggest that Sodom was a place of general sexual license, this trio of sins is a typology of evil for the rabbis rather than a textual interpretation.[14] Later in the middle ages the depiction of Sodom as a place of general sexual license appears in the *Midrash Tanhuma,* a tenth-century midrashic compilation.[15] Lot chose the plain of Sodom as a residence precisely because the Sodomites were sexually promiscuous. Lot's attraction to the sexual looseness of the city is proved by his willingness to offer his daughter to the crowd. "Ordinarily a father lays his life down to protect his daughters; this one gives them over to the mob to be sexually abused."[16]

I have found only one early rabbinic text that specifically refers to sex between men as among the crimes of the Sodomites. *Avot de-Rabbi Nathan* is an expansion and commentary on Mishnah Avot most probably written in the late second or early third century.[17] This commentary of Rabbi Nathan has been preserved in two manuscripts, one deriving from Babylonia and the other from the Land of Israel. In the Babylonian text there is no reference to homosexuality. In the Babylonian version the sins of Sodom were general sexual promiscuity, profanation of God's name, and the Sodomites hatred of one another. The version of the text edited in the Land of Israel lists two sins of the Sodomites, general sexual promiscuity and murder, and then as an addendum adds *mishkav zakhar,* sex between men, to the list. The difference between these two versions of *Avot de-Rabbi Nathan* offers us a unique opportunity to see how the cultural contexts shaped different portrayal's of Sodom's sin. Babylonia was largely unaffected by Roman culture and its institutionalized forms of same-sex male relations. It simply did not occur to the rabbis living in Babylon to identify Sodom with sex between men. However, the Jews living in the Land of Israel were under the political domination of Rome. In many Judean cities Jews lived side by side with pagan Romans and were forced to address Roman sexual mores, which included an acceptance of pederastic associations between adolescent boys and men.

This association of Sodom with sex between men, while virtually ignored by later commentators, does appear somewhat obliquely in the twelfth century in Italy. In one of the latest midrashic texts, the *Midrash Sekhel Tov* edited by Menahem ben Solomon, we find Lot's plea to the mob recast as a sermon. "Thus the Lord exhorted the sons of Noah saying, 'and a man shall cleave unto his wife and they shall be one flesh.' (Gen. 2:24). The verse says, 'unto his wife' and not unto a male because two males cannot become one flesh."[18] The author of this midrash is not cataloging the sins of Sodom as were the rabbis of the talmudic period. His problem is a different one. He wants to understand why, prior to the giving of the Torah, same-sex relations would be considered problematic, especially for non-Jews. In doing so he carries us back to the creation story. What interested Menahem ben Solomon was not the character of the people of Sodom but how a prohibition in Leviticus, yet to be revealed, related to non-Jews.

The Seven Laws of Noah

The Torah was given to the Jewish people and intended as a unique covenant with a unique people. While other traditions have taken the Hebrew Bible's revelation as a piece of their own sacred literature, Jews have understood its claim on them as exclusive. No one else is duty bound to keep the law. In the beginning of the covenantal journey in the Book of Genesis, Abraham is told that if chooses to leave Ur and follow God, he will become the father of a great people through whom "all the families of the earth shall be blessed" (Gen. 12:3). The mission of this people is to be a "light unto nations," not to impose its own unique covenant with God on them.[19] Non-Jews were explicitly not expected to fulfill all the demands of the Torah.

However, even if the Mosaic covenant was exclusive, goodness and righteousness surely were not. Even before the covenants with

Abraham and Moses, the Bible has a good deal to say about moral values. Eventually a tradition developed that prior to the covenants of Abraham and Moses, God had indeed made a covenant with the children of Noah. There were seven laws that the children of Noah had been given. While the list was not well defined initially, the rabbis of the Talmud eventually settled on the following seven: injunctions against idolatry, murder, sexual immorality (uncovering of nakedness), theft, blasphemy, and cruelty to animals (tearing off an animal's limb to eat while the animal is still alive), and the duty to set up just courts of law.[20]

The reference to "uncovering nakedness" is vague. Some rabbis have interpreted the violation as incest because the "uncovering of nakedness" appears specifically in the context of incest violations. However, others have translated the term as "sexual immorality" in general in order to include adultery and male-male intercourse. It was assumed, at least by later sages, that in addition to incest, both adultery and *mishkav zakhar,* male-male intercourse, were among the sexual prohibitions enjoined upon the sons of Noah. The *Midrash Sekhel Tov* discovers *mishkav zakhar* in the Genesis narratives, and the *Midrash Yalkut Shimoni* discovers it in a passage from the Book of Ezekiel.[21]

While the medieval Jewish commentators surely knew of these few sources, they ignored them in favor of the dominant rabbinic approach to Sodom. Rabbi Moshe ben Nahman of the twelfth and thirteenth centuries (known by the acronym RaMBaN) could not have been clearer in his association of Sodom with human cold-heartedness and cruelty. He adds that such base qualities bear dangerous consequences, especially for those who dwell in the Land of Israel.

> Their intention was to prevent people from traveling through their territory . . . because they thought that since the land is beautiful, like a heavenly garden, many will come (to live there) and they despised charity. Lot, however, was wealthy, so they accepted him when he came to them and requested residence among them, and perhaps they received him out of honor to Abraham. . . . According to our sages they [the people of Sodom] had every bad quality, but their judgment was sealed on this sin because they did not strengthen the hand of the poor and downtrodden, and they were consistent in this sin more than others. As well, every other nation

in the world extends kindness to neighbors and to the poor, so, [in contrast,] there was not among all the peoples any that compared to Sodom in cruelty. . . . Know that the judgment of Sodom is an expression of the greatness of the Land of Israel; since Israel is the inheritance of God, it does not suffer men of hateful deeds (*anshei toevot* from the Hebrew word *toevah*, abomination). Since the land [in the future after Israel settles it] will completely throw out people because of their abominations, it already vomited out this nation because they were more evil than any other, both to heaven and to people.[22]

Perhaps the most telling demonstration of the dominant rabbinic view is how the Sodom story was translated directly into law, not in relation to sexual vice but in relation to possessiveness and callous indifference. From their conceptual understanding of Sodom the sages of the Talmud developed the legal category of *middat Sedom,* meaning Sodomite character or conduct. Someone who refuses to offer help to another in need when the generosity costs him nothing is, in halakhic terms, behaving like a Sodomite. A man, for example, who owns a property that is vacant and unused and who denies another person temporary use of it, even though such use costs the owner nothing, is a Sodomite. This rule was strong enough to provide the court with the prerogative to force a person to benefit others when it causes him no loss.[23] The Jewish court is empowered to enforce such a costless generosity on an individual in order to ensure that no Jewish community becomes like Sodom.

Given the evidence, it would appear that the predominate Jewish reading of Sodom does not portray it as a place of homosexual license. In the few sources where male homosexual relations do appear, they are part of a depiction of exploitation, violence, selfishness, and cruelty. Where there was no such social referent, the sin of Sodom was universally understood as inhospitality.

Following this interpretation of Sodom as a place of inhospitality, a contemporary Bible scholar, Derrick Sherwin Bailey, has suggested that even the request of the townspeople to "send the guests out so that we may know them" is ambiguous enough to cast doubt on the sexual nature of their intentions. According to Bailey, Lot had violated the norm of the place by inviting in strangers without permission of the city's elders. What the crowd is demanding at the door is simply that the guests be brought outside so that the townsfolk "might know" who they were. The crowd had gathered to challenge Lot's right to invite strangers to his home without getting approval first. This, Bailey suggests, demonstrates that the sin of Sodom was one of inhospitality rather than sexual immorality.[24]

Bailey has a hard time explaining Lot's offer of his virgin daughters. He claims that "the surrender of the daughters was simply the most tempting bribe Lot could offer on the spur of the moment to appease the hostile crowd." Trying to square the representations of Sodom as a place of inhospitality with the overt sexual threats of the crowd, Bailey fails to make the connection between forced intercourse and Lot's violation of the city's rule of refusing entry to wayfarers. Both are ruptures of boundaries, the former of the body and the latter of the body politic, the city. The clamor of the crowd is motivated, not by sexual desire per se, but by a cruel measure-for-measure retaliation that one who breaches the city's armor is himself breached.

In order to read this story as a story of inhospitality one must think about homosexuality in terms very different from our own. We associate men who engage in anal intercourse with a certain set of erotic desires. But there is nothing in the story about sexual desire. The story is about a city that wants to discourage brotherly care when it comes to outsiders. Newcomers with wealth, like Lot, may be admitted. But transient strangers are not welcomed, and the poor are utterly shunned. Outsiders who have availed themselves of the city's shelter unlawfully and those members of the community who have broken the rules of membership by welcoming such strangers are threatened with rape, not as a sexual act, but as a means of brutal humiliation and punishment. This is what the Sodomites mean when, after Lot refuses to hand over his guests, they say, "The one who came as a stranger is going to tell us what is right and wrong!"[25]

Sodom is not a place of promiscuity, or if it is, that problem is not the one that most concerns God. It is a place where the citizens, like a band of thieves, have made a pact not to prey on one another in order to permit themselves to prey openly on outsiders. Abrahamic sociality treats all passersby as brothers. Welcoming the traveling stranger into one's home is the proof of the brotherhood of all and the root of civilization. By replacing predation with cooperation and care, people build trust in one another and learn to work together. Sodomic sociality is not brotherhood narrowed to the group, but selfishness expanded outward to include the citizens of a city. While it may claim only to prey on outsiders, because its very root is fear and hatred and not love, eventually it preys on itself.

It is important to remember that Lot's social contract prioritized his male guests over his daughters. Lot translated Abraham's ethic of brotherhood in bluntly patriarchal ways. For Lot the rule of no predation between men (all men are brothers) did not exclude male predation of women. Lot revealed in the offer of his daughters to the crowd how much he had learned from his neighbors. The Sodomites marked "us and them" along territorial lines. Lot seems to have expanded the territory of filial duty to include all men but having done so, redrew the line between the genders.

In a prophecy of doom Ezekiel compared Jerusalem to Sodom and claimed that Jerusalem had become worse.[26] It is not sexual desire that brings down divine wrath, but the absence of human relatedness. By Ezekiel's time Sodom was a city of example, the epitome of a society without empathy, a city of wolves.

So where is Sodom? In the language of Ezekiel, Sodom is anywhere there is arrogance and greed resulting in the abandonment of the poor and the needy. In the language of the rabbis, Sodom is where sexual acts are tools of cruel domination and hierarchy, where beds for wayfarers are devices of torture designed to eradicate human difference, where compassion and love are made illegal and those who cross the lines are murdered . . . there is Sodom.

3

Leviticus

Ever since I began to quietly self-acknowledge my homosexuality, I cringed to hear my shame read aloud on the Day of Atonement. The afternoon service of Yom Kippur includes reading aloud the portion from Leviticus 18 delineating the sexual prohibitions, among them the stark prohibition against sexual relations between men.

My emotions accompanying the reading have changed through the years. At first, I felt guilt and contrition. Later, I felt a deep sadness for being caught up in gay desire, and I would petition heaven for understanding. After the reading, I would sob in my corner seat of the shul, acknowledging the pain of those verses on my body and spirit. I have tried to connect myself with Jews of countless ages, listening in shul to their deepest feelings of love and desire turned abhorrent, ugly, and sinful. Finally, listening has become, in addition to all else I might feel, a protest.

I have never missed the afternoon service on Yom Kippur. Never did I leave the synagogue to avoid this gut-wrenching reading. It never dawned on me to walk out. Over the years I developed a personal custom of standing up during the reading. Because I have always spent Yom Kippur in the seriously prayerful Orthodox environments where tears are common enough, no one ever took much notice when, wrapped in my kittel (a white cotton robe worn all day Yom Kippur and in which pious Jews are buried when they die) and with my tallit (prayer shawl) over my head, I stood up for a single portion of the Torah reading and sobbed. In time, as my self-acceptance grew, the tears stopped, and in their place was a stoic rising to my feet to hear the unfair accusations of a heavenly court against me.

On Yom Kippur 1996 I took my submission/protest one step further. I decided that it was not enough to stand up. I wanted to have the aliyah (to be called up to the Torah) for the reading of those very verses. I arranged with the shammes that I would have the proper aliyah, and when it was time, I went up the bimah in the center of the shul. My heart was pounding as I climbed the steps to the table where the scroll is read. I felt as if I were standing on top of a mountain in a thunderstorm. My head was swirling as I looked out at the congregation seated around me. The men standing on each side of me at the podium were intent on their jobs, oblivious to me. Before me was the scroll.

It is hard to express the feeling of standing before an open Torah scroll. The Torah scroll possesses the highest level of sanctity of any object in a synagogue. If it is dropped, the whole congregation must fast. To stand there before the scroll as it is rolled open is both intensely intimate and public. I have studied this scroll for years. On Simchat Torah I have danced with it. I kiss it weekly as it passes through the congregation on Shabbat. The plaintive and magisterial melody of the reading on Yom Kippur is both ominous and comforting. I say the blessing, the scroll is rolled opened, and I feel as if my arms too have been rolled aside and my heart is exposed.

I hold on to one of the handles of the scroll for balance. I am surprised to find the words ominously poetic. Thou shalt not uncover the nakedness of thy father's wife, the nakedness of thy sister, the nakedness of thy daughter-in-law. And then it comes. "Thou shalt not lie with a male as one lies with a woman, it is an abomination." To my surprise, when it is read, I no longer feel pain or threat or even accusation. I feel strangely empowered. In exposing myself to this verse, it has become exposed to me. At that moment I grasped that this verse has, in a sense, never been understood. Until those whose bodies and souls have been tormented by it, who have suffered for years under its weight, are among its legitimate interpreters, how could it possibly give over its full meaning?

We have arrived at the threshold of the text that, perhaps more than any other, has defined attitudes toward same-sex sexual relations in Western society. Our presence here may seem to many like a masochistic exercise. The Leviticus text is no longer read on Yom Kippur in most gay synagogues for this reason. But while I do not wish to minimize the pain of the thousands before us who were tormented by these bits of ink and parchment, I believe these words to be a site of reckoning and of potential redemption. The Hebrew name of the Book of Leviticus, Vayikra, roughly meaning, "And the Lord called." So, let us imagine that we are now all called upon to stand before the open scroll, to read, and to be read.

Introduction to the Book of Leviticus

The Book of Leviticus lacks the narrative sweep of the other books of the Bible. It is primarily a law book—indeed, the sages call it *Torat Kohanim,* the priest's handbook. Throughout the Middle Ages and still today in very pious communities, children begin their study of Torah with Leviticus. As odd as this curricular decision might sound to contemporary ears, Leviticus was thought to be the perfect beginner's introduction. The book contains the largest collection of core Jewish ideas and more laws than any other book of the Torah. The middle book of the Hebrew Bible, it was considered both a literary and a philosophical fulcrum of Jewish faith. In the middle of this middle book is chapter 19, the holiness code, beginning with what may be the organizing theology of the Torah itself: "You shall be holy for I the Lord your God am Holy."

The midrash explains the curricular decision with a jarring comparison. "Let the pure (children) come and study the pure (rules of sacrificial purity)."[1] Children have no sin; sacrificial lambs have no blemish. The comparison evokes the story of the binding of Isaac, child of Abraham and Sarah, replaced on the altar by a ram caught in a thicket by its horns. Since the end of sacrificial worship in Jerusalem, the study of the Torah (and Leviticus in particular) and daily prayer have stood in place of blood expiation on the altar. The succession of replacements moves from Isaac, to a ram, to Temple sacrifice, to the study of Leviticus. It appears that teaching a child Leviticus, for the sages, is a repetition of the saving of Isaac, who was replaced by a ram, which was replaced again by a retelling of the story. The first words of Torah taught a child are perhaps then a ritual of protection.

The Book of Leviticus expresses another kind of protection as well. Following Exodus as it does, Leviticus is the culmination of redemption. God has redeemed his people from Egypt by signs and mighty wonders and has revealed his Law to them at Mount Sinai. At the end of the Book of Exodus, God bestows on his people a miraculous in-dwelling of the divine presence in the finished tabernacle. The Book of Exodus essentially ends with these words: "When Moses had finished the work, the cloud covered the Tent of Meeting, and the Presence of the Lord filled the Tabernacle" (Exod. 40: 33b–34). The achievement of a human society in which God's presence can dwell is presented as the fulfillment of the creation itself, a retroactive justification of the divine initiative to create humanity.

However, nothing is more fragile than human achievement. The success of the project easily becomes a primary anxiety. God's presence among the people would need to be secured with a careful attention to purity of heart, mind, and body. The Book of Leviticus immediately follows the achievement of human-divine intimacy at the end of Exodus with instructions about the various sacrifices and rules necessary to ensure God's constant nearness to them. The book is concerned with preserving the purity of the people because the Land of Israel spews out those who defile her, as it spewed out the Canaanites.[2] God does not tolerate impurity, injustice, and immorality among the chosen people and in the Promised Land. The difficulty with this formulation is not the demand for virtue and justice, but their relationship to the body. Just what is impurity?

The Body

The body is central to the moral map Leviticus spreads out over society. Our lives revolve around the vulnerabilities of the body, its pains and travails, its satisfactions and pleasures. For Leviticus being is always embodied being. Consequently there are no sharp distinctions between ethics and physical purity. The separation between the life of the body and the life of the spirit is a task that Christianity carried forward from the Greeks.[3] For ancient Israel everything was related. So, in chapter 19, the central chapter of Leviticus, the concerns range from justice in the courts to not eating the fruit of trees until after their third year of growth, from universal concerns like loving your neighbor as yourself to ritual concerns like not weaving wool and linen together and not consuming blood. Juxtapositions appear haphazard. The prohibition against giving one's daughter over to harlotry is cited directly before the command to honor the Sabbath. The mix of concerns, the breadth of contexts, and the repetition of "I am the Lord" following nearly every paragraph communicate that God's concern is for the totality of human existence, body and spirit, self and community. From eating to work, from sex to speech, life is overfilled with meaning. The values embodied in Leviticus, for all their strangeness to our contemporary ears, are supremely Jewish. We are, in the words of Sander Gilman, a people of the body.

The prohibition of male homosexual relations is found in chapters 18 and 20 of Leviticus amid other laws of sexual morality. I will begin the task of making sense of the verses in question and their context here and continue in later chapters of the book. Before we embark on the reading, however, it is important to add a very Jewish caveat. While the tradition refused to relegate scriptural passages into a distant and irrelevant past, it also refused to read the Torah as if it meant and has always meant only one thing. The Torah is black fire upon white fire, which bears specific and different meanings depending on the living-reading-observing community. In the first century the schools of Hillel and Shammai differed greatly on many issues and often had completely opposing interpretations. The rabbis claimed that "both these and those are the words of the living God."[4] If two opposing understandings of Scripture can both be the word of God, there must be no final reading of any verse. All verses in the Torah are pregnant with multiple meanings, some on the surface, others more deeply hidden, and some yet unborn.

Traditional reading demands that one approach the verses in Leviticus as covenantal duty. That we ought to be committed in advance of our reading to uphold the verses in question is not to say that we know in advance what they actually forbid or require us to do. Even though they may have meant something particular in the past, they also speak today. As the psalmist teaches, the Torah is given "today—if you will hearken to his voice" (Ps. 95:7).

Exegesis

Those unfamiliar with Jewish reading of Scripture may find the barrage of questions that follow most unusual. Questions are a hallmark of Jewish spirituality. They are a great cultural paradox in that they both destabilize and secure social norms. Questions tend to spread power around; they are a democratizing force. Comfort with questions conveys a fundamental trust in the good sense of people and particularly in the goodwill of governing authorities. Autocrats hate questions. We train children at the Passover seder to ask why because tyrants are undone and liberty is won with a good question.

It is for this reason that God loves it when we ask why. We celebrate challenging the Torah to make sense and above all to be a defensible expression of divine goodness. When we ask good questions, the Torah is given anew on Sinai at that very moment. As we read the verses from Leviticus, let us make no assumptions in advance in regard to their meaning. Later we will need to engage in a fuller analysis of these verses from the vantage point of their possible purposes. For now let us read as if the Torah were given today.

A review of the whole of chapters 18 and 20 will be helpful before embarking on this task. Be aware that I have translated those verses holding more closely to the original Hebrew than most standard English translations. I have done so in order to give a full sense of the possibilities within the Hebrew text.

> And with a male you shall not lie the lyings of a woman: it is a *toevah*. (Lev. 18:22)

The verse is full of puzzles. First, what does "the lyings of a woman" mean? Second, why is the phrase necessary at all? The verse might have very simply read, "You shall not lie with a man." Third, what does *toevah* mean, and what does it add? It is often translated as "abomination," but what is meant in the Hebrew is not so clear. At the end of chapter 18 all the prohibitions of the chapter are lumped together and called the *toevot* of the inhabitants of Canaan on account of which the land spewed them out. If they are all considered *toevot,* why then is male-male sex specifically called *toevah?*

The Lyings of a Woman

The meaning of this phrase is difficult to decipher because this language does not occur in any other context of the Bible. While in no other place do we read of the "lyings of a woman," a parallel phrase sheds some light. The phrase "the lying of a male" *(mishkav zakhar)* is found in the Book of Numbers. Women who know the "lying of a male" are experienced in intercourse. The "lying of a male" is apparently what a woman experiences in intercourse, that is, the penetration of the vagina.[5] If this phrase is the reverse of our phrase in Leviticus, then we have found a possible meaning. The "lyings of a woman" *(mishkeve ishah)* would mean what a man experiences in intercourse with a woman, that is, the engulfment of the penis. Men then commonly know the "lyings of a woman" *(mishkeve ishah),* and women the "lyings of men" *(mishkeve zakhar).*[6] Consequently the verse reads, "And you shall not lie with a male in the way you lie with a woman," that is, in a way that involves the engulfment of the penis in penetrative intercourse.

But if so, then might not the modifying phrase seem redundant? In other words, why isn't "you shall not lie with a man" sufficient to convey the prohibition of male-male sexual intercourse? Why must the text tell us that lying with a man means inserting a penis into his body as one does with a woman? Is not that conveyed by the word *lie?*

Just as in English the verb *to lie* is used quite straightforwardly to mean "reclining, lying down, or sleeping." However, while *shokhev* can mean "to lie down," when it takes a direct object, as in this verse, it has a meaning similar to the English of "bedding" someone. It may be that the Torah wishes to make perfectly clear that it is not referring to two men reclining on the same couch or sleeping in the same bed. The unusual nature of the context perhaps forces the text to make it perfectly clear that it is speaking of an act of sexual penetration. A man generally experiences the lyings of a woman (engulfment of his penis) with a woman. By describing male-male sexual intercourse as the "lyings of a woman with a man," the verse sharpens the sense of gender substitution. A male subject must not do to another male an act ordinarily done to a female.

The verb may well be related to the Hebrew word *shekhovet,* "seminal emission," or as biblical scholar Jacob Milgrom has suggested, "penis."[7] If so, then the verb is clearly describing active penetration. While the common understanding of the verse "Thou shall not lie with a male as one lies with a woman" has been taken to refer to both active and passive partners, given the meanings of *shokhev,* it would appear that the verse directly refers only to the active partner engulfing his penis in the body of another man.

According to this analysis the verse prohibits one, and only one, sexual practice between men, namely, anal intercourse, and speaks specifically to the active partner. There is no mention of any other behavior that this verse would prohibit.[8]

Abomination

The remaining philological problem is the word toevah, usually translated as "abomination." The word in the Hebrew Bible is used in different contexts to mean different things. It appears first in Genesis when Joseph invites his brothers to dine with him, and we are told that the Egyptians do not eat with Hebrews because doing so is hateful *(toevah)* to them.[9] It is clear from this context that the idea of *toevah* is not unique to Hebrews. Every people has its own list of things that it finds contaminating or distasteful.

In the Book of Exodus Moses tries to persuade Pharaoh to permit the Hebrews to travel three days from Ramses to celebrate their sacrificial holiday in the desert. "If we sacrifice the *toevah* of the Egyptians before their eyes (in Ramses) will they not stone us?"[10] Here the word *toevah* refers either to the sheep, which may have been hateful to Egyptians (we already know from Gen. 46:34 that the Egyptians despised shepherds), or to the slaughter of a sheep that may have been an Egyptian sacred animal, which would be a hateful thing to do.

In various books of the Bible, food prohibitions, idolatrous practices, magic, sexual offenses, and ethical violations are all described as *toevah.*[11] The unifying concept common to all the various uses might convey the idea of offensiveness. A *toevah* is something that offends the accepted order, ritual or moral.[12] The verb form of the word is synonymous with *hate* or *abhor*. In some contexts the meaning of the word is closer to moral indignation, in others to a visceral disgust, and in yet others to mere social rejection. *Toevah* has a much stronger meaning when the behavior in question is not just hateful but specifically hateful to God.[13] That which God finds offensive is not merely a matter of taste.

The sense of the verse ought now to be relatively clear.

ve'et zakhar	And a male
lo tishkav	you shall not bed (sexually penetrate)
mishkeve ishah	(engulfing one's penis) as in the lyings of a woman
toevah hi	it is abhorrent

Biblical law required the death penalty for two men caught engaging in anal intercourse when observed by two eyewitnesses. We have no way of knowing if a Jewish court in biblical or rabbinic times ever punished two men with the death penalty. Jewish courts lost their power to apply capital punishment after their loss of sovereignty. In practice, for the sages, the death penalty was a didactic matter. Following the destruction of Jerusalem, there is no record of anyone ever receiving such a punishment at the hands of any Jewish court for a sexual crime.

In one instance the Talmud reports the accidental discovery of two men engaged in sexual relations by a well-known third-century rabbi, Rabbi Yuda ben Pazi. Rabbi "Yuda ben Pazi once went up to the attic in the study hall and saw two men having intercourse. They said to him, 'Rabbi, make note that you are one and we are two.'"[14] This audacious source tells us that when it came to prosecuting sex crimes, the likelihood of two kosher witnesses (family members were not acceptable witnesses) able and willing to testify that they saw two people in the midst of an illicit sexual act was nil.

As unlikely as prosecution may have been, the punishments for sexual violations are amply prescribed in chapter 20 of Leviticus. The punishment for male-male intercourse is listed among them. "If a man lies with a male the lyings of a woman, the two of them have done an abhorrent thing; they shall be put to death—their bloodguilt is upon them" (Lev. 20:13).

The most interesting discrepancy between the two verses is that in chapter 18 only the penetrating party is addressed, while in chapter 20 both the parties are addressed. The sages found this inconsistency troubling. How is it that a punishable crime in chapter 20 has no warning in chapter 18? While this may seem like a technical question, it will prove to be important in understanding the concerns of Leviticus.

To summarize, in chapter 18 one finds the prohibitions and in 20 a review of the same prohibitions (more or less) along with their punishments. The verse in chapter 18 prohibits the active but not the passive party in a consensual sexual engagement. The verse in chapter 20 adds that both parties have committed a *toevah* and are liable for punishment. So the question is: How can the text punish in chapter 20 what it had not prohibited in chapter 18?

According to Rabbi Ishmael in the Talmud, the prohibition in regard to receptive sexual intercourse is found in another verse in Deuteronomy.[15] "No Israelite woman shall be a female prostitute *(k'deshah),* nor shall any Israelite man be a male prostitute *(kadesh)*" (Deut. 23:18). The word *k'deshah* appears in other places in the Bible in reference to a prostitute who camps by the intersection of roads to attract her johns (Gen. 38:21). According to R. Ishmael, both words, *kadesh* and *k'deshah,* refer to pagan cult prostitution, in which both men and women would be available to male celebrants for ritual sexual relations.

R. Ishmael cites another verse that helps to make his case. In the first Book of Kings, we read that during the reign of Rehoboam in Jerusalem "they built for themselves shrines, pillars, and sacred posts on every high hill and under every leafy tree and there was also a *kadesh* in the land, so they were imitating all the *toevot* of the nations that the Lord had dispossessed before the children of Israel" (1 Kings 14:23–24). R. Ishmael understands male-male intercourse from Leviticus to be the epitome of *toevah.* Thus, when the verse says that a *kadesh* was living in the land and directly afterward we hear of *toevot,* we should be in no doubt as to what the *kadesh* was doing. In any case male prostitutes, according to this view, would be specifically employed, as are female prostitutes, to serve in a receptive capacity.[16]

This reading of the prohibition suggests that male intercourse was directly associated with pagan religion. While the claim has its merits, recent research has raised serious doubt about the practice of cult prostitution in Near Eastern religion. Even if such sexual rites did occasionally occur, historically speaking, there is no evidence that male prostitutes were available for homosexual intercourse. Since cult prostitution was primarily a fertility rite, it seems more likely that such prostitution would have been heterosexual.[17]

Rabbi Akiva differs with Rabbi Ishmael. He finds a way to read the single verb *tishkav* in Leviticus chapter 18 in two ways. In Hebrew the active and passive forms of the same verb can sometimes be written using the same consonants. In this case, *lo tishkav,* the active form of "you shall not lie (sexually penetrate)," can be vocalized as *lo tishakhev,* meaning "you shall not be laid (sexually penetrated)." Since the sentence reads perfectly well with either vocalization, Rabbi Akiva concludes that both are included in the prohibition.[18]

This rabbinic exploration into active and passive sexual roles offers an interesting and important insight. The verse in Leviticus according to both R. Ishmael and R. Akiva is about active, rather than passive, partners. In other words, the central prohibition–the one concerning which there is no doubt—is that of penetration. The receptive party's guilt is interpolated into the prohibition in one way or another, but he is not the main focus of the interdiction. This is particularly remarkable because in many societies men who penetrate other men are not considered deviant. It is receptive men who violate the given social order by playing a woman's role in sexual intercourse. Whatever the reason or reasons that undergird the prohibition in Leviticus, the text appears to be concerned primarily with the man on top, the penetrating partner, and only in a derivative fashion with the receptive partner.

Early Christian law emphasized the receptive partner. The New Testament takes its language directly from Greek sexual typologies. There were *arsenokoitai,* who enjoyed penetrating their male sexual partners, and *malakoi,* who enjoyed being penetrated by others.[19] Soon after the Roman Empire became Christian in 313 C.E., those convicted of sodomy were burned at the stake. For more than two hundred years only the passive, penetrated partner of a couple engaging in homosexual intercourse was put to death. By 533 C.E., the active penetrating partner was added to the statute and if convicted also suffered the death penalty.[20]

So far, then, we have a law prohibiting a man from sexually penetrating (or being penetrated by) another man anally. This interpretation of the verse results in a number of surprising conclusions. First, there are a variety of ways that men can pleasure each other sexually. If the prohibition is defined by anal penetration, then a whole array of sexual engagements between two men, ranging from kissing onward, would not be formally prohibited. Second, the centrality of the penetrating party in Leviticus portrays a very different set of cultural prohibitions than have been normative in other societies. Third, homosexuality, that is, same-sex emotional and physical desire, is not prohibited in Scripture. Actions are prohibited, not psychological states or sexual desires. Fourth, there is an enormous omission in the text: the Torah does not prohibit lesbian relationships.

Regarding the latter, the rabbis of antiquity were aware of such relationships, and while they could find no specific scriptural prohibition, they did prohibit such contact between women on the level of rabbinic enactment. If Scripture did not bother to prohibit such relations, why did the rabbis invent a prohibition of their own? The next chapter will address this biblical silence and the rabbinic effort to find nonetheless some direction on the matter from within the Torah.

4

Lesbian Omissions

Unlike its very strong reference to sex between men, the Torah gives no hint anywhere that sex between women is a particular problem. The absence of any attention to lesbian relations is not because what females did was inconsequential per se. Concerning bestiality, for example, the text very clearly states both what men and what women are forbidden to do with animals.[1] It appears that the silence on lesbian sex is more basic. Lesbian sex simply does not include a penis, and only sexual acts involving penile penetration were under the legislative scrutiny of the Torah.

While lesbian sexual relations are missing in the Torah, they do appear, if rather obliquely, in the Talmud. In the absence of a scriptural prohibition the rabbis explored the meaning of sexual contact between women in the context of the sexual propriety of Temple priests.

Priests in ancient Israel were subject to a host of extraordinary demands placed upon them in light of their sacred role in Temple service. Among the laws unique to priests is one limiting their choice of marriage partners. Leviticus 21:7 tells us that a priest may not marry a woman who is a *zonah*, literally meaning a prostitute. Despite the apparent clarity, there were multiple rabbinic traditions in regard to the treatment of the *zonah*. While Rabbi Akiva did indeed read *zonah* as a prostitute, Rabbi Eliezer defined the term more widely, to include a single woman who had premarital sexual relations. According to Rabbi Eleazar, a woman who had a single encounter with an unmarried man would afterward be disqualified from marrying

86

a priest. Despite the fact that Rabbi Eliezer's opinion in regard to heterosexual promiscuity and the priesthood was ultimately rejected by his colleagues, his view of lesbian relations determines the law in the case below.[2]

> Rav Huna said: Women who rub against each other *(nashim hamesolelot)* are prohibited to marry a priest. And even according to R. Eliezer, who says that when a single man has intercourse with a single woman she becomes a *zonah* (who is no longer fit to marry a priest), that is true when the premarital sex was with a man, but sex with a woman is mere indecency. (BT Yevamot 76a)

Rav Huna tells us that *nashim hamesolelot,* women who "rub their sexual organs against each other," have engaged in a form of sexual promiscuity and so are disqualified from marrying a priest.[3] R. Eliezer does not agree with R. Huna's stringency. According to R. Eliezer "rubbing" with a woman is mere indecency, and while not praiseworthy, it does not render a woman unfit to marry a priest. The law is decided against R. Huna that lesbian relations are "mere indecency."

R. Huna might have gotten some support for his position that lesbian sex is indeed considered sufficient to disqualify marriage to a priest from another source. In Shabbat 65a we are told that, Rabbi Abba ben Abba, commonly referred to in the Babylonian Talmud as the father of Shmuel (Abbahu d'Shmuel), would not let his two daughters sleep next to each other. Since we are not provided with an explanation, the Talmud attempts to interpolate Abbahu d'Shmuel's reasoning.

> Abbahu d'Shmuel . . . did not let permit [his daughters] to lie down together. Might this be a support for R. Huna, who says that women who rub with each other are disqualified for the priesthood [i.e., marriage to a priest]? No. He held that they should not become accustomed to [sleeping with] an alien body.[4]

Unsure of Abbahu's rationale for not allowing his daughters to sleep together in the same bed, the Talmud offers two possibilities. The first is that he agrees with R. Huna that "rubbing" would disqualify them both for marriage to a priest.[5] R. Abbahu was from a prestigious family of priests, so this suggestion would not seem wholly unfounded. However, the Talmud offers another, more plausible explanation. Abbahu d'Shmuel wasn't concerned that his daughters would engage in sexual behavior with each other. He was worried that the comfort of sleeping next to a warm body would bring them to desire a man and so they would be easily seduced.

From these two halakhic sources it would appear that lesbian sexual relations are indecent but do not constitute a punishable violation of either biblical or rabbinic law. Since there is no other classical rabbinic source on the issue of lesbian sexual relations, it would seem that the law should be clear.

This would have likely been the case had it not been for a single midrashic text and a medieval commentary that put it to unprecedented use. Leviticus 18, the chapter that delineates the sexual violations and proscribes intercourse between men, begins with an exhortation not to copy the customs of the surrounding pagans. The text and its commentary follow:

> You shall not copy the practices of the land of Egypt, where you dwelt, or of the land of Canaan, to which I am bringing you. You shall not follow their laws. My regulations you are to do, my laws you are to keep by following them; I am YHVH your God. (Lev. 18:3–4)

> "You shall not copy the practices of the land of Egypt . . ." Can it be that they [the Israelites] must not build buildings or plant crops like they [the Egyptians or Canaanites] do? The Torah teaches . . . "You shall not follow their laws," this means only the practices that were given legal force from the time of their fathers and their fathers' fathers. What would they do? A man would marry a man, a woman a woman, a man would marry a woman and her daughter, and a woman would be married to two men. It is about these customs that it is added, "in their statutes you shall not go."[6]

This text from the *Sifra,* the Midrash-Halakhah on the book of Leviticus, says nothing concerning sexual relationships between two women per se. It speaks only about marital unions.[7] Whatever import this text may have in regard to contemporary same-sex marriage, it would appear to say nothing in particular about the sexual relations themselves. This would have likely been the standard ruling had it not been for the medieval philosopher and halakhist Maimonides.

Maimonides integrates the two sources cited earlier (Yevamot and the *Sifra*), and reads the practice of "women who rub" against each other as an example of "the ways of Egypt." In doing this he has categorized lesbian sex as a violation of biblical weight. While little in the rabbinic material invites such an expanded reading, this view was carried into the succeeding codes of Jewish law.[8] The following is the full text from Maimonides' Code of Law.

> It is forbidden for women to rub against each other; it is among the "ways of the Egyptians," about which we were warned in Leviticus 18:3 and about which our sages expounded, "What would they (the Egyptians) do? A man would marry a man, a woman would marry a woman, and one woman would marry two men. While the behavior is prohibited, one does not punish it with lashes because no specific biblical prohibition has been violated and no sexual intercourse took place at all. Consequently, such women are not prohibited from marrying a priest because of looseness, and neither is a [married] women prohibited from remaining with her husband [after a same-sex extramarital affair] because this behavior is not formally considered sex. It is, however, appropriate to punish such women with lashes imposed [not by the Torah but] by the court since they have violated a prohibition. A man ought to be exacting with his wife on this matter and should prevent her from associating with women known for this, not to permit those women to visit her nor her to visit them.[9]

While in his code Maimonides legitimates a court punishment for public lesbian behavior, in another source, his commentary on the Mishnah, he says that no punishment is warranted, even under rabbinic auspices.[10] Maimonides' concluding statement is also rather telling. This admonition does not appear in any of the rabbinic sources and is likely original to him. Husbands must be watchful. They must prevent their wives from any association with women known for such behavior. One finds nowhere in the sources any warning to wives to watch out for their husbands' "associations" with men, even though homosexual violation for men was a much more serious offense. Wives must be under surveillance, despite the fact that sex between women is not adultery. It would seem that, for Maimonides, the problem of female sexual relations is fundamentally an issue of male disempowerment. Maimonides seems to be shaping a policy that prevents single women from becoming lovers of women, eases their way into marriages, keeps them in marriages when they cheat, and warns their husbands to prevent such dalliances in advance, if they suspect them.

Rabbi Judah ben Nathan (Rivan), one of Rashi's sons-in-law, suggests a rather bizarre interpretation of the original text in Yevamot that underscores the problem of male disempowerment.[11] He argues that *nashim hamesolelot* are not, as Rashi and Maimonides claim, women who rub their genitals together. They are women who receive the seed of their husbands and exchange it with each other.[12] If this practice is meant instead of genital rubbing, then Rav Huna disqualifies women who are interfering with the male lineage by sharing their husband's seed with each other. For both Maimonides and Rivan, the problem of female sexual relations is that they threaten men, and particularly their husbands. Either women are contorting the lines of paternity, or they are enjoying sexual play without their male partners. In either case male virile power, represented by semen or by a penis, is undermined. While no "other man" has trespassed, and thus no adultery has occurred, men have been replaced.[13]

When the issue of lesbian relations is raised, Orthodox rabbis are ready to admit that the Torah contains no admonition against sex between women. However, since Maimonides' ruling was taken into the legal canon, rabbis have a means by which they can formally describe both male and female homosexual relations as biblical prohibitions. And despite the fact that the older and more compelling talmudic material describes such relations as "mere indecency," Maimonides' ruling cannot easily be ignored. Since many Orthodox authorities treating lesbianism tend to follow Maimonides' lead, more clarity on that prohibition would seem to be in order.

Against Copying the Gentiles

Rabbi Joseph ben Solomon Colon (known as the Maharik) writes that the prohibition against copying the gentiles falls into two categories: the customs of gentiles that are of no practical benefit and those customs that are public expressions of sexual immodesty. Any practice having independent value was immediately permitted no matter from where it came. Copying the architecture, cuisine, or music of the gentiles was not a problem. Only imitating practices having symbolic (or expressly religious) rather than pragmatic value was prohibited. In regard to sexual behavior, again only the symbolic forms of public representation were considered problematic.[14] For this reason marriage customs rather than private sexual customs are identified. A number of brazen or immodest sexual practices between husband and wife might be discouraged, but they are not considered "copying the gentiles," because they are private. Private sexual practices, immodest or not, are not a violation of this rule. Given this understanding of the prohibition, sex between women in the privacy of their home would simply not qualify as a problem.[15]

However, even a public expression of a lesbian partnership, for example, a commitment ceremony in a synagogue, may not violate the rule. In the 1930s Rabbi Yehiel Weinberg, the head of the Hildesheimer Rabbinical Seminary, treated the law against imitating gentiles in a rather modern context.[16] A halakhic scholar of both yeshiva and university training, Rabbi Weinberg responded to many halakhic inquiries bearing directly on the challenges to Orthodoxy in the modern world. In the volume of his collected responsa, the *Seridei Esh,* he entertains the following question: "Is it permissible to celebrate a bat mitzvah?" It might appear a strange question, but such ceremonies, when they were first introduced, were challenged on just these grounds of imitating gentiles. While gentiles do not have bat mitzvah ceremonies for their daughters, the innovation of a new life-cycle event motivated by desire for parity between boys and girls was considered an import from Christian contexts.

Rabbi Weinberg claims that the general rule not to imitate gentiles is given to the wise scholars of every age to apply to their circumstances on the basis of their judgment.[17] He adds that the prohibition is only relevant when there is a specific intention to imitate non-Jews. Someone who behaves in the same manner as non-Jews but does not do so to appear like a non-Jew violates no prohibition. Rabbi Weinberg permits the practice of bat mitzvah because it is done for its independent value and not for its apparent similarity to Christian custom.

Given this distinction, one would be hard pressed to define lesbian relations or even lesbian commitment ceremonies as imitating gentiles. Many of the most vocal lesbian activists have been Jewish. It would seem very odd to claim that Jewish lesbians were finding each other, making Jewish homes together, and celebrating their unions with the specific intent of imitating non-Jews.

Lastly, the subjective ground of the prohibition is part of its very definition. According to Weinberg, the wise scholars of every age are to apply the general prohibition against imitation of non-Jews "on the basis of their judgment" and "in accordance with the prevailing circumstances." Given both the power of the "wise scholars" in this halakhic ruling and the demand on them for a blatantly contemporizing assessment of Jewish identity and distinctiveness, the rule becomes contingent on context. In different communities there will be different senses of what crosses the line from Jewish to non-Jewish. The rule then functions in a circular way to support a community's already existing boundaries.

In communities where lesbian life is so totally unknown and foreign that it appears to be a licentious import from immoral neighbors, the "out of the closet" lesbian and surely the public "marriage-like" commitment ceremony might very well be seen as "copying the gentiles." In those communities where engagement with the larger world is more extensive, where homosexuality is no longer seen as an immoral sexual practice imported from the gentiles but as a widely dispersed cross-cultural human variation, the prohibition would disappear even in regard to such celebrated unions.

The social contextuality of this law is brought home forcefully in the custom among some Babylonian scholars of arranging for themselves an evening companion when traveling to foreign cities.

> Rav, when he would travel to Darshish, would announce: Who will marry me for a day? Rav Nahman, when he would travel to Shechanzib, would announce: Who will marry me for a day?[18]

In the discussion that follows this text in the Babylonian Talmud, the rabbis are troubled, not by the legitimated promiscuity that it describes, but by the problem of incest. Potential children of such one-night-stand marriages might meet each other and marry, not knowing that they were actually siblings. The rabbis resolve the problem by suggesting that since these two great sages, Rav and Rav Nahman, were renowned, their children would be told with pride who their father was, and so, knowing their parentage, they would be able to avoid incest. The custom of "marriage for the night" was a well-known Babylonian custom of well-to-do traveling business-men. That it was not seen as a violation of "copying the gentiles" suggests that despite its rather public expression of sexual permis-siveness under a fig leaf of formality, it was not regarded as particu-larly gentile.

The circularity of the argument is again apparent. Jewish distinc-tiveness is communally determined and then undergirded by the rule against "copying the gentiles." If this Babylonian custom, de-spite its sexual permissiveness, was deemed legitimate, then the gen-eral biblical demand for Jewish distinctiveness should hardly pro-hibit the inauguration and celebration of a committed lifelong love relationship between two women.

One of the most renowned and respected contemporary halakhic authorities in Israel today, Rabbi Eliezer Waldenberg, writes that les-bian relations are not prohibited biblically, that such relations are "mere indecency" and at most prohibited rabbinically.[19] He appears to downplay the seriousness of sex between women, referring to it as playful touching. Most importantly, he makes no mention of Maimonides' concern with "copying the gentiles" either in regard to lesbian sexual relations themselves or in regard to marriage between women. While Waldenberg may not have been focusing on the issue of marriage in this responsum, it is remarkable that he does not find it necessary to hedge his leniency on lesbian relations themselves with a clear prohibition of public marriage ceremonies.[20]

Procreation

As we will see in more detail later, same-sex relations caused at least two kinds of anxieties: about what such relations do and about what they cannot do. For men we have seen that same-sex intercourse is of itself, for reasons not disclosed in the text, abominable. For women we have seen that there is no direct biblical concern at all with lesbian sexual relations. However, for both men and women same-sex rela-tions fail to accomplish what heterosexual relations can and often do accomplish. In the first chapter of Genesis God blesses the human couple: "Be fruitful and multiply and fill the earth." Later we will address the problem of reproduction for men, but even if lesbians might be permitted sexual relations, what about the duty to procreate? Surprisingly, the tradition determined that men are obligated to marry and procreate, but women are not.[21] While the verse in Genesis appears to address the newly created male and female couple, the active obligation falls only on men.[22] Women may have instinctual and cultural pressures to produce progeny, but the law does not require that women marry and become mothers. It may seem counter-intuitive (and surely the social reality was often quite different), but formally speaking women are free to choose to enter or not to enter the normative family context.

So far we have shown that, while the rabbis deemed lesbian relations immodest, there is no biblical prohibition against lesbian sex and no obligation for women to marry or to reproduce. Given that lesbian relationships are not expressly forbidden in the Torah, an astonishing insight emerges. The Hebrew Bible is not particularly interested in homosexuality. *Homo*sexuality, that is, sexual desire and activity between members of the *same* sex, is not the concern of Leviticus. Sameness does not seem to be the problem, for were it so, then surely two women engaging in sexual relations would be as problematic as are two males. This fact alone ought to focus our attention on the specifics of what happens in male-male sex that is seen as abominable, and not upon homosexuality.

The question that we are left with is, Why should a single act between men be prohibited? What is wrong about sex between men that sex between women does not entail? Why is anal intercourse between males so abhorrent in the eyes of God in the first place?

In the third section of the book, "Rationales," we will address just this question in detail in order to better understand the prohibition, its various contexts, and the directions available for reconsideration of its implementation. However, before we explore the prohibition further, it behooves us to see how same-sex experience found expression in biblical and rabbinic society and literature. There was no possibility of legitimated extramarital or coupled homosexual relations in any ancient or medieval Jewish society. Men were expected to desire and marry women, and women were expected to desire and marry men. Given the clarity of this social expectation, it will be interesting for us to explore some of the different ways same-sex experiences found expression in Jewish historical, literary, and legal materials despite the unambiguous acceptance of the prohibition.

Evidence

5

Princely Love

Neither in the Bible nor in the Talmud are there any openly homo-sexual love stories. However, expressions of love between men that are erotic without necessarily being overtly sexual are evident in a handful of places. Unfortunately, even the meager evidence of male same-sex love is not found in regard to women. Aside from the scant halakhic material in the Talmud and parallel rabbinic works, there are no traces of erotic love between women. While lesbians suffer total erasure in the various traditional texts in which evidence of same-sex love might be found, a committed love between two women, albeit chaste, is celebrated in the Book of Ruth, which will be discussed at the end of this chapter.

The first and most celebrated story of same-sex love between men is that of Jonathan, the young prince of Israel, and David, the acolyte, warrior, and singer of songs. The rabbis idealized the love between Jonathan and David. Love that exists outside the bounds of mutual benefit, they say, is eternal. Love dependent on benefit and, in particular, love based on lust for sexual pleasure, is very short lived. They offer examples of each kind of love: The epitome of in-tensely burning and quickly evaporating love is the love of Amnon for his half sister Tamar, whom, in his frenzied passion, he rapes. Once his lust is spent, he spurns her (2 Sam. 13:1–19). The epitome of eternal love, a love unqualified and independent of worldly bene-fit, is the love of David and Jonathan.[1]

By this comparison the sages appear to be trying to erase any sus-picion of erotic investment between David and Jonathan. However, in doing so they also leave us wondering exactly how the love between two men is greater than the love of a man for a woman. The Greek philosophers also thought that love between men was more noble and lasting than the love between men and women. The juxtaposition of Amnon's love of Tamar and the love of Jonathan and David seems to point in two directions, toward the differences and the similarities between these two couples.

Intense homophilia was very familiar to the rabbis of antiquity. In the social world of the Babylonian academies, young men engaged in the study of Torah were expected to form deep and abiding affections for their fellow students. Throughout the Talmud there are famous rabbinic couples, *havrutot,* whose combative sparring in the study hall is rendered as a profound and intimate love. In *Avot de-Rabbi Nathan* we learn that one ought to acquire a friend with whom "to eat and drink, read and study, sleep and share secrets of Torah and personal secrets."[2] The love between these comrades-in-arms was understood as an outgrowth of their shared commitment to something beyond them both, the revealing of God's will through the study of Torah. This sort of love is eternal because there is nothing to disappoint, no rise and fall of attraction, in short, no hot desire and deflating climax to make love volatile. But despite the rabbinic insistence on the platonic nature of this biblical friendship, the narrative description of Jonathan and David's relationship in the Books of Samuel is guardedly but surely erotic.

Jonathan and David meet in the very first verse of chapter 18 of 1 Samuel. The young shepherd, armed with a few smooth stones and a sling, has just felled the great Philistine giant, Goliath. He is taken to Saul, with the Philistine's head in his hand. Saul has no idea who this youth is and asks for his father's name. David responds that he is the son of Jesse the Bethlehemite, and as he finishes speaking, we are witness to Jonathan's intense reaction.

> When [David] finished speaking with Saul, Jonathan's soul became bound up with the soul of David; Jonathan loved David as himself. Saul took him [into his service] that day and would not let him return to his father's house. Jonathan and David made a pact because [Jonathan] loved him as himself. Jonathan took off the cloak and

tunic he was wearing and gave them to David, together with his sword, bow, and belt. (1 Sam. 18:1–4)

We are told twice of Jonathan's reaction to David when they first meet. Immediately Jonathan's soul became bound up with the soul of David; Jonathan loved David as himself. Indeed, both father and son seem to be smitten with David. Saul immediately takes David into the royal house, refusing to let him return home to his father. The juxtaposition of Saul to David's father suggests that David is adopted into the royal family. Jonathan and David make a pact, and then Jonathan takes off his vestments and weapons and dresses the young David.

As the story progresses, David achieves great military stature. His success in the battlefield eclipses not only Jonathan but Saul as well. Saul's love of David turns quickly to jealousy and suspicion as David's fame and reputation among the people rises. In fits of anger Saul's jealousy turns murderous. Saul tries many times to do away with David, to pin him to the wall with spears, or to bring about his death in other ways. Jonathan defends and protects David, which infuriates his father.

After Jonathan helps David escape his father's clutches on a new moon feast, Saul flies into a rage against Jonathan. "You perverse and rebellious son! I know that you have chosen the son of Jesse to your own shame and the shame of your mother's nakedness!" (1 Sam. 20: 30). Saul rages in this scene not at David, but at Jonathan. David makes Saul feel embattled and threatened, but his own son raises in him feelings of disgust. Jonathan's disinterest in his own welfare, his refusal to compete with David for honors, and his unmanly love of the man who will, if not stopped, take his throne repulses Saul. Indeed, Saul understands everything correctly.

Saul is disgusted with Jonathan's naive disregard of the mounting threat David poses to his political future. Apparently unaware of the machinations around him, Jonathan wants everyone just to get along. Saul has tried to hide from Jonathan his earlier attempts to murder David. But now he reveals everything, not only his love of David turned to hatred, but his disgust for his own son. Saul plainly sees that Jonathan has no care for the royal office he might someday hold. Jonathan's act of dressing the young David in his own princely clothing the moment that they met expressed both Jonathan's instantaneous love and his wish, conscious or not, to divest himself of his royal identity. Saul is right. Jonathan is unconsciously in league with David and so rebellious, in love with David and so perverse.

The language of the verse clinches the argument that Jonathan's love for David cannot exclude the sexual. Jonathan's choice of David is associated not only with rebellion, but with his own shame and the shame of his mother's nakedness. The phrase "mother's nakedness" in this context is not easily understood. The Hebrew word for nakedness here, *erva,* is the word used in Leviticus and elsewhere to express sexual violation. To uncover nakedness is to have illicit sexual relations. Add to this that the first of Saul's insults to Jonathan is that he is perverse. Jonathan has chosen David in a perverse and shaming way that offends his mother's nakedness. Saul is not offended by a platonic friendship, but by his son's perverse, shameful, and naked love of David.

A last bit of evidence, given the language just described, is very evocative. In his rage at Jonathan for his shameful and perverse choice of David, Saul demands that Jonathan bring David to him for execution. Jonathan rises to defend David, innocently asking what David has done to deserve to be put to death. Saul, frustrated with his clueless son, does the unexpected. He throws a spear at Jonathan. The text does not seem to worry that perhaps Jonathan might have been injured by the attack. There is no statement to the effect that Saul missed. We are led to believe that Saul had no intention of really hitting Jonathan. If so, what was the demonstration about? It could be pure rage and nothing more. However, it could be more pointed than just blowing off steam. Could it not mark his rage at Jonathan's lack of male virtue by having chosen for himself a male to love? If so, the violent gesture could be demonstrating what real men do. Real men, for Saul, penetrate women in love and men in battle. Or perhaps the lodging of a spear in the wall behind Jonathan was meant as a taunting threat on the order of "If you want to be penetrated by a man, then I will penetrate you!"

While our attention was initially focused on Jonathan and David, Saul is actually the central character of the story. He is the fulcrum not only for the history of the kingship but also for the fate of Jonathan and David. Why did Saul, on meeting David for the first time, take him into his service and not permit him to return to his father's home? Is the juxtaposition to "his father's home" a way to signal that Saul's motives were fatherly? Or is it simply that Saul, like Jonathan, had been charmed by the young David? Did he see Jonathan's reaction to David? Perhaps he hoped to provide a stalwart and courageous friend for his son, whose mettle he doubted. Or maybe Saul was expressing an unconscious wish to have a son who would make him proud, unlike Jonathan, who did not.

Eventually Saul's fatherly love of David puts him at odds with his own interest in Jonathan's succession. Saul comes to realize that David's immense popularity poses a threat to Jonathan's future and even to his own. As the plot thickens, Saul is caught wavering. Repeatedly he sets out to destroy David and returns repentant of his mistrust. David attempts to prove his loyalty to Saul in a dramatic moment. Saul has gone to relieve himself in a cave where, coincidentally, David is hiding. David cuts off the corner of Saul's robe to prove to him that were his intent to depose the king, he could have killed him easily. Temporarily Saul is convinced, but later his fears are renewed that as long as David lives, Jonathan will not sit upon his throne. Saul appears to be caught in a bind, loving and hating Jonathan, loving and hating David.

From the day they meet, when Jonathan takes off his robes and dresses David, to the day he dies and is eulogized by David, the text presents Jonathan's love of David as something ominous and beautiful. The rabbis consider it to be a love without dependency, pure and perfect. Unlike the lust of Amnon for Tamar, which ends with hatred, the love of Jonathan for David is eternal. While the story drips with obvious homoeroticism, there is no evidence of any physical intimacy between them.[3] There is, however, also no evidence in the language that would absolutely preclude such a relationship either.

The most poignant moment in the story is when Jonathan and David make a pact. David will be waiting for Jonathan to signal with arrows if it is safe to return to the palace or not. Jonathan still hopes that his father's rageful fits are over and discovers in the previously described outburst that they are not. As planned, Jonathan signals

David that he must leave. When the servant lad accompanying Jonathan had been dismissed, David and Jonathan have a moment to say their farewells. "Just as the lad had gone, David arose from the mound and fell on his face to the ground and bowed three times, and each man kissed the other and wept for the other; though David the longer" (1 Sam. 20:41).

When, at the end of the story, Jonathan dies in battle, David speaks his poetic lament for his beloved Jonathan.

> How the mighty have fallen
> In the thick of battle—
> Jonathan, slain on your heights!
> I grieve for you, my brother Jonathan.
> You were most dear to me.
> Your love was wonderful to me,
> More than the love of women.
> (2 Sam. 1:25–26)

Much has been made of David's comparison of Jonathan's love to the love of women. It is unlikely that David is expressing an erotic love for Jonathan at this moment. He admits that Jonathan was very dear to him, but no more. He remembers Jonathan's love of him as more selfless and giving than the love he received from the women in his life. It was, as we have noted earlier, Jonathan who loved David. David has the sort of magnetic personality that draws friends and supporters, lovers and defenders, and, of course, jealous enemies. But as ordinary as it is for David to draw lovers around him, he does not love back so easily. Even in his romantic entanglement with Batsheva, the text never speaks of his love. He is adored, fawned over, worshipped in song and lore, but David never seems to be passionately in love with anyone, except perhaps God.[4]

The story would seem to make the most sense if Jonathan were gay, but David not. Jonathan is, after all, the son who disappoints his father in just the ordinary ways. Though he manages in battle, we find him not very aggressive or interested in military prowess. He doesn't think strategically. Moreover, he is smitten at first sight by the young David and immediately dresses him in his own clothing. The erotics of this gesture are difficult to explain away. Lastly, his love of David is deemed perverse and shameful by his father.

It is, of course, quite possible to read the story totally outside any sexual meaning. The actions might all be explained by political intrigue and friendship. While such a reading is possible, it avoids a more direct and obvious power in a narrative in which love is mentioned over and over again regarding a relationship between two men.

For lesbians, there is no biblical parallel to David and Jonathan. However, many women have found a great deal of comfort in the story of the companionship of Ruth and Naomi. Unlike what we have seen in the text of the Books of Samuel, there is no hint of any erotic tie between the women. Still, Ruth's care and devotion for Naomi have been employed by lesbians seeking to ground their experience in text, as a biblical touchstone.

Naomi's husband and two son's die, and she is left with her two Moabite daughters-in-law. "Orpah kissed her mother-in-law farewell, but Ruth clung to her" (Ruth 1:14). The language of the text parallels Adam's description of male-female attachment, following the creation of Eve. "Therefore a man leaves his father and mother and clings to his wife, so that they become one flesh" (Gen. 2:24). Immediately after the narrator of the book describes Ruth's tie to Naomi as one of clinging, Ruth delivers her famous speech: "Wherever you go, I will go; wherever you lodge, I will lodge; your people shall be my people and your God my God. Where you die, I will die, and there I will be buried. Thus and more may the Lord do to me if anything but death parts me from you" (Ruth 1:16b–17). The line is so evocative of marital intentions that it has been almost universally included in contemporary Jewish lesbian commitment ceremonies. Ruth commits to a bond that is explicitly about a lifelong companionship, "till death do they part."

The recovery of fragments from David and Jonathan, from Ruth and Naomi for our purposes is not to say that either of these biblical pairs were lovers. Instead, it is to show that erotic pull and committed love between people of the same sex were acknowledged in our sacred tradition.

6

Rabbinic Heroes

The fascination with the young David that captures Saul, Jonathan, and eventually all of Israel is not independent of his handsome appearance. While male physical beauty was hardly of central importance to the sages of the Talmud, there were some rabbis who, among their other qualities, were famous for their beauty. Rabbi Yohanan is the prime example of the beautiful rabbi.

> Rabbi Yohanan said, "I have survived from the beautiful of Jerusalem." One who wishes to see the beauty of R. Yohanan should bring a brand new silver cup and fill it with the red seeds of a pomegranate and place around its rim a garland of roses, and let him place it where the sun meets the shade, and that vision is the beauty of R. Yohanan.
>
> Is that true? But haven't we been taught by our master that "the beauty of Rabbi Cahana is like the beauty of Rabbi Abbahu. The beauty of Rabbi Abbahu is like the beauty of our father Jacob. The beauty of our father Jacob is like the beauty of Adam." [If R. Yohanan is so beautiful] so then, why isn't he mentioned [in this list of beautiful rabbis]? R. Yohanan did not have splendor of face (i.e., a beard).[1]

R. Yohanan was so ravishing, we are told, that he would sit outside the mikvah so that women leaving from their monthly ritual bath would see him. Women would gaze on him on the way to their husbands (with whom they had not been intimate for nearly two weeks) so that during coitus they would have his dazzling visage in their minds and so would conceive children as beautiful and as learned as he.[2]

Perhaps what makes R. Yohanan's beauty less threatening to everyone is that he has, particularly by Roman standards, a boyish appearance. R. Yohanan's beauty was delicate and hairless. He was missing the outward sign of male maturity, the beard. The image of crimson wine, pomegranate seeds, and rose garland is a mysterious way to describe R. Yohanan's beauty. The repeated dark reds speak of passion and intensity. The images evoke a highly androgynous beauty, just the sort of youthful beauty that an expectant mother might wish to transfer to her child of either sex. It is a beauty that not only inspires women to produce beautiful children but also, on one occasion, invites a sexual assault from a passing gladiator. The following story is one of the most evocative and tragic romantic tales in the whole of the Talmud.

> One day R. Yohanan was bathing in the Jordan. Resh Lakish saw him and jumped across the Jordan after him [placing his lance in the Jordan and vaulting to the other side]. When R. Yohanan saw Rabbi Shimon the son of Lakish, he said to him, "Your strength for Torah!" He replied, "Your beauty for women!" He said to him, "If you repent, I will give you my sister who is more beautiful than I am." He [RL] agreed. He [RL] wanted to cross back to take his clothes, but he couldn't. He [RY] taught him [RL] Mishnah and Talmud and made him a great man.[3]

Resh Lakish in the story is a Jewish gladiator who vaults over the river to rape an unsuspecting bather. The bather turns out to be R. Yohanan, the sage. In the standard version of the story, we are left not knowing whether Resh Lakish thinks that the bather is female or male. We have already been told that R. Yohanan had features that might have made him appear feminine, especially at a distance. However, it seems just as reasonable to suggest that Resh Lakish saw a dazzling naked man bathing in the Jordan and vaulted over the river for a pederastic conquest well within the ordinary prerogatives of a Roman gladiator. We have just been told that R. Yohanan was boyish looking, tremendously beautiful and hairless, a potential object of desire for an adult Roman male.

In either case Resh Lakish sheds his heavy gladiatorial vestments, surely hopeful of a sexual conquest, and pole vaults over the river to find neither a woman nor a delicate boy, but the famous scholar R. Yohanan. Seemingly unflustered by the intrusion, the rabbi comments on the virile power of his would-be attacker with a brief statement, "Your strength for Torah," meaning, "Your manly power could be put to better use in the study of Torah." R. Yohanan's calm and his interest in drawing this brigand into the coterie of Torah scholars suggest that it must have been immediately apparent to R. Yohanan that the young man before him was Jewish. If so, it might very well be that the vaulting athlete was himself as naked as the bather and so recognizable as Jewish by his circumcision.

The wise rabbi does not criticize nor reprimand. He merely suggests that if the young man wishes a conquest, then the conquest of Torah is more valorous than gladitorial conquests. Resh Lakish does not respond to this point and instead—unable to take his eyes off the beautiful R. Yohanan—says to him, "Your beauty for women!" Again a brief expression, this retort can be read in two very different ways. "Your beauty is for women" might mean "only a woman should possess such beauty" or alternatively "your beauty should be properly used for seducing women; let's go!"

In this terse dialogue between the two men, it appears that each is belittling the manhood of the other. R. Yohanan is marking Resh Lakish as a gentile-Jew who is less than a full man because real men study Torah. Resh Lakish is marking R. Yohanan as a man-woman because real men are not beautiful objects of desire but aggressive sexual predators. Daniel Boyarin has masterfully explored the overlap of gender and politics in this story.[4] He suggests that the narrator of this talmudic story has constructed a dramatic encounter between the rabbi and the gladiator, thus juxtaposing the epitomes of masculinity in the rabbinic and the Roman cultures.

The progression of R. Yohanan's responses to Resh Lakish is also of import. R. Yohanan had originally intended to address the masculine power and aggression of his intruder by assuring him that these masculine arts ought to be deployed in Torah study ("Your strength for Torah!"). Once Resh Lakish makes clear that his interest is in beauty and sex with women ("Your beauty for women!"), R. Yohanan understands that he must now address the topic of desire. He responds that if it is a beautiful woman that Resh Lakish wants, he can arrange that too. R. Yohanan has a sister who is even more beautiful than he. He offers to the gladiator his sister's hand in marriage, if Resh Lakish will abandon his brigandage and follow him to the academy.[5]

The critique of Roman masculinity is not that it is aggressive per se, but that its aggression is played out in the wrong arena. Jewish masculinity is won in valorous contests fought with words. The wise students of Torah engage upon a textual battlefield, tongues in place of swords, subduing a feminine Torah, whose secrets they uncover. While the Torah will not be taken without her suitors dueling over her, such contests over real women are not necessary. Resh Lakish is assured that he does not need gladiatorial aggression to get sex. He will not have to renounce sex to renounce rape. Sex will be provided for in a sanctioned marriage. He will not need his lance to be a husband and father; an ordinary penis will do.

When Resh Lakish agrees to the bargain, immediately he cannot vault back across the river to get his clothes. His lance no longer works. The garments of his prior identity are irretrievable. The symbols of Roman mastery, lance and toga, are relinquished for the study of Torah and marriage with a nice Jewish girl. The story peaks when Resh Lakish is taught Mishnah and Gemara and becomes "a great man."

If the story ended here, it would simply be a paean to the rabbis' masculine ideal transforming physical violence into debate, substituting marriage for sexual aggression. However, as Boyarin deftly points out, the rabbis critique their own gentler and kinder form of masculinity and its ideals by reporting a story that, despite its lack of physical violence, ends in death. In order to understand this text a single detail regarding the laws of ritual impurity should be understood. Ritual impurity can only adhere to completed vessels. Until the object is finished, it cannot become impure, for example, by contact with a corpse. The following discussion is about when weapons would be considered "finished" and thus susceptible to impurity.

> Once they were disputing in the study house: "The sword and the lance and the dagger, from when can they become impure?" R. Yohanan said, "From the time they are forged in the fire." Resh Lakish said, "From the time they are polished in the water." R. Yohanan said, "A brigand is an expert in brigandage [i.e., tauntingly:

"You should know! Weapons are the tools of your profession."]."
[RL, hurt and angry,] said to [RY], "How have you benefited me?
There [among the thieves] they called me 'Master' and here [among
the scholars] they call me 'Master'!" [RY] "I have benefited you by
drawing you close, under the wings of the Divine Presence!" R.
Yohanan became utterly dejected [as a result of which] Resh Lakish
fell ill. His sister [RY's sister and now RL's wife] came to him [RY]
and cried before him [asking him to entreat heaven for the life of
her husband, Resh Lakish]. She said, "Look at me!" He did not pay
attention to her. "Look at the orphans!" He said to her, "Leave your
orphans; I will give life." (Jer. 49:11). "Do it for the sake of my wid-
owhood!" He said, "Place your widow's trust in me." Resh Lakish
died, and R. Yohanan mourned him greatly. The rabbis said,
"What can we do to comfort him? Let us bring Rabbi Eleazar the
son of Pedat, whose traditions are brilliant, and put him before
him." Every point that he [RY] would make, he [the new student]
said, "There is a tradition that supports you." R. Yohanan said, "Do
I need this one? The son of Lakish used to raise twenty-four refuta-
tions, until the matter became completely clear, and all you can say
is that I say good things?" He used to go and cry out at the gates,
"Son of Lakish, where are you?" until he went mad. The rabbis
prayed for him, and he died.[6]

The debate in the study hall is over weapons.[7] It is here that our
two rabbis tragically renew their debate on violence and words of
Torah. R. Yohanan's sarcastic remark, "a brigand is expert in brigandage," may have been delivered as a sharp personal attack or as a
teasing jest. We would have no way of knowing. Likewise, it is possible that in reply Resh Lakish was merely expressing disappoint-
ment at having won the debate on a technicality, the advantage of
his gladiatorial experience. However, as the tension mounts, it seems
more likely that he was deeply hurt by what he experienced as a public humiliation by R. Yohanan. R. Yohanan shames him by suggesting that despite appearances, Resh Lakish is still a brute and a brig-
and. He replies to this, "Fine, then I will act like a power-driven
brute, and I tell you that in regard to real power, you have not benefited me at all!" Where the misunderstanding begins does not really
matter. By the end both men are personally insulted and deeply
hurt. Most important is that R. Yohanan has taken to heart Resh
Lakish's biting critique that Torah scholarship is not so different

from gladiatorial prowess. Both are mere power games of men seeking to be called "master" by other men. R. Yohanan is wounded deeply and curses him.

R. Yohanan's curse does its damage, and Resh Lakish falls ill. The sister of R. Yohanan (the wife of Resh Lakish) comes to beg her brother to prevent her husband's death. At first he does not even pay attention to her. He was ready to marry her off without asking her in advance and now seems ready to see her widowed without a bit of consideration. His apparent cruelty here has been difficult for traditional commentators. How could the great sage and scholar R. Yohanan be so cold and heartless? One wonders if, all along, R. Yohanan has been jealous of his sister. She is, after all, the one who lives most intimately with Resh Lakish. Indeed, R. Yohanan does appear to be acting like a spurned lover. His sister comes to him because she loves her husband and wants to save him. The fact that she gets nowhere with R. Yohanan attests either to his utter rejection of her subjective interests (which we have seen before) or that her tearful entreaty only further incites a very jealous man to rashness.

When Resh Lakish dies, R. Yohanan is inconsolable. He blows up at the brilliant student who is provided him in lieu of Resh Lakish. He cannot endure the agreement and praise that the new acolyte showers on him. He misses his intellectual opponent who challenged every one of his statements and so engaged him to clarify matters down to the last detail. He wanders the streets, calling out his name. As in a Shakespearean tragedy, he jealously causes his love's death and is driven mad by the loss.

Whether or not R. Yohanan was homosexual is neither knowable nor very important. What is important is that the rabbis who recorded this text were unafraid to write such a deep and moving story about a famed and venerated pair of rabbis, despite the obvious character flaws it would expose. The story rejects the Roman male virtue of physical aggression but admits that even in the world of the rabbis men can die of wounds they inflict on one another. It demonstrates that the kinder, gentler men can still impose their will on women, albeit in less overtly violent ways, and that verbal repartee between men can at times be no less bloody than physical sparring.

The intensity of this teacher-student love relationship has strains from Greek philosophic culture. There were ample models from the Hellenistic world both to lend a dramatic credence to this story and to teach a lesson. The author may have wanted to warn young rabbinic scholars of the dangers of Greek pedagogic models, even if by doing so he diminished R. Yohanan's stature.

Highlighting the powerful emotional attachment between these two scholars is a remarkable comment on the verse we encountered in the first chapter. When the *adam*'s loneliness motivates God to create a life partner for the lonely *adam,* the Hebrew word used to convey the idea of partner is *ezer k'negdo,* literally a "helper *(ezer)* opposite or against him" *(k'negdo).* To explain the tension between the two parts of this expression, Rabbi Mordechai Joseph Leiner of Izbica, a Hasidic master we will encounter again later, uses the relationship of R. Yohanan and Resh Lakish as a model. The helpful opposition that Resh Lakish provided for his teacher raised the level of R. Yohanan's thinking. Two minds open to each other and willing to be challenged always achieve greater clarity. This is just the kind of helpful opposition the Torah has in mind for married couples, says Rabbi Leiner. Just as the rabbis use Jonathan and David to demonstrate "love with no ulterior motive," Rabbi Leiner employs R. Yohanan and Resh Lakish to demonstrate the ideal of "helping opposition" in marriage.

The story does suggest that R. Yohanan was smitten with Resh Lakish, first with his powerful body and then with his aggressive mind. R. Yohanan becomes obsessed with the man he compelled his sister to marry. There is little to explain R. Yohanan's brusque rejection of his sister's tearful entreaties. The cold response makes little sense unless underneath the dialogue one hears the voice of an embittered and jealous man saying, "If I can't succeed with him as my student, then you can't have him as your husband." Even though the suffering is wrought of his own hands, the image of the illustrious scholar wandering the streets crying out for Resh Lakish by his nickname, "Bar Lakisha, Bar Lakisha, where are you?" is heartrending.

7

The Queer Middle Ages

Despite the fact that the verses in Leviticus were universally understood within the developing canons of Jewish literature and law to prohibit male sexual relations, in real life there were men who fell in love with men. Not only did such relationships occur, but in rare instances such love affairs were recorded in dramatic, if somewhat coded, literary accounts. The story of David and Jonathan and that of Rabbi Yohanan and Resh Lakish demonstrate not so much that love between men occurred commonly, but that its representation in sacred literature was not vilified or silenced completely. This next set of voices carries the same theme into the Middle Ages in an even more graphic and demonstrative fashion.

Muslim Spain from the tenth to the middle of the twelfth century was a very unusual haven for the embattled Jewish communities of Europe. When the Moors crossed the straits of Gibraltar and invaded Visigothic Spain, Jews became their instant allies. The tolerance of the Omayyads turned Spain into a refuge, and Jews from all over Europe immigrated to Spain to benefit from the opportunities. The real Jewish cultural revival began at the beginning of the tenth century, when Spanish society offered to Jews broad educational opportunities and remarkable cultural and political access. Jewish and Arab scholarship and culture flourished and were mutually influenced by each other. Such an opportunity for social and intellectual openness and for sustained mutual engagement between Islam and Judaism has not happened since.

Poets and men of letters were among the elite of Spanish

intelligentsia, and there were many new poets writing in Arabic and Hebrew on both secular and religious themes. Among the love poems written by both Muslims and Jews are a sizable selection of homoerotic poems. While some of the poems are quite racy, most of them are ordinary love sonnets, often of unrequited or hidden love. The only difference is that the love object in them is a young man, often called the fawn.

For many years the scholarly last word on these poems has been Chaim Shirman in his *Hebrew Poetry of Spain and Provence,* published in 1954. Shirman writes somewhat contradictory things on the topic of the medieval love poems. He claims at first that they are stylistic works written as a competitive challenge to create in Hebrew poems similar to Arabic poems of the times. He suggests that the erotic subjects of the secular poems were contrived and had no relation to reality. They were creative attempts to prove that Hebrew was a language equally suited to poetic tasks. Songs of this sort were sung at parties in Spanish Muslim culture, and Spanish Jews, who loved parties, generated their own party songs.

However, Shirman then demonstrates that the subject of the love of youths was unique among subjects. If Jews were merely mimicking the stylistic writing of Arabs, then other topics unique to Arab poetry should have been borrowed for similar reasons. There are many Arabic hunting songs, and none among the Jews, who did not hunt. Arabic songs speak of camels, lions, and horses, animals unfamiliar to Jews and not found in Jewish poetry. Even war songs were common among Arabs, and only rarely does one find them in Hebrew.[1] Consequently the songs of the love of men, which do appear in Hebrew, ought to be seen as expressive of authentic feelings rather than mere competitive play with Arab poets.

Shirman acknowledges that among the expressions of Arab culture supposedly foreign to Jews, only male love was put to verse by the Hebrew poets. However, he cannot follow the force of his own argument and ends up insisting that these poems were a symbolic genre having no base in real experience. At one point he even suggests that the Hebrew poets writing of male love were actually writing about women and substituted men for the love object, which he also claims to find among some Arab and Provençal poets.

However, the proof is in the pudding. The following two poems were written by two of the most famous medieval Jewish scholar-poets, Moshe Ibn Ezra and Judah HaLevi. Both men were independently well respected for their scholarship as well as their poetry. Moshe Ibn Ezra wrote a great many liturgical poems, or *piyyutim,* that are scattered in various prayer books. Judah HaLevi was not only a prolific poet, the author of some 800 poems and 350 liturgical *piyyitim,* but a popular philosopher as well. The story of the friendship between these two Hebrew men of letters is in itself intriguing.

Late in the tenth century Judah HaLevi passed through Cordoba and entered a poetry contest. He won the contest by imitating a stylistically complicated poem by the then renowned Moshe Ibn Ezra. Ibn Ezra, impressed with the young poet's talent, invited him to come live with him in Granada. During HaLevi's stay in Granada, Ibn Ezra became his patron, supporting him in the luxurious style of wealthy Granadan Jews. Despite the twenty-year difference in their ages, these two Spanish poets sustained a lifelong friendship. However, as the following poems seem to suggest, neither of these men was immune to the kisses of a beautiful man.

MOSHE IBN EZRA

My heart's desire, my eyes' delight:
the hart beside me and a cup in my right hand!
Many denounce me for loving, but I pay no heed.
Come to me, fawn, and I will vanquish them.
Time will consume them and death will shepherd them away.
Oh, come to me, fawn, let me feast on the nectar of your lips
until I am satisfied.

Why, why would they discourage me?
If it be because of sin or guilt,
I am ravished by your beauty—and God is there!
Let your heart not be swayed by the words of my tormentor,
that close-minded man.
Oh, come put me to the test!

He was enticed and we went to his mother's house.
There he bent his back to my heavy yoke.
Night and day I alone was with him.
I took off his clothes and he took off mine.
I sucked at his lips and he suckled me.

115

But once his eyes stole my heart,
his hand fastened the yoke of my sin,
and he looked for grievances.
He raged against me and shouted in fury,
"Enough! Leave me alone!
Do not drive me to crime, do not lead me astray!"

Oh, do not be unrelenting in your anger, fawn.
Show me the wonders of your pleasure, my love.
Kiss your friend and fulfill his desire.
If you wish to revive me, then give life;
but if you would instead kill—then kill me.

JUDAH HALEVI

Look at me, my fawn, look!
Take full note of my misery
lest I fill with sorrow . . .

Drip, drip, drip goes my blood,
my life in your hands.

Let your heart be compassionate to the downcast,
who cannot eat and cries when you rage
and waits for your love to return . . .

Manna, manna, manna for my hunger,
give my daily wage.

If you rejoice in my lovesickness,
so here are my cheeks,
abuse me then, afflict me . . .

No, no, no disgrace,
just the casualties of innocence.

I have fought this miser of the heart,
and were he just a bit afraid of me
then perhaps sleep might come and I would . . .

Fly, fly, fly in my slumber,
I would dream double.

I would ask for his honeycomb lips,
reddening like the setting sun
my eyes transfixed on his form . . .

How, how, how does this man from Aram
color his lips so ruddy?

His song ploughs my heavy heart,
he sings to awaken my fire.
Enough, my love, drink from my mouth.

Bas, bas, bas befumi [Kiss, kiss, kiss my mouth],
Wa-da' sawadak ya 'ammi. [Put aside your black mood, my friend].[2]

These two poems are among the most beautiful of the love poems to youths, but they are by no means unique. Scores of such poems can be found in the collections of Shlomo Ibn Gabirol, Shmuel HaNagid, Abraham Ibn Ezra, and the two authors under discussion, Moshe Ibn Ezra and Judah HaLevi.

In the poem by Moshe Ibn Ezra we are given no reason that the lover should be reviled by others for his love, but indeed he is. Many denounce him for his love of the youth, but he pays no heed. He promises the youth that he will vanquish their detractors, that death will shepherd them away. He argues for the goodness of their love. The erotic nature of the love is more than obvious in the third stanza. After the lover's tryst the youth cannot bear his feelings of guilt and he rages at the lover. The youth accuses the lover of driving him to crime, of leading him astray. The lover insists that only close-minded men would mistake what they feel for each other as sin and, in the melodramatic manner of lovers, begs his beloved to revive him with a kiss or to kill him.

This is not a poem about platonic friendship, nor is it a love poem to a woman who has been cast as a boy for reasons of delicacy. The love is erotic, and the threats to the love are the common threats to same-sex loving.

The poem by Judah HaLevi is more delicate but includes similar themes. He begs his young fawn to relent, to have compassion for his lovesickness. He, too, would prefer abuse to neglect and insists that there is no disgrace in their loving. In the last lines he dreams of his fawn's honeycomb lips and implores the young man to drink from his mouth. The triple word repetitions throughout the poem mark the pleading of the lover.

The last two lines of a strophic poem of this period are called a *kharja*. Typically it finishes a Hebrew poem with a couplet not in Hebrew but in a mixture of Romance and Arabic languages. Following the more formal Hebrew text, *Bas, bas, bas befumi*—"Kiss, kiss, kiss my mouth"—has an urgency and intimacy that seems to say, "Enough with the sweet talk, just kiss me!"

These poems and others like them demonstrate that homosexual practice did indeed exist in the Middle Ages. While homoerotic poems of this sort were virtually nonexistent among Jews in any other time or place in Jewish history, they still attest to the existence of same-sex love in a particular medieval culture despite the clear rabbinic opinions on the matter. The writing and publication of such poems open up the possibility that such relationships may have existed, albeit in more closeted forms, in other less culturally open periods and places as well.

The authors of these poems do not theorize about the meaning of their experience. They do not try to make sense of it in terms of the received tradition. They trust their feelings and do battle with their enemies in the name of love. Though they were all men of learning and piety, in these works they were not scholars but lovers. The exception to this rule appears two hundred years later in Provence in a poem by a medieval writer who, in a rather unusual way, attempts to make sense of his feelings in light of the meanings of gender in his world and in light of the law as well.

Medieval Gender Bender

In a little book by the thirteenth-century pietist Kalonymus ben Kalonymus of Arles is found one of the most startling queer texts of the Jewish Middle Ages. The book is titled *Even Bohan* and includes in its introduction a few pages of amazing gender-bending writing. The original writing in Hebrew is highly stylized and somewhat repetitive. The spaces between paragraphs signify that lines have been left out of the following translation in order to simplify and slightly compress the piece.

> What an awful fate for my mother
> that she bore a son.
> What a loss of all benefit!
> Cursed be the one who announced to my father:
> "It's a boy! . . .

Woe to him who has male sons.
Upon them a heavy yoke has been placed, restrictions and constraints.
Some in private, some in public,
some to avoid the mere appearance of violation,
and some entering the most secret of places.

Strong statutes and awesome commandments,
six hundred and thirteen.
Who is the man who can do all that is written,
so that he might be spared?

Oh, but had the artisan who made me
created me instead—a fair woman.
Today I would be wise and insightful.
We would weave, my friends and I,
and in the moonlight spin our yarn,
and tell our stories to one another,
from dusk till midnight.
We'd tell of the events of our day, silly things,
matters of no consequence.
But also I would grow very wise from the spinning,
and I would say, "Happy is she who knows how to work with combed
    flax and weave it into fine white linen."

And at times, in the way of women,
I would lie down on the kitchen floor,
between the ovens, turn the coals, and taste the different dishes.
On holidays I would put on my best jewelry.
I would beat on the drum
and my clapping hands would ring.

And when I was ready and the time was right,
an excellent youth would be my fortune.
He would love me, place me on a pedestal,
dress me in jewels of gold,
earrings, bracelets, necklaces.
And on the appointed day,
in the season of joy when brides are wed,
for seven days would the boy increase my delight and gladness.

Were I hungry, he would feed me well-kneaded bread.
Were I am thirsty, he would quench me with light and dark wine.
He would not chastise nor harshly treat me,
and my [sexual] pleasure he would not diminish.

Every Sabbath, and each new moon,
his head he would rest upon my breast.
The three husbandly duties he would fulfill,
rations, raiment, and regular intimacy.
And three wifely duties would I also fulfill,
[watching for menstrual] blood, [Sabbath candle] lights, and bread.

Father in heaven, who did miracles for our ancestors with fire and
    water,
You changed the fire of Chaldees so it would not burn hot,
You changed Dina in the womb of her mother to a girl,
You changed the staff to a snake before a million eyes,
You changed [Moses'] hand to [leprous] white
and the sea to dry land.
In the desert you turned rock to water,
hard flint to a fountain.

Who would then turn me from a man to woman?
Were I only to have merited this, being so graced by your goodness.

What shall I say? Why cry or be bitter?
If my Father in heaven has decreed upon me
and has maimed me with an immutable deformity,
then I do not wish to remove it.
And the sorrow of the impossible
is a human pain that nothing will cure
and for which no comfort can be found.
So, I will bear and suffer
until I die and wither in the ground.
And since I have learned from the tradition
that we bless both the good and the bitter,
I will bless in a voice, hushed and weak,
Blessed are you, O Lord,
who has not made me a woman.[3]

For a writer at the end of the thirteenth century, this is a rather
astonishing piece of self-expression. Of course, Kalonymus writes his
polemic against maleness and in praise of femaleness against the
backdrop of a society that strongly does exactly the opposite. This
being so, it is tempting to read him as a transgendered person struggling against his given body and its meanings. His use of the Hebrew
word *muum,* meaning "deformity" or "blemish," to describe a penis is
astounding in a cultural frame that so profoundly valorized maleness.

However, it might also be possible to think of Kalonymus as an example of how homosexual desire plays out in world that cannot name it. Might it be that for Kalonymus the only way to make sense of the desire to be loved by a man is to fantasize being a woman? Where only two genders exist and each with a particular desire, then the desire for a man might very well be articulated as a desire to be a woman. Whether this religious writer was transgendered, homosexual, or just remarkably sexually fluid, what is certain is that he was unafraid to articulate his desire that God change him miraculously into a woman. He fears none of the demotion. He longs for the life of a woman in spite of (or perhaps because of) its disempowerments. His paean to womanhood articulates the burdens of male identity along with the great emotional richness of a woman's life (even or especially) in a man's world.

The poem includes some telling talmudic references. Oblique references to talmudic texts were a necessary device for the medieval Jewish writer. More than a stylistic flourish, the use of talmudic references was a way to connect one's thoughts with the authorities of the past while demonstrating one's erudition at the same time. The references in the quoted selection having to do with bread and wine are actually sexual metaphors borrowed from a rather bawdy talmudic text: "Rabbi Judah said in the name of Rav: The men of Jerusalem were vulgar. One would say to his neighbor, 'On what did you dine today [whom did you bed today]? On well-kneaded bread [a married woman] or on poorly kneaded bread [a virgin]? On white wine [a light-skinned girl] or dark wine [a ruddy one]? On a wide couch [a wide-figured woman] or on a narrow couch [a slim one]? With a good friend [a beautiful woman] or a bad friend [homely one]?'"[4]

Bread and wine, we are told, were common euphemisms for the bedding of different sorts of women. This being so, it is odd for Kalonymus to employ them. His motive cannot be to demonstrate his knowledge or borrow authority from such a crude source. It appears, however, that Kalonymus had a very different agenda. Speaking as his fantasized woman-self, he actually turns the text inside out. Rather than representing the multiple ways by which men are sexually pleased, bread and wine become the multiple ways that the bride gets her young groom to sexually please her. Kalonymus moves the metaphor from the multiple partners that men want to the multiple techniques (with one partner) that women want.

His closing on the blessing that men are to say each morning, "Blessed are you, Lord, who has not made me a woman," is riveting. The early sages determined that a number of morning blessings were integral to the experiences of arising in the morning. Opening one's eyes was like seeing for the first time, stretching was like being released from prison, dressing was like being clothed by God, as were Adam and Eve. At the start of this morning ritual, focused on thankfulness, one finds the following blessing articulated not as an affirmation, but as a negation: "Blessed are you, Lord our God, ruler of the universe, who has not made me a woman." Much later, a blessing for women was fashioned that articulated an acceptance of the status of womanhood: "Blessed are you, Lord our God, ruler of the universe, who has made me according to his will." This blessing for women is written in the form of a *tsiduk ha'din,* a prayerful vindication of a painful divine judgment.[5] Similar to what one says when sad tidings are heard or when a loved one dies, "Blessed is the true Judge," this blessing calls on women to righteously accept the less than desirable condition of being a woman.

Kalonymus again turns the tables on the rabbis in their gender hierarchy. He reinterprets the blessing assigned to men and designed to remind them of their privilege and shapes it as a *tsiduk ha'din,* a quiet acceptance of a painful divine decree.

Bending the Gendered Blessings

The privilege of male identity seemed ordinary to me during my early twenties. But as I began to encounter and then address my gayness, in my late twenties, I began to understand that male privileges were primarily reserved for heterosexual men. Slowly I began to protest the blessing.

First, I insisted that it be said quietly, out of concern for hurting the feelings of women. Boasting about male privilege in female company might very well be a violation of a rabbinic prohibition of showing off in front of those less fortunate. One is not permitted to demonstrate in any outward way one's advantage among the disadvantaged. Such a public blessing might very well be "mocking the poor," or *loeg larash*.[6] Later, in my thirties, I refused to say the blessing altogether out of my growing feminist sympathies. Toward the end of my thirties I decided I needed a more positive practice than silence.

For nearly ten years now I have adopted the blessing that women say. The choice was motivated by the possibility that a man's adopting a woman's blessing was the best solution to the problem. It valorizes feminine experience and usage, serves as a queer practice by the gender inversion, and articulates what gay people in particular but also anyone, might rightly feel, which is that God has made us all as we are, and in this we are blessed. A translation true to the original Hebrew would read: "Blessed are you, Lord our God, who has created me just as he wished me to be."

Kalonymus rereads the traditional blessing's intent and also inverts its meaning. It was meant to affirm male identity as richer; he has it meaning the perfect opposite of this. It is remarkable that Kalonymus does not distinguish between his inner experiences and his religious strivings. He did not have the option of a sex-change operation to fix his deformed body and make it match his inner spirit. He also could not openly express homoerotic love, if that was motivating his desire to be a woman. But he could reread a blessing and invest it with its opposite meaning. It is just this sort of relationship between experience and practice toward which I am aiming. Like Kalonymus my sense of self leads to the rereading of the received tradition and the discovery of new and even contradictory meanings. In the time of Kalonymus he bravely transformed what was a blessing of privilege for most men into what was for him the humble acceptance of a harsh reality. I have decided to actively remake what was for most women a humble acceptance of a harsh reality into a profound and expansive blessing.

As we move to the legal material, it will be important to remember that law, like text, can be a rigid frame that permits a wide array of meanings, even contradictory ones, to exist inside its structure simultaneously. From here we are ready to move to the legal material, beginning with the construction of a single authoritative law code in the sixteenth century, the *Shulhan Arukh*.

8

The Legal Literature

The *Shulhan Arukh* is the basic code of Jewish law. Written in the sixteenth century, it still serves as the authoritative foundation for contemporary halakhic deliberation. Rabbi Joseph Caro of Safed, the primary author of the *Shulhan Arukh*, does not properly cite the prohibition of sexual intercourse between men in the code, which has been claimed to demonstrate "the virtual absence of homosexuality among Jews."[1] The opposite would appear to be the case.

The *Shulhan Arukh* does address the issue of same-sex relations obliquely by repeating the talmudic assumption that Jews were generally not suspected of *mishkav zakhar* (homosexual anal intercourse). In the absence of any such suspicion men were formally not prohibited from contact or seclusion with other men. Despite the Talmud's general assumption, R. Joseph Caro adds, "Since in our times the sexual degenerates have increased, there is reason to avoid privacy that might welcome physical intimacy with males."[2] This remarkable stringency of discouraging any two males from being alone together behind closed doors is likely a product of a very unusual community.

The *Shulhan Arukh* was written in the hills northwest of the Sea of Galilee in the city of Safed. Following the expulsion from Spain in 1492, many Jews seeking refuge found their way to Safed, bringing with them an esoteric mystical tradition. By the middle of the sixteenth century Safed had become a center of Jewish mystical life and literary creativity. In response to the exile a number of spiritual brotherhoods developed in the town, made up of men who shared great intimacy with one another. It is possible that erotic ties between men were not uncommon, especially among those in close-knit spiritual communities.[3] Whatever the meaning of the lacunae, sufficient real-life circumstances must have existed for R. Caro to invent a stringency not conceived of before him in any source.

The stringency of the *Shulhan Arukh* that discouraged the seclusion of two males was rejected by most of Caro's contemporaries. Rabbi Joel Sirkes of the sixteenth century claimed that Caro's stringency applied only to his locality or perhaps only to Jews of Sephardic communities who "were licentious in regard to this sin." In eastern Europe the rule was not applicable and might only be observed as a "pious custom." He adds, however, that two men ought not to sleep together in the same bed and that it was proper even to protest this practice when it occurred.[4]

In eastern Europe during the sixteenth century there was very little concern about these issues. Rabbi Shlomo Luria, author of the *Yam Shel Shlomo,* is even more lenient than Sirkes.[5] Disagreeing with Sirkes, he argues that it is completely permissible for two bachelors to sleep in the same bed under the same blanket. What emerges from these materials is the difference between various social worlds in regard to same-sex contact in general. In Sephardic contexts the rules were more suspicious of men, in eastern Europe much less so. When temptations were deemed high, legal fences were created to limit opportunities. When temptations were deemed relatively low, the legal fences, if any were erected, were low.

The famous mystic of Safed, Rabbi Isaac Luria (called the ARI), who lived roughly during the same period as the author of the *Shulhan Arukh,* offered to those who asked him a method of atonement for the sin of lying with men. Luria's material on this matter was transmitted orally to students and was intended as spiritual advice for those who desired the fullest sort of repair, *tikkun,* from sin.

The material was not included in any halakhic work of his age or any other until the dawn of modernity. A nineteenth-century scholar, Rabbi Joseph Hayyim ben Elijah al-Hakham from Baghdad, was the author of the *Ben Ish Hai,* a brief summary of practical Halakhah, which remains popular to this day among Sephardic Jews. In a collection of his responsa the editor records a question from a penitent young man seeking healing-atonement for having had sex with a man.

> And furthermore he [the penitent sinner] asked [R. Joseph Hayyim] about the healing-atonement *(tikkun)* for lying with a man. Our teacher the ARI [R. Isaac Luria] of righteous and blessed memory wrote that he should fast two hundred and thirty-three fasts and roll in the snow. The student wanted to know, if he fasted in the winter two hundred and thirty-three fasts expecting to roll in the snow during this time [but could not because] in the end there was no snow, would it help to roll in the snow later when it was available, or was he required to roll in the snow during the fasts? Moreover, he asked, if the *tikkun* of rolling in the snow worked even after the fast period, then perhaps the fasts alone were enough? Also, what if the snow had melted in one place and become water and he bathed in it, would this be sufficient or not?[6]

Rabbi al-Hakham encourages the penitent to find snow if he can or at least to rub his hands with snowlike frost nine times during the fast period. Bathing in the melted snow, he deduces from the words of the ARI, is acceptable as well. While the context is rather extreme, Rabbi al-Hakham actually takes a lenient position on the matter, permitting a symbolic form "snow rolling" in place of the real thing.

Such practices of penitential self-inflicted suffering have become alien to most Orthodox Jews today. It would be very rare to find, even among Hasidic rabbis steeped in mystical doctrine, a master encouraging his disciples to perform the prescribed two hundred and thirty-three fasts for the sin of sleeping with a man.

It is important to note that mortification of the flesh rarely went beyond fasting or minor sufferings such as sleeping on the floor with no mattress or pillow or, as we have seen, the rather outlandish practice of rolling in the snow. It is interesting as well that the mystical healings from the Middle Ages were designed not as halakhic responses to sins, but as spiritual ones. The idea of rolling in snow is found nowhere in the Talmud and was apparently invented by mystical pietists in Middle Ages. That such extralegal spiritual healings should be advised in the mid-nineteenth century as a quasi-halakhic duty suggests that private sin and personal healing had taken on a more public form just as homosexuality was finally addressed in the scientific discourses of the times. Until then those who knew of the Lurianic *tikkun* and chose to do it did so quietly. In the 1860s not only did this sort of question arrive at the desk of Rabbi al-Hakham, but it was deemed a matter of sufficient significance and public value to be printed in a volume of his responsa. While the idea of observing two hundred and thirty-three fasts seems rather extravagant, for a sin whose biblical punishment was death, a penalty carried out in the Middle Ages by some Christian courts, the absence of more serious censure is rather astonishing. When measured against masturbation at eighty-four fasts, sex between men appears to be a more severe sin of a similar category.

Evidence of the existence of lesbian relations, as noted earlier, is even more difficult to find. The most telling source is one we have already encountered. Maimonides, in another extrahalakhic stringency, tells us that "a man ought to be exacting with his wife on this matter (erotic relations with women) and should prevent her from associating with women known for this, not to permit those women to visit her nor her to visit them."[7] The policing of a wife's activities in regard to same-sex relationships with a suspicious eye toward their potential erotic content is not found anywhere in the earlier rabbinic literature. Maimonides must have had firsthand experience with this problem for him to add a caution of his own. It is also very interesting to discover that in the time of Maimonides certain women were "known for this," meaning their penchant for sex with other women.

Responsa Literature

Before we get more involved in the world of medieval responsa, a few words about the literature are in order. Responsa literature is the general name given the body of legal literature that developed following the close of the Talmud. In Hebrew the literature is called *she'elot u-teshuvot,* literally meaning "questions and answers." The leading halakhic thinkers of every age and place responded not only to real-life questions of individuals but to the pressing legal issues of the moment. The literature is a very helpful historiographic tool for discerning what Jews were doing and thinking from the early Middle Ages on. What emerges most clearly for us from this literature is that homosexual relations were only rarely addressed in the responsa.

It should be noted that much of the real life of Jewish communities was not well suited to the question and answer format. This sort of case-law literature responds mainly to anomalous situations rather than to ordinary ones. Most often it was a unique situation or an unusual opposition of competing values that demanded the attention of halakhic decision makers. Occurrences that defied easy categorization—acts, persons, objects, and time frames that for one reason or another were ambiguous—were opportunities for rabbis to display the depth and breadth of their learning. These texts were often designed as educational resources for the more learned community members. Among their purposes was to provide a way for rabbis to demonstrate their erudition and to publicize the rulings by which their communities were religiously governed.

On more rare occasions responsa were written polemically in response to new and challenging social, economic, scientific, or cultural realities that called for a revisiting of traditional norms. Sometimes these changes were met with resistance, sometimes with accommodation.

The dearth of responsa on the topic of homosexual relations should not be surprising. It is reasonable to assume that instances of homosexual behavior that did arise would only very rarely have reached the desk of a halakhic authority. Jewish courts, with extremely rare exception, did not have the option of capital punishment for any crime, including sexual crimes. Without that option less formal means of dealing with sexual misconduct were employed. While capital punishment of sexual misconduct was effected in Christian courts, throughout the Middle Ages it was considered treason for a Jew to deliver another Jew to a Christian court.

Lastly, family matters often stay closed within the sanctuary of the home. Until private behaviors affect questions of communal policy, they are unlikely to be made public. Even when such problems were brought to the attention of rabbis, because the prohibitions themselves were unchallenged, solutions were most often sought in an informal human relations mode rather than a legal one. Consequently the sexual deviance of a member of medieval Jewish society would not necessarily involve matters that a court would address. As we will see, only when such deviance affected the safety of children or the functioning of the communal fabric was it raised as a problem. Otherwise, no formal legal actions were generally sought or taken.

The few responsa regarding homosexual relations that do exist will help to demonstrate that medieval Jews addressed the occurrence of same-sex sexual relations with little of the anxiety that our society associates with homosexuality. While no premodern responsa offers overt permission for homosexual relations, they are surprisingly free of the kind of panic that homosexuality has inspired in Western culture. These texts help to show that contemporary religious authorities wishing to uniquely censure homosexual sexual relations are less traditional than they think.

It is important to mention that according to some scholars the responsa that do deal with male same-sex relations say little about what we today call "homosexuality." For nearly twenty years the debate has raged among historians of different sorts. Were there homosexuals before the late nineteenth century, or is the birth of sexuality itself and the homo-hetero divide a feature of modernity? The question is an important one if we are to make any generalizations from the responsa material to our own time.

According to the "constructionists" Michel Foucault and David M. Halperin, the homosexual is a modern invention. According to the "essentialists" John Boswell, Wayne Dynes, Fredrick Whitam, and Robin M. Mathy, there were homosexuals in premodern history despite the absence of clearly demarcated terms of identity such as "gay" or "lesbian."[8] Language is a problematic tool in this regard, because reality never quite fits in the procrustean beds that we use to reflect it. The very categories we use can impute more substantiality and clarity than actually exist and most always miss the nuances. Moreover, the availability of categories directs the efforts of social ordering and can reify one set of distinctions over another. According to this argument, the division of people along a hetero-homo divide invents an "identity," a type, that does not actually exist any more than an essential difference exists between people who like the taste of sardines and those who don't. If gastronomic appetite does not make a kind of person, why should sexual appetite?

However, others have claimed that while different cultural expressions of same-sex desire did emerge in different social contexts, the consistent desire of some people for same-sex emotional and physical companionship has been a consistent phenomenon throughout history. Suffice it to say that whether or not people could have so described themselves as homosexuals in the modern sense, there were always people who preferred to have genital contact with members of the same sex. What the responsa will show is that the phenomenon of sexual relations between members of the same sex did occur, but such relations were generally thought of as indistinct from any other violation of the Torah's code of behavior.

In most of the responsa dealing with same-sex relations one finds very little to mark the violation as particularly heinous. There appears to be no grandiose fear nor any diabolic connotations associated with this particular sin. It was deemed a sin like any other. Most of the responsa that touch at all on the issue of homosexual relations address it in terms of its communal consequences. Members known to have engaged in homosexual sexual contact might very well lose certain legal rights, might be deprived of certain sorts of work, but they were not drummed out of the community. They were deviant members of the community, but members just the same.

Rabbi Joseph ben Moshe, the fifteenth-century Ashkenazi author of the *Leket Yosher,* was asked if it is permissible to teach Torah to a boy who has violated the prohibitions against lying with a male *(mishkav zakhar)* and against stealing.[9] The question deals with an actual situation and was likely posed by a teacher of the boy. The problem for the teacher is a tradition that Torah should not be taught to the wicked. R. Joseph ben Moshe answered that since the boy can repent of even such grave sins, the learning might be considered helpful in that regard. In fact, the fundamental question that the *Leket Yosher* seems to be addressing is whether *mishkav zakhar* is a sin like any other, for which one can repent, or an evil condition that offers no real hope for repentance.

It is tempting to wonder whether the issue was a doubt concerning the sin of *mishkav zakhar* itself, the nature of its hold on a young boy, and the extent of his capacity to change. The *Leket Yosher* concludes, on the basis of conviction rather than empirical evidence, that the sin is an ordinary one. It is principally impossible for a sin to be essential to a person. Sins are by definition pathologies of behavior, given to change.

Rabbi Eliyahu ben Hayyim, a Turkish scholar of the sixteenth century and author of the *Mayim Amukim,* addressed the issue of a *shaliah tzibbur* (a role similar to a modern-day ritual director/cantor) who had been fired from a teaching position in another small town because he was suspected of sexual indiscretions, including his engagement in *mishkav zakhar.*[10] The responsum is most concerned with the nature of the accusations, how founded in fact or in mere gossip they were, and what kind of evidence and due process would be necessary to remove a communal servant from his post. The responsum ends with no final determination because of the lack of sufficient substantiating evidence.

Several responsa from the sixteenth through the nineteenth century focus their attention on the legitimacy of the legal testimony of a person who violates *mishkav zakhar.* The laws governing who is and who is not a proper witness in general disqualify a person who is a willful violator of the law. These responsa are evidence that individuals known to have engaged in same-sex sexual activity were considered functionally to be members of the community, even while they were not upstanding citizens.

One of the most outrageous responsa concerns the sexual exploits of a fellow named Moshko. The background story involves a young man, Joshua ben Abraham, who grabs two friends, Judah bar Isaac Cohen and Moshko Cohen, to come along with him to the home of a young woman, Palori, daughter of Rabbi Joseph. Joshua calls to her, and when she comes out, he gives her a gift and says, "Take this for the sake of marriage." Before the two witnesses, the young woman responds by taking the gift but says nothing. However, as the story proceeds, we discover that the whole affair was seen, if at a distance, by others. The various witnesses offered confusing accounts of exactly what happened, what the boy said specifically, and if the girl said anything at all. According to one witness the girl refused his proposal but took the gift anyway. The question posed to Rabbi Samuel di Medina of Salonika of the sixteenth century was to determine the validity of the marriage. Those bringing the question to R. Samuel were apparently hoping to invalidate the marriage.

Among the mitigating factors of the case was the character of one of the witnesses, Moshko, whose sexual exploits are brought to light in detail. The responsum includes the witnessed reports of not less than six different occurrences of sexual intercourse between Moshko and other young men.[11] For example, one of the witnesses, a certain David bar Nissim, testified that he and a merchant ventured to the edge of an orchard to ask the owner to sell them some fruit when they spotted Moshko and another young man in the midst of sexual intercourse. When the couple realized they had been seen, they ran away in different directions with their pants undone.

The responsum ends by roundly disqualifying the wedding on a number of grounds, the most important of which was the rejection of Moshko's legitimacy to serve as a witness to the original marriage ritual. While some medieval authorities permitted (explicitly in regard to marriage ceremonies) the testimony of someone suspected of sexual violation, most did not. Thus, R. Samuel felt confident to rule that the woman was never married and was permitted to marry whomever she wanted. Despite the many witnesses to Moshko's exploits, Rabbi Samuel does not raise the question of formal prosecution or punishment of Moshko.

Private sin, in this instance, comes to bear on the public domain in the courtroom. A very interesting case of this sort is found in the eighteenth-century responsum, *Mishpat Yesharim,* of Rabbi Raphael ben Mordechai Berdugo from Morocco.[12] The case concerned two men who were accused of being sexually involved. Such an accusation only came to the attention of the rabbi because the two were accused before they were scheduled to testify in a particular case and so disqualified before they could give evidence in court. In order to be able to testify, the two men claimed to have repented and submitted themselves to a punishment of flogging. The author of the responsum spends most of his effort proving the legitimacy of such a process of repentance even when it is clearly motivated by a desire to legitimate an upcoming testimony. His attention in the responsum is focused not so much on the nature of the particular sin as on the problematics of the process of repentance in general, which might legitimate an otherwise disqualified testimony.

In the middle of the nineteenth century, Rabbi Joseph Saul Nathanson of Poland responded to a case of sexual abuse.[13] Two young men testified that when they were children, a schoolteacher had sexual intercourse with them. The responsum addressed the problem of removing the teacher from his duties and even banning him from the profession on the basis of the testimony of the young men. The technical question at hand was whether two witnesses could testify legally to an event that had happened before they had come of bar mitzvah age. Rabbi Nathanson responded that such testimony could not convict for the death penalty. However, since what was at stake was the right of the teacher to continue teaching, an area of social rather than purely legal concerns, the testimony should be granted legitimacy. His reasoning was that in circumstances as secretive as sexual acts with minors, the testimony of the violated child is the best testimony that one is likely to get.

The nineteenth-century Iraqi scholar Rabbi Joseph Hayyim ben Elijah al-Hakham addressed a similar question in regard to authenticating a signature on a signed contract.[14] One of the contracting parties, again a teacher of children, had been accused years before of having sexual relations with a young boy, and since that time the young man had come of age. The problem was that the only person able to verify the signature of the teacher, and in doing so confirm the validity of a contract, was this same person, now a grown man. Having admitted to the fact that he and the teacher had once had sexual relations, his own legitimacy as a witness was in question. We are informed in the responsum that the alleged sexual relations occurred before the boy was nine years old. According to al-Hakham, since sexual relations with a boy under the age of nine years and a day are prohibited rabbinically and not biblically (this alarming fact will be addressed in chapter 13), his testimony is not disqualified because only a violation of a biblical law has the power to disqualify testimony.

What emerges from these responsa is that homosexuality existed and was dealt with. It was considered significant to the legal system when it interfered with the web of communal enterprises such as testimony in the courts or suitability for leading prayers or teaching children. The individuals addressed in the literature are sinners who have violated a prohibition, but they are not thought to be particularly threatening to the society. That belief essentially prevailed until the modern era.

In none of these responsa do we find the kind of horror and contempt that appears in the contemporary period. In none of the responsa do we find any distinction offered that might portray homosexual relations as a more horrifying sin than Sabbath violation. Indeed, public violation of the Sabbath was one of the sins that could actually deprive one of membership in the community, something that a sexual violation could not do. Sabbath observance was the most potent of social markers; it was, in effect, a sign of Jewish identity. Anyone publicly violating the Sabbath was deemed, in function if not in fact, a gentile. This assessment did not apply to the men discussed here who were known to be repeat offenders of the law against male sexual contact. We read in these responsa about an ordinary sin. It is only when we come to the modern period that we find sex between men moving from sinfulness to willful corruption and from prohibition to taboo.

9

Rav Moshe and the Problem of Why

"Thinking again?" the Duchess asked, with another dig of her sharp little chin. "I have a right to think," said Alice sharply, for she was beginning to feel a little worried. "Just about as much right," said the Duchess, "as pigs have to fly."

Lewis Carroll, *Alice in Wonderland*

In many social worlds asking certain questions would be considered traitorous, bait for the enemy. Such questions no one is permitted to ask. In my first year at Yeshiva University, a fellow student asked such a question. He wanted to know whether the whole received tradition, written and oral, had actually been given at Sinai. The rabbi's answer was "Well, where do you think you are, young man? The Reform rabbinical seminary?" Like the "wicked son" at the Passover seder, the questioner was responded to in anger and disdain.

Certain questions demonstrate that the questioner is marginal to the community. He would have never made it out of Egypt. They mark one as an outsider precisely because insiders don't ask this sort of question. And such threatening questions are not unique to traditional environments. They can be asked in the boardroom, in the university classroom, and in the halls of state. One infraction might be ignored, but repeated commitment to asking an inappropriate why is an invitation to social marginalization and potentially to eviction from the community.

The most dangerous questions are those that, like the question of the Yeshiva student, are not merely outside the social frame but are commonly associated with competing social or political movements or ideological frameworks. The threat to the rabbi at Yeshiva University was not merely a question out of his frame of reference, but a question that smelled of the religious opposition, Reform Judaism.

In our moment, to ask why two people of the same sex ought not be permitted to build a life together has become the epitome of such a question in the Orthodox community. This was not always so. The law against homosexual relations for nearly two thousand years was a rule like any other. Over the last two generations liberal governments, psychologists, and even clergy of some denominations have legitimated what was once deemed to be criminal, pathological, or at the very least immoral behavior. The increased public presence of gays and lesbians in day-to-day life, the rising political demands for equality and legitimacy, and the support that gay liberation has garnered among liberal Jews have turned the question into a threat and raised the stakes enough to demand a response from a great American Orthodox scholar, not merely on homosexuality, but on the very legitimacy of asking why.

Rav Moshe

Rabbi Moshe Feinstein, warmly referred to as Rav Moshe in Orthodox circles, is important to our inquiry for two reasons. First, he was one of the greatest and most innovative American halakhic authorities of the last century, unafraid to take bold positions on many contemporary issues. Second, his gut response to homosexuality will serve as a foil to our endeavors to understand the biblical prohibition. Despite his utter rejection of the question "Why does the Torah prohibit homosexual intercourse?" we will nonetheless engage this question in the next four chapters.

Rabbi Moshe Feinstein was born in Russia in 1895 and served as a rabbi in Russia until he moved to the United States in 1937. Under his leadership the yeshiva he headed, Mesivtha Tifereth Jerusalem in New York, became a leading center of Torah study in America. He was a leading halakhic authority of American Orthodoxy, and his responsa, which were widely circulated, are considered authoritative in Orthodox communities around the world. Many of these responsa deal with modern social and technological problems. He died in 1986, though his influence in print through his written responsa is as strong as ever in the Orthodox world.

In the 1970s, a Swiss publisher found a previously unknown manuscript of a Torah commentary attributed to the revered Rabbi Yehudah HeHasid of Regensberg, a German pietist of the twelfth century.[1]

Publication had begun when Rabbi Daniel Levy, concerned about certain "heresies" that he had found in it, sent a copy to a number of religious authorities. Rabbi Feinstein and others tried to halt the publication of the book, claiming that it was a forgery. While the publisher was willing to amend passages here and there to assuage Rabbi Feinstein and others, he insisted on the authenticity of the text and refused to stop publication. In the end the attempt to bury the manuscript failed. It was published, and despite the fact that it was virtually banned from the yeshiva world, the scholarly community has regarded it as authentic.

Among the alleged heresies found in the Torah commentary of Rabbi Yehudah is his comment on the prohibition in Leviticus of homosexual intercourse in which he addresses its rationale.[2] Here Rav Moshe makes his opinion known concerning the legitimacy of asking why.

> When the manuscript was sent to me by Rabbi Daniel, I saw in it another matter. The wicked had intended to weaken the prohibition of male homosexual intercourse, first by the question of why the Torah had prohibited it. In itself this is a great evil that weakens the prohibition for the wicked ones who have this ugly craving, which is so detestable that even the nations of the world know that there are no abominations like it. It needs no reason since it is an abomination, despised by all the world. All understand that transgressors of this sin are corrupt and not members of civilization at all. And when the reason is sought for this prohibition, the asking of such a question removes [from the prohibition] all the obscenity, shame, and disgrace, and completely disparages it. Moreover, his rationale [for the prohibition] is to ensure that men marry women and fulfill the commandment to reproduce [be fruitful and multiply]. This explanation only further weakens the prohibition. It is as if he is saying that there is no sexual prohibition at all except as a support to the positive command to reproduce, which is not considered a very serious matter by the world. It is prohibited to publish this, just as if it were heresy, since it reads a Torah text in a fashion contrary to the Halakha. Because errors like this in other places in the book can be found and because there is no one who can read through the book carefully from the beginning to the end [to remove such material], it is prohibited to publish even one word from it, according to my opinion.[3]

The diatribe of this responsum is caustic and painful. However, putting that factor aside for the moment, one must admit that politically speaking, Rav Moshe is right. Reasons undermine taboos. As I read this responsum for the first time, I had a very unsettling feeling. I realized that I was doing exactly what Rav Moshe feared would be done. Among my central tasks in writing this book is to ask why male homosexual intercourse is prohibited in the first place and then to theorize about the prohibition in ways that shed new light on it, its meaning, and application. According to his description, my work would seem to be an elaborate justification of vice, an attempt to halakhically rationalize sexual license.

What makes Rav Moshe's diatribe most pointed is that he is a conceptual thinker. He uses formal halakhic language in reaching his decisions but always decides on the correct form by considering the values content. Generally speaking, the enterprise of halakhic decision making cannot help but assume rationales in the process of interpreting, balancing, and nuancing traditions. Rav Moshe was hardly against considering strategic content questions for the purpose of determining the application of a law. For some reason it seems that this prohibition was unique. Rav Moshe, no doubt, felt true revulsion and horror at the thought of men having sexual relations. The strength of his response comes from his fear that if the law were to be explained, a sense of natural revulsion might be lost.

Rav Moshe makes it clear that there can be no ordinary scenario for male-male desire. Since taboos when violated shake the foundations of the earth, the only motive for crossing them must be wanton destructiveness for its own sake. In another responsum he suggests that homosexual desire is not desire at all. There can be no understanding of the experience of homosexuals because the desire for male homosexual sex is contrary to desire itself. Being without any human purpose, it must be rooted in an anarchic rebellion against God.

> Since the lust for male sex is against the essential (heterosexual) desire and even the wicked do not lust for this in particular, a person has such a craving because it is a prohibited thing and the evil inclination *(yetzer hara)* seduces him to rebel against the will of the Holy One, blessed be he.[4]

While Rav Moshe was often pained at the neglect of observance reflected in the questions that came to his door, he never prohibited an attempt to provide reasons for the observance of other *mizvot*. He certainly knew of the plethora of English books aimed at justifying and explaining the commandments to a nonobservant readership. The violation of the Sabbath laws or the marital laws (of abstinence during and shortly after menstruation) was no longer sufficiently taboo to inspire such horror. They could be supported with rationales marshaled in their defense and popularized in dozens of books. Male homosexual sex, however, was for him a living taboo, and he did not want it to slip into the realm of the explainable.

The Dangers of Demystification

Rav Moshe is not alone. The claims of those who actively oppose any weakening of religious or public sanction against homosexuals are most often without reason. The reasons when offered give the impression of being beside the point. Rarely are they contingent, and rarely does it matter to those who offer them. They use the Bible as their justification because it is not a reason but an authority for their horror.

Hester Prynne and her lover brought on themselves a ruination because they violated a taboo. Since the days of the Puritans, adultery has slipped out of the realm of taboo into the realm of rational, purposeful prohibitions. What was once a crime inspiring murderous passion is now more commonly seen as a private matter between two people, a violation of confidence, a disloyalty. The movement of adultery from a cultural taboo to an interpersonal contractual violation has contributed to the sense that rationalizing biblical sexual mores results in the weakening of the family unit.

Many who oppose the removal of sodomy legislation and the protection of the rights of homosexuals perceive homosexual inclusion as a palpable danger. The legitimation of gay sexuality is understood as just the kind of social dissolution that would bring ruin in its wake. A taboo is different from a prohibition in a number of ways, the most significant of which is that a taboo violation brings ruination not only to the perpetrators but to the collective as a whole.

Rabbi Feinstein's diatribe against asking why is another version of a very familiar tactic in antigay politics. President Clinton's "don't ask, don't tell" political solution for gays in the military was also the prohibition of a question. It, too, was motivated by irrational fears. Keep gayness secret and the new recruits will not have to wonder who is showering next to them. Among antigay religious groups a similar theme appears. Gayness must not be legally acknowledged in any way. Keep gay sex secret and it will remain shameful. Keep it covert and maybe only the infested pockets of Sodom and Gomorrah will burn. "Don't ask, don't tell" is a containment policy. Let the truth out, open the doors of the closets, reveal the lesbians kissing in our parks, the gay men in loving embrace on our streets, and the skies will open up ablaze over us all.

So how does one respond in a meaningful way to a taboo? One way, of course, is to insist that the whole frightful mess is superstitious hogwash. There is no curse, no ruination, no cosmic blight attendant to homosexual sex. A demystification of sexuality in general and of gay sex in particular seems imperative in order to proceed thoughtfully toward understanding.

However, as a religious person I am caught at this juncture, unable to chase away the old sacred narratives that map a holy and mysterious world and replace them with objective data. Demystification, or disenchantment, as Peter Berger would call it, is one of the calling cards of the modern era.[5] When mystery and transcendence are washed away and only the scientifically observable and the bureaucratically definable are left, we are perhaps easily freed from our demons; however, we are also deprived of a spiritual life. Where there is no wonder, no mystery, no meandering, no sense of a Presence hiding in the wings, then life is deprived of its deepest meanings.

And, of course, it is no surprise that sex is one of the things that we have the most trouble demystifying. Even though contraceptives have disengaged sex from inevitable life making, we still feel that the sexual experience is much more than can be accounted for by the physiology of orgasmic release. Sex is always a matter of the soul. The Jewish mystics believed that sexual desire did not originate in the person but was sent down from above.

It remains for us, then, to explore the tools of demystification, in this case the un-tabooing of a prohibition, in the service of knowledge, in a way that will not exile us from a holy world. The rabbis of the first and second centuries aimed their efforts at just such a paradoxical goal. They invented a way of thinking and talking about Scripture that unhinged certainties, opened up multiple meanings, and, by doing so, demystified the biblical law—and then they turned around and remystified it by finding, inside their conversational Torah study, the very workings of the divine.

Reasoning the Commandments

Thinking about the possible reasons for commandments, despite the speculative nature of the endeavor, is important in two ways. First, reasons help us to think more deeply about the possible good the Torah is seeking to achieve. By clarifying the various possible benefits that the fulfillment of the commandments might bring about, we are better equipped to implement them. Until we grasp the reasoning of a law, its attempt to achieve the good in some way, we cannot effectively apply it to varying situations.

Second, seeking the understanding of a scriptural law is a spiritual path for grasping the mind of the Law Giver, for knowing and ultimately loving God. Even more powerfully, the good reasons behind the laws of the Torah assure us of God's love for us. The law is not a tool of divine control, but a gift of divine love. In the *Ethics of the Fathers,* the sages teach that God gave the Torah to Israel out of love. They add that a love greater than this was shown to the people of Israel when God made known to them that the Torah was not merely divine legislation, but *"a teaching of the workings of goodness."*[6] Reasons make known to us the workings of goodness in the law.[7]

Not in Heaven!

We are about to embark on a journey into a way of thinking about sacred text and by extension, God, that may be unfamiliar to many readers. While we have met many rabbis on our way already, the next four chapters will focus almost exclusively on rabbinic literature. It will be helpful for us to know a bit more about these unusual men and their times before we sit down to learn with them.

Jewish scriptural traditions that had abounded from time immemorial were dislocated and tattered by the Roman War. After the destruction of Jerusalem and its Temple in the year 70 C.E., Rabbi Yohanan ben Zakkai moved the center of Jewish spiritual leadership to the town of Yavneh, a town on the coastal plain. In Yavneh great traditions were gathered as old and young scholars sifted through memory. The gathering reinforced some received traditions and placed others in doubt. The encounter also brought new intellectual and spiritual energies into the mix as these survivors of the war with Rome struggled to make theological sense of the catastrophe. The war generated two responses, one to remember and preserve what was lost and the other to engage with the tradition in more creative and energetic ways.

Perhaps the most famous of the Yavneh debates involves two representatives of these two postdestruction responses, an extreme preserver, Rabbi Eliezer, and his innovator opponent Rabbi Joshua.[8] An argument ensues surrounding a particular sort of oven and its purity (the details of which are unimportant for our discussion). R. Eliezer says that the oven is pure, while the sages are not convinced. When the sages, clearly in the majority, are ready to vote, R. Eliezer rallies miracle after miracle to demonstrate the truth of his received tradition.

> They taught: If he cut the [earthenware] oven into rings and separated each ring with sand, R. Eliezer declares it pure; the sages declared it impure. . . . On that same day R. Eliezer provided them all (the) arguments in the world, but they did not accept them from him."
>
> He said to them: "If the Halakhah agrees with me, let this carob tree prove it." At which point the carob tree was torn a hundred cubits out of its place (and some say four hundred cubits). They said to him: "No proof can be brought from a carob tree!" Again he said to them: "If the Halakhah is as I say, let the aqueduct prove it." Whereupon the water in the aqueduct flowed backwards. They said to him: "No proof can be brought from an aqueduct!". . . .
>
> He then said: "If the Halakhah agrees with me, let the heavens prove it!" [Whereupon] a heavenly voice declared: "What do have against R. Eliezer, the Halakhah agrees with him everywhere!"
>
> R. Joshua rose to his feet and declared: "It is not in heaven!" (Deut. 30:12)
>
> What did he mean by "It is not in heaven!"? R. Yermiah said:

"Since the Torah was given at Mount Sinai, we pay no heed to heavenly voices, for you have already written in the Torah at Mount Sinai: 'incline after a majority.'" (Exod. 23:2)[9]

R. Eliezer is incensed by the Yavneh court's willingness to vote when he has a reliable tradition on the matter. Possessing the miraculous powers of a prophet, he pulls out all the stops and finally gets heaven to intervene on his behalf. R. Joshua's audacious response to the heavenly voice is groundbreaking. God is told that the Torah is no longer in his possession. He has given it to human beings, and it is now in their hands to debate and then to decide the law according to the majority opinion. God is held accountable to what is written in his Torah, overruled, in effect, by his own law "to incline according to the majority." The story takes one theological step further in the epilogue that follows.

R. Natan met Elijah and asked him: "What did the Holy One, Blessed be he, do in that moment?" He [God] laughed [with joy] and said, "My children have defeated me, my children have defeated me."[10]

A laughing God who takes pleasure at his children's independence embodies a powerful new theology. The age of prophecy is over. The Torah is not in heaven, but in the hands of the wise of every generation whose responsibility it is to implement the law in their own moment by majority decision. This story portrays a revolution in theology by which the divine authority is not in a single received meaning of the text but in its very letters, black fire upon white fire, given over fully to the interpretation of human beings.

The responsibility for developing the oral Torah, declares R. Joshua and his followers, is charged to the mundane, worldly sensibilities of the human learner. The covenant of learning, of Torah study, is understood by the Yavneh court as founded on a sharp demarcation of divine and human authorities dividing between "the word and meaning, between text and understanding, between interpretandum and interpretans."[11] Or as Daniel Boyarin puts it, "Meaning is not in heaven, not in a voice behind the text, but in the house of the *midrash,* in the voices in front of the text. The Written Torah is the Torah which is written and Oral Torah is the Torah which is read."[12]

While the innovators carried the day in Yavneh and throughout much of the Babylonian Talmud as well, the tension between preservation and innovation did not disappear. We will begin our inquiry into the verses in Leviticus with a methodology associated with innovators. Asking why and seeking reasons for the written word is at the very heart of the Yavneh legacy. After our exploration of rationales we will return to a preservationist sensibility, the possibility that the law is beyond our rationalizing, but for the moment let us ask the question outright:

Why does the Torah prohibit intercourse between men?

In the following four chapters, four distinct rationales for the prohibition in Leviticus will be presented, each with differing grasps of the problem of male homosexual relations and each inviting very different analyses and policy implications. They are:

1. The rationale of reproduction. The law prohibits a form of sexual expression that by definition cannot produce a child.
2. The rationale of social disruption. The law prevents husbands from abandoning their wives for sexual adventure with men.
3. The rationale of category confusion. The law prohibits a form of sexual intercourse that confounds the categories of maleness and femaleness.
4. The rationale of humiliation and violence. The law prohibits a form of sexual expression that is, by definition, driven by power, control, and domination.

Rationales

10

The Rationale of Reproduction

"'Therefore shall a man leave his father and mother and cleave to his wife, and they shall become one flesh' (Gen. 2:24). . . . [T]hey shall become one flesh through offspring in which their flesh is united into one."

Rabbi Shlomo ben Isaac

Why should the Torah prohibit male sexual intercourse? The first and most commonly offered rationale is that God made sexual desire so that men and women would produce offspring. If the intended purpose and ultimate raison d'être of sex is reproduction, then nonreproductive sex might be seen as a problematic abuse of sexual pleasure. Any uses of sexuality that contravene the procreative purpose by seeking other goods of sexuality to the exclusion of procreation would be proscribed. The twelfth-century pietist we encountered in the last chapter, Rabbi Yehudah HeHasid, offers just this rationale for the prohibition in Leviticus.

> Why did the Torah prohibit sexual intercourse between males or between humans and animals? All this is in order that men marry women and fulfill the command to be fruitful and multiply. And even though [this prohibition of male intercourse] carries with it capital punishment and the duty to procreate is just a positive command, the Torah deemed it necessary to [prohibit male intercourse so strongly in order to] guard the law [of procreation] by erecting a [legal] fence around it.[1]

Rabbi Yehudah's unassuming question already challenges a number of assumptions. First, as noted in the previous chapter, the question demonstrates that the prohibition against sexual intercourse between men is not self-explanatory. Male intercourse is not prohibited because it is intrinsically hateful or disgusting. There is a purpose for the Torah's legislation against such acts. Just by asking the question in this open fashion, R. Yehudah has prepared us for a purposive law aimed at some rational good rather than a gut response to depravity.

The purpose of the law in Leviticus according to R. Yehudah is to support and protect the duty to marry and have children. Before we explore the implications of Rabbi Yehudah's rationale for the prohibition of homosexual relations, it makes sense to clarify the mitzvah of procreation.

Reproduction

After the creation story in the Book of Genesis the world is a vast garden with two human inhabitants. God blesses the human pair with the famous words: "Be fruitful and multiply and fill the earth" (Gen. 1:28). However, this blessing becomes a duty when, after the devastation of the flood, it is repeated as a charge to the sons of Noah.[2] The rabbis of the first century read this text in Genesis as a duty for males to produce at least one son and one daughter.[3]

The rabbis of the Talmud added to this biblical law a rabbinic duty "to settle the world." They derived this duty from the words of Isaiah, "Not for void did he create the world, but for habitation did he form it."[4] Because of the risk of infant mortality, the limit of two was deemed fundamentally insufficient. Moreover, replacing oneself is not adequate if the goal is to contribute to and extend the world's human habitation. Rabbi Joshua carries the duty even further and actively rejects the Mishnah's claim that two children are enough. "If a man has married in his youth, let him also marry in his old age. If a man has had children in his youth, let him have children in his old age."[5] The duty to reproduce continues unabated from youth to old age. Rabbi Joshua's position has been actively adopted by ultra-Orthodox couples, who commonly have eight or more children.

Interestingly, the Halakhah excluded women from the duty to reproduce and offered various reasons for doing so.[6] The midrash on Genesis seems to suggest an anxiety that if women were commanded to procreate, they could easily fall prey to a well-intended promiscuity.[7] Others suggest that women do not need to be commanded to reproduce because their instinct for bearing children is already strong enough.[8]

The duty to reproduce was surely related to the threats to survival in the ancient world. Children in our social world are consumers; for the ancients children were producers, necessary for the family economy. For the family, tribe, and nation under threat, population increase is always a boon. While the ancients may well have been persuaded by the simple demands of economic survival, the rabbis saw the commandment to reproduce as an extension of divine creativity and an affirmation of the essential goodness of the world.

In the first chapter of Genesis each completed stage of the process is "good." When the cosmos is finished, "God saw everything that God had made and behold it was very good" (Gen. 1:31). By creating new life we become partners with God in the creation celebrated as "very good." More pointedly, the duty to procreate affirms that human life is good. To enjoy life was thought to be an obvious duty, to reject its joys and pleasures a blatant rejection of the creator.[9] "A man will have to give account on the judgment day for every good permissible thing that he might have enjoyed and did not."[10] If life is a precious gift, then how can we not feel a deep gratitude to our ancestors and a profound responsibility to repeat the kindnesses we received from them by producing a new generation of children?

Parenting joins us not only in the efforts of creation but also in the ongoing caretaking that follows. Like God we do not create and walk away. The ordeal of rearing children was understood as a moral education, a crucible of maturity and compassion.[11] We are taught that no rabbi was accepted to serve on the high court, the famed Sanhedrin of Jerusalem, unless he had already fathered and reared children. The experience of parenting was deemed central to the development of a self-sacrificing and compassionate personality.

Lastly, mystical reasons were adduced to explain the command. Some mystics claimed that the messiah could not come, and with him the perfect world, until all the souls created in the beginning and stored up in heaven had been born, lived, and died. The original Adam, according to the *Zohar*, is a treasure chest of souls waiting to be born. If so, then procreation becomes a way to hasten the coming of the perfection of the end of days.[12]

As important as reproduction is, Jewish tradition offers little if any support for the claim that reproductive capacity is necessary for legitimate sexual expression. In the context of marriage, sexual intercourse is permitted with pregnant, nursing, and menopausal women. A mishna in Yevamot did press the concern of reproduction to the point that after ten years of a childless marriage a man ought to divorce his wife, but later authorities actively overturned this position.[13] The sages were not eager to end happy marriages because a couple failed to reproduce. In response to the mishna, Rabbi Idi tells a beautiful story of barren love.

A couple had been married for ten years and had not been blessed with children. Because they had not yet fulfilled the duty to procreate, they agreed to divorce. They went to Rabbi Shimon bar Yohai, who failed to dissuade them. He bid them to make a feast for their separation just as they had done for their wedding. At the feast the husband asked his wife to choose whatever precious treasure she desired most from his home and return to her father's house. At the end of the feast the husband, having drunk too much wine, fell asleep, and at midnight he awoke to find himself with his wife at her father's house. "How did I end up here?" he asked. She responded, "Did you not bid me take the most precious treasure for myself from your house? You are my most precious treasure." And, of course, they lived happily ever after.[14]

In the seven wedding blessings recited under a huppah at a Jewish wedding, the theme of reproduction is alluded to in the third blessing. "Blessed are you, Lord our God, ruler of the universe, who . . . established from within humanity *(adam)* a building for eternity. Blessed are you, Lord, creator of the human being *(adam)*."[15] Overwhelming this subtle reference to future generations, the seven blessings are filled with the exuberance of the physical and emotional fulfillments of love. "Blessed are you, Lord our God, ruler of the universe, who . . . brings intense joy and exultation . . . who gladdens the beloved companions as they were in the Garden of Eden . . . who created joy and gladness, groom and bride, mirth and song, pleasure and delight, love and fellowship, and peace and companionship."[16]

However, the weakness of the argument from procreation aside, the use of the duty to reproduce as a rationale for the prohibition of male homosexual relations, whether by ancients or moderns, opens up some very interesting questions. First, why should legislation be necessary to ensure that men marry and have children? Isn't this what most people ordinarily do? Second, of all the legislative ways to encourage marriage, why would the prohibition of male sexual relations be foremost? What R. Yehudah does not elucidate is the nature of the countermotivation to marriage and family. One is struck with the possibility that R. Yehudah assumed that men are not ordinarily heterosexual. Were they, then there would be little use in prohibiting homosexual outlets that few would care to pursue. According to this rationale men are at the very least bisexual, if not omnisexual. This being so, humanity is in need of the prohibition of male intercourse to ensure the survival of the species. It is remarkable to discover in a medieval text that ordinary men are held to have desires for other men that, if permitted, would be rampant. According to R. Yehudah it would appear that male bisexuality is the problem that the prohibition comes to solve.

However, there is another way to read R. Yehudah. It is possible that the motivation of men to have their sexual needs met with other men rather than with women turns less on the inherent bisexuality of most men than on the enormous investment that sex with women entails. This reading of R. Yehudah would suggest that heterosexual partnership leading to marriage and children is in danger without the law because men would ordinarily prefer sexual expressions that are less cumbersome. Do away with the prohibition of same-sex sexual expression and most men will simply choose a form of sexual release that obligates them in no real way toward a partner, a community, and—with the absence of children—the future of the tribe. According to this reading, if society allows men to find sexual release with other men, then the necessary sexual pressure for ordinary heterosexual men to marry would be compromised.

Reuven Kimmelman of Brandeis University has echoed this rationale for the prohibition of same-sex sexual expression.[17] Given the impact of contraception on contemporary sexual behavior, this particular argument seems a bit absurd. To propose that straight men trying to avoid the responsibilities of family would prefer to have sex with men rather than use a condom with a woman strains the imagination. Furthermore, the notion that men will always seek the least committed form of sexual gratification doesn't hold up.

While the availability of nonreproductive sex has made it possible for many to postpone marriage, the desire for marriage and family making has not abated.

Wasting Seed

The rationale of procreation is supported not only by the biblically mandated duty to reproduce but also by rabbinic legislation against the wasteful emission of semen, called *hotzaat zera levatalah*.[18] The Mishnah (Niddah 2:1) states: "Every hand that frequently checks [for genital emissions]: in women, it is praiseworthy but among men you should cut it off." (It is important to keep in mind that rabbis often employed hyperbole to support a tradition not expressly mandated by scripture.) Women are deemed praiseworthy for checking frequently to see if they have begun their menstrual flow, in order to know when they must refrain from intercourse with their husbands. However, why men should not touch their genitals frequently is not quite so obvious. Early rabbinic material explains that touching with one's hands body orifices or open wounds can lead to bad health, but the more common explanation was that a man ought not to touch himself lest he arouse himself sexually and ejaculate.[19]

As the discussion in the Babylonian Talmud unfolds, two distinct problems appear: the problem of self-arousal and the problem of a wasteful emission of semen. The difference between these two interpretations of the mishna is significant. Self-arousal was understood as a problem of pleasure and self-control having nothing per se to do with semen. The wasting of semen, on the other hand, was construed as a misappropriation, a misuse of the body and its powers. There was a good deal of difference of opinion on these matters between rabbis living in the Land of Israel and those living in Babylona, but the most important distinction is found between the early and later strata of the text.

Michael Satlow has demonstrated that the material prohibiting the waste of semen in the Babylonian Talmud was created entirely by the editors of the Talmud. While earlier rabbis (especially those in the Land of Israel) inveighed against self-arrousal, only in the latest editorial layer of writing does the discourse move to the waste of seed.[20] Satlow adds that editing of the Talmud in Babylonia took place during the heyday of Zorastrian religion and that the Zoroastrians were known for their very severe views on the wasting of seed. If Satlow's analysis is correct, then the concern with wasting semen would not be a feature of Tanaitic or Amoraic tradition.[21]

The power of editors, however, can be decisive. The halakhic codifiers followed the lead of the redactors and prohibited both self-arousal and wasting semen. The most severe formulations of the rule against wasting seed are found in the mystical tradition. The *Zohar*, the primary textbook of Jewish mysticism, describes masturbation as "a sin more serious than all the sins of the Torah."[22] While this was considered grossly hyperbolic by many halakhic authorities, the expression crept into the authoritative law code, the *Shulhan Arukh*, and as such could not be easily ignored.[23]

The destruction or wasting of seed is cited as the central problem of male homosexual relations by a famous medieval work by Rabbi Aaron HaLevi of Barcelona. The *Sefer HaHinnukh*, or "book of education," composed in the early fourteenth century is a catalog of the 613 commandments along with material on their legal structure and rationales. Here is the particular rationale offered for commandment number 209, the prohibition for men not to have sexual relations with men.

> The source of this commandment is that God desires the settlement of the world, which he created, and so he commanded [men] not to destroy their seed by intercourse with males, for this is indeed destruction. It effects neither offspring nor the fulfillment of the command to pleasure one's wife *(mitzvat onah)*.[24]

For R. Aaron HaLevi, male homosexual relations fail to accomplish either of the two legitimate goals of sex, producing offspring and pleasuring a wife. Either would be sufficient. Were a man to pleasure his wife and not be at all able to reproduce, his semen would not be wasted. Waste does not mean that *every* drop of semen must be able to fertilize an egg. It means that it is located in a heterosexual relationship that includes both desire for reproduction and ongoing sexual fulfillment of both parties. Masturbation and male intercourse are both blatant violations of the rule because they cannot result in progeny and they are not a mutually pleasurable part of heterosexual marital life.

A common and erroneous biblical source cited in regard to masturbation is the story of Onan in Genesis 38:4–10. According to the Bible, Onan's sin was not spilling seed per se, but his failure to discharge his duty as a levirate husband. The levirate law described in Deuteronomy 25:5 permits a unique override of a law of incest when one of two brothers dies before fathering any children. Normally a sexual relationship between a man and his sister-in-law, even after the brother's death, was considered incestuous and forbidden (Lev. 18:16). But if the brother died before producing a child, his surviving brother was urged to marry the widow to produce a child that would be heir to the deceased brother. Onan was all too willing to enjoy intercourse with Tamar, his deceased brother's wife, but he did not really want to sire any children in his brother's name. Onan was punished because he was a sexual opportunist. He took advantage of the levirate law, had relations with Tamar, and then pulled out before ejaculation to avoid impregnating her. There is little in this source to support a general biblical prohibition on nonprocreative seminal emission.[25]

Still, there were authorities who tried to sustain the idea that the prohibition against wasting seed was indeed of biblical authority. One medieval opinion held that the prohibition of wasting seed was fully entailed in the biblical duty to reproduce.[26] Another opinion suggested that prohibition might be subsumed under the general prohibition against destructiveness *(baal tash-hit)* in Deuteronomy 20:19.[27] The need to find a biblical authority was so great that it has been suggested that the law was orally transmitted to Moses on Sinai.[28] However, the dominant view has been that of Maimonides, who determined the prohibition to be rabbinic and not biblical.[29]

The prohibition against spilling seed did not prevent an active sex life between married couples even when pregnancy was impossible. As mentioned earlier, intercourse is permitted with pregnant, nursing, postmenopausal, or sterile women, and anal intercourse between a man and his wife is also generally permitted.[30] Unlike the sodomy laws that have persisted from medieval times in Christian and modern secular states, rabbinic laws held that sodomy between husband and wife was a legitimate marital relation.[31]

The decisive lenient position in regard to "waste of semen"

within the context of heterosexual marriage was proposed by Rabbi Isaiah ben Mali di Trani.[32] His position is that everything depends on intent. If the husband's intent is to avoid pregnancy so that his wife's beauty is not marred or because he simply does not want to fulfill the command to reproduce, then he "wastes his seed" in any manner of nonreproductive ejaculations. But if his intent is to spare his wife physical hazard or even if he simply intends his own pleasure, as long as the ejaculation is part of ongoing marital relations and is not designed to avoid pregnancy altogether, it is permitted.

While men were discouraged from marrying women unable to produce children, such marriages were permissible because they served the purpose of pleasure and mutuality. This being so, it appears that nonreproductive sexual relations are permitted if there is no active rejection of childbearing and such relations are part of a mutually pleasurable marital relationship. While pleasure alone allegedly did not suffice to legitimate sexual activity, mutual pleasure was central to the very definition of marriage.

In the halakhic discourse contraception has generally been permitted when a wife's health and well-being are at stake. For this purpose the diaphragm has been widely permitted (based on a similar talmudic contraceptive device called a *mokh*), while the condom has been roundly prohibited. The reason for this distinction is that the diaphragm leaves the vagina open for "free unimpeded contact and the release of sperm in full physical pleasure and 'in the flaming ardor of passion' (Song of Songs 8:6)."[33] With a condom, however, a man does not "cleave to his wife, becoming one flesh" because there is no flesh-to-flesh contact.[34] The tradition was understood not merely to tolerate pleasure but to require that "body derive pleasure from body" *(guf nehene min-haguf)*.[35] It is a remarkable feature of traditional Jewish sexual ethics that it views the condom as problematic, not especially because it interferes with reproduction, but because it interferes with the mutual pleasuring, body to body, of a heterosexual couple.

Gay Men and Reproduction

Are gay men obligated to reproduce? Rabbinic authorities are split on this issue. Some have suggested that with or without desire, a man is duty bound to marry and reproduce. In a summary of the Orthodox position on homosexuality, Rabbi Dr. Alan Unterman, a lecturer in comparative religion at Manchester University and a congregational rabbi in Manchester, writes: "[I]t is not demanded that one should be sexually attracted to members of the opposite sex, but it is demanded that, attracted or not, one should still get married and have children."[36]

However, according to Rabbi Chaim Rapoport, advisor to the chief rabbi of England on matters of Jewish medical ethics, a gay man who is "completely homosexual" is exempt from the duty to reproduce and in most cases should not marry. In response to Rabbi Untermans position on the matter, Rabbi Rapoport says that the Jewish commitment to marriage and procreation should be sustained "where the potential for a healthy and stable [heterosexual] marriage exists." However, "those unable to find a suitable spouse or who are constrained by mental or physical incapacity are exempt from fulfilling this commandment."[37] He bases his position on the solid halakhic ground that in regard to positive commandments, a person need not exhaust all possibilities. In order to fulfill a positive command such as the duty to "be fruitful and multiply," a person need not expose himself or herself to health hazards or trauma.

Another argument could be offered on the basis of the opinion of Rabbi Joseph Engel, the head of the High Jewish Court of Cracow in the early 1900s. He writes that while duress does not free a person completely from his or her duties to other human beings, God does not demand compliance in the absence of freedom. "God does not act imperiously with his creatures, to demand fulfillment from those who cannot fulfill."[38] In regard to the duty to reproduce two separate commandments are involved, as we have seen in the preceding discussion: a duty to "be fruitful and multiply" from Genesis and a separate duty to "settle the earth," from Isaiah's affirmation that God created the world for habitation (Isa. 45:18). If one cannot by reason of duress fulfill the first duty, he is completely exempt. The second duty, as understood by Rabbi Engel, is a responsibility to humanity rather than to God. To actively contribute to the shared enterprise of human civilization remains despite one's condition of duress, but this obligation may be fulfilled in other ways.

Excluding gay men formally from procreation may have a secondary benefit in regard to other halakhic concerns. According to Rabbi Jacob ben Meir Tam, the leading French authority of the twelfth century, a person not commanded to "be fruitful and multiply" is not commanded concerning the prohibition of wasting seed.[39] Spilling seed is only a problem for those men who are formally responsible for having children. According to this opinion, since gay men are not obligated to marry and bear children, the problem of spilling or wasting seed may very well be irrelevant to their sexual ethics.

If gay men are not duty bound to reproduce, and if in the absence of that duty, there is no rabbinic problem in the destroying of seed, then it would appear that as long as gay men do not have intercourse, they are violating no prohibitions, rabbinic or otherwise. Moreover, if such is the case, then the prohibition of male anal intercourse itself cannot be explained by the rationale of procreation since gay men have already been relieved of that duty.

While the rationale of reproduction has been used by many to explain the prohibition in Leviticus, it is clear that it does not hold up to scrutiny. However, despite the weakness of this rationale, a contemporary Jewish philosopher, David Novak, has attempted to revive it.[40] Novak claims that the fundamental purpose of sex is procreation and that since homosexual relations are by definition a rejection of procreation, such relations ought to be rejected. He acknowledges three legitimate purposes of human sexuality: pleasure, mutuality, and generativity.[41] However, he claims that only when an act accomplishes all three aims can it be considered "natural." Because Novak knows that Jewish law permits sex between heterosexual partners who cannot reproduce, he insists that gay sex "by design does not intend children." Sterile couples have an "unintended impediment" to procreation, while gay couples have an "intended impediment." Because only heterosexual acts can accomplish all three purposes, natural law would sanction no other use of the sexual organs. While Novak's arguments are far from convincing and poorly supported by the sources, he raises issues that bear addressing.

Novak claims that gay sex by design does not intend children. Whatever Novak means by attributing intentionality to gay nonreproductivity, he is not supported by the experience of gay people.

Since the biological simplicity of heterosexual reproduction is not available to homosexuals, many lesbian and gay couples are opting to build families in other ways. Whether by surrogacy or adoption, homosexuals are choosing to be parents, despite the social, economic, and legal difficulties. Gayness is no more an automatic intentional rejection of procreation than is straightness a sworn promise of it.

The strangest element of Novak's argument is his dependence on a version of natural law to ground his argument. He claims that because nature intends men and women to produce children even if they cannot, the form of the union of such couples is in concert with family and generation and is thus permissible. Gay unions are by design "contra naturam," against nature, no matter what the couples personally might wish.

While Christianity was in need of a natural law, it is doubtful that Jews ever subscribed to such a notion.[42] For Jews nature is an expression of the divine, but it cannot command; that is God's prerogative alone. Nature, for Jews, is a precious context, but not a normative ideal.[43] Perhaps the best example of this view is circumcision. In this case the unnatural state is commanded. Greeks found this Jewish custom most reprehensible because it tampered not only with nature but also with natural beauty. What is considered "nature," however, is always culturally linked. What for Jews was most "natural," for Greeks was the epitome of the violation of nature. There is no unmediated appeal to nature. Nature is a text that can say almost anything we want it to say while appearing to have said nothing but what is evident.

Even more worrisome are the abuses of the idea of a natural law. The "natural-unnatural" dichotomy is very easily mapped over the inside-outside categories of any society. Natural is us; unnatural is them. Such a definition of nature has grounded racial stereotypes and has been used by the most oppressive regimes to justify their violence. European anti-Semites of the last century thought Jews to be a violation of nature. The non-Jewish advocates for the emancipation of Jews in England and France claimed that what appeared to be the "natural" diseases of the Jews were induced by the social degradations to which they were subject. Others insisted that these corruptions were innate and that no emancipation would correct them. In the same vein, the argument that grounds heterosexuality in nature and then describes homosexuality as unnatural is a mere cover for a culturally embedded prejudice.

In fact, the argument could very well be turned on its head. Homosexuality might easily be described as a naturally occurring variance that appears in 5 to 10 percent of the population of most societies. The reliability of homosexual orientation across cultures has puzzled those evolutionary anthropologists who believe that homosexuality is associated with a particular gene. How could a gene that inhibits reproduction survive natural selection? Some scientists have suggested that the gene controlling homosexuality was sustained, despite the lack of reproductive incentive, because families in which homosexuals are born may fare better because at least one of the children is available to help care for and support the other siblings and their families.[44] It may be that a gay brother or sister increases the genetic success of an individual who possesses the recessive gay gene. Whether this logic stands up to scrutiny or not, homosexuality might very well be as natural as left-handedness and perfect pitch.

Bruce Bagemihl, a biologist and researcher at the University of British Colombia, has discovered more than 450 species in which scientific observers have noted homosexual or transgendered behavior.[45] Drawing on a rich body of zoological research spanning more than two centuries, Bagemihl's research shows that animals engage in all types of nonreproductive sexual behavior. While the evidence from animal behavior doesn't legitimate corresponding human behavior, it makes it unmistakably wrong to claim that same-sex courtship, sexual relations, and pair-bonding are, formally speaking, unnatural.

Novak makes another outrageous claim in regard to nature. He claims that since the genitals were obviously created for the purpose of generation, any other use of them ought to be considered illegitimate and proscribed. What he does not explain is why the Creator should take offense at human ingenuity and expansiveness. It is hardly obvious that organs created for a central purpose may not be used for any other. We have a mouth for eating, without which we cannot survive. We do many things with our mouths that are for our pleasure or amusement alone, without which we can survive. We speak, sing, laugh, and kiss with our mouths. Because these forms of communication are secondary to the mouth's usefulness in eating hardly makes them immoral. Why then should using our sexual organs for communication and relationship be any more morally problematic? What we do with our bodies beyond necessity is a large part of what makes us human. We are innovators, always pushing the boundaries of our physical context. Nature surely did not mean us to fly, but because our imagination and ingenuity is boundless, we now soar higher than the birds.

Novak concludes his argument with the audacious claim that "any situation in which family life is absent, especially when that absence is intended, takes a toll on one's humanity."[46] One can much more persuasively claim that forcing a homosexual person into a heterosexual marriage that would accomplish the motive of reproduction but not the motives of pleasure and personal communion would take an even greater toll on one's humanity and that of others.

In the Absence of Desire

That reproduction is necessary for the survival of humankind is obvious. While the mitzvah was taken seriously, its fulfillment was not understood as a technical matter independent of human relationships. The rabbis, of course, had experience with men who did not want to marry. It seems that celibacy was common enough in the first and second centuries, and that worried the sages. They were very insistent that students of Torah not put off marriage indefinitely. In the Land of Israel rabbis preferred their students to learn Torah first and then to marry. In Babylonia students were encouraged to marry first and then learn.[47] However, try as they might, they could not convince one of Rabbi Akiva's prized students, Ben Azzai, to marry.[48] One gets the feeling from the following text that he is being coerced by his colleagues into voicing a halakhic opinion on a profound failure in his life. The blessings and warnings offered to Noah following the deluge ground the rabbis' discussion, so they are cited first.

> Whoever spills the blood of *adam* (usually translated "man"), by *adam* will his blood be spilt, for in the image of God did he make the *adam*. So then, be fruitful and multiply; abound on the earth and increase on it. (Genesis 9:6–7)

It is taught:

Rabbi Eliezer says: Anyone who does not engage in producing children, it is as if he spills blood. As it is said: "He who spills the blood of *adam,* by *adam* shall his blood be spilt," and later it says, "So then, be fruitful and multiply."

Rabbi Jacob said: It is as if he diminishes the image of God [in the world]. As it says: "for in the image of God did he make the *adam*" . . . and afterward . . . "So then, be fruitful and multiply."

Ben Azzai said: It is as if he both spills blood and diminishes the image of God, since it says [after both phrases], "So then, be fruitful and multiply."

They said to Ben Azzai: There are those who learn well and fulfill well, those who fulfill well but do not learn so well, [it appears that] you learn well but do not fulfill very well.

Ben Azzai said to them: What shall I do? My soul lusts for Torah and likely the world will be sustained by others.[49]

Ben Azzai defends his bachelorhood with a very strange claim: What can I do? In rabbinic circles this would seem to be a laughable contention. The Torah commands many things that one might not want to do. That a mitzvah is uncomfortable or difficult is hardly an excuse. His explanation is even more puzzling. Why would lusting for the Torah preclude marriage and children? Do not his colleagues also spend most of their time and energy in the study of Torah? Why should his love of Torah free him, but not his colleagues, from the command to reproduce?

The answer must be that he is leaving the embarrassing truth out. His lust is *only* for Torah. He simply does not desire women. The language of *heshek* is one of passion. Ben Azzai is claiming that he has no passion for a woman. Of course, this is begging the question. Who says that one needs passion in order to marry and have children? If the rabbis were to have answered him, which they did not, then they might have said, "Well then, marry without passion." If the Sabbath must be kept with or without passion, why should reproduction be different? Of course, the answer is that unlike the Sabbath, reproduction is not a mitzvah that one can accomplish alone. The command to reproduce is not a technical one, some objective act to perform. This mitzvah entails interest in a certain kind of physical loving relationship. Ben Azzai is saying that without the necessary sexual desire for a woman the mitzvah of reproduction simply cannot be fulfilled. He gets away with his "What can I do?" because the sages understand that desire cannot be manufactured by the will, and that without at least some desire the resulting marital relationship would be painfully cruel and exploitative.

Ben Azzai ends his statement with another important point. "It is likely that the world will be sustained by others." He accepts that his life is not the ordinary state of affairs, and he assures the sages that his failure to marry and procreate will not endanger the world. There will be plenty of others who will generously populate the world. It is an aggregate task to be achieved by those who can.

Perhaps Ben Azzai is also saying that there are other ways to establish and secure the world. While society needs children to continue its work, it also needs many other people to tend to the needs of growing children. Ben Azzai is suggesting that while he lacks the desire for a woman, which has world-building consequences, his desire for Torah can be seen as equally world building. Lastly, the expansion of the modes of generativity has always made a great deal of sense for those unable or not fortunate enough to produce children. The multiplication of the ways by which individuals might consciously nourish and sustain the world and care for its future beyond reproduction and parenting seems absolutely crucial for human prosperity.

There are at least three ways to consider Ben Azzai's attitude to the command to procreate. It is possible that when he doubles the crime, he is playing along with his colleagues' game of hyperbole. To support the observance of injunctions not generally taken so seriously, the rabbis often provided their own hyperbolic framings. Since the Torah offers no biblical punishment for failing to reproduce, the rabbis may have worried that people might easily take such a failure too lightly. To strengthen the duty and heighten its seriousness the rabbis speak about the cosmic consequences of not procreating.

Or perhaps Ben Azzai understands that his colleagues were harping on his own disregard of the injunction by enlarging this particular sin of omission to cosmic size. If so, his joining in may just be a way to play a bit with them, before he defends his life's choices.

It seems most likely that instead of either of these intentions, he is articulating a very conservative position in regard to the command to procreate. While R. Eliezer describes the one who refuses to procreate as a murderer, and R. Jacob as one who diminishes God in the world, Ben Azzai insists that both are right. Not to reproduce is a rejection of both humanity and God. Ben Azzai does not weaken the normative power of a rule that he cannot fulfill. He actually increases it! Ben Azzai has no ideological stance against the primary value of the heterosexual family. He believes that our duties to God and to one another generally outweigh personal preferences of all sorts. He simply explains how, since his heart works in another way, it is best for him to nourish the world in another way.

His argument with his colleagues is a different one. This particular duty, says Ben Azzai, is not like others. Reproduction is not a mechanical duty but a relational one. It assumes a desire for physical and emotional intimacy with a partner of the opposite sex on the part of every man and woman. In such a context the law to be fruitful and to multiply is in force. Without such a desiring context the mitzvah simply cannot be fulfilled. Neither can the law command the manufacture of desire. Either it is there or it is not. The duty to reproduce, enmeshed as it is in the sharing of one's body and heart, is a full-fledged duty for those whose sexuality desirously carries them into the arms of the opposite sex.

Ben Azzai sustains a social and religious norm, even though for very personal reasons he cannot fulfill it. He has no desire to generalize from his experience. He models for us the possibility of supporting the communal norm of heterosexual marriage and reproduction while being excluded from both by the desire of one's own heart. However, he reminds us that the commandment of generativity ought to include ways other than baby making to express concern and nourish the world.

The rationale of reproduction is a significant challenge to non-reproducing individuals and couples to find alternative ways to care for and sustain the world. However, it does not justify the forcing of homosexuals into heterosexual marriage, nor does it ground the rejection of same-sex partnerships for gay people. Indeed, the policy that would most sensibly emerge from the value of reproduction and family making would be one that supports and encourages homosexuals to fulfill in whatever ways possible the duty to "settle the world." A healthy, just, and creative society has many jobs that are better suited to men and women not involved in the tasks of family caretaking. Many of the most creative members of society, artists and writers, academics and scientists, have been childless people. Ben Azzai reminds us that people who build lives without children and who instead are devoted to the care of the world in other ways can be assured that "the world will be continued by [the reproduction of] others."

Lastly, according to the Torah, the earth was made in order to be a sanctuary for life and in particular a habitation for human life.[50] The commandment to have children is considered important because through it the world is continued and developed.[51]

What then if the very existence of the world required new thinking about human reproduction? What if the planet could not tolerate uncontained human population growth? If the world is no longer sustained by increased population but diminished and even imperiled by it, might there not be reason to reconsider the duty to reproduce?

The expression "be fruitful and multiply" in the story of Genesis is in fact more like a blessing than a commandment. A few verses earlier in the creation story the fish and birds were given the same divine blessing. Surely to them it was a blessing and not a command. The Hebrew could be read quite naturally as: "Be fruitful and multiply so that you fill the earth!" on which we might add our own midrashic point, "and not that you overfill it!"

Leviathan

In the first chapter we discovered that both the great lights and the great sea monsters were unstable pairs, each spelled with a missing letter in their plural endings. Just as with the great lights, God was forced to correct an unforeseen problem of twos.

> Genesis 1:21–22: And God created the great sea monsters . . . and said, be fruitful and multiply. Rashi: Two equally large fish, and in the words of the midrash this is the Leviathan and its mate. For God created the male and female and then killed the female and

salted it away for the righteous in the future to come, for were they to reproduce, the world could not endure them.

On the fifth day of creation the sea creatures and the birds were created and commanded to be fruitful and multiply. The great sea monsters posed a particular problem in the plan. Were the two sea monsters permitted to multiply, their progeny would destroy the world. Reproduction, which normally sustains and furthers life on earth, can be a grave danger for the world.

Most traditional rabbinic authorities have not treated the dangers of overpopulation very seriously. This is so for two rather obvious reasons. Minorities generally look suspiciously on any grand plans to limit the birth rate. Small populations tend to experience their relative growth as a sign of cultural success and their diminishment as a deep threat to their social viability and political clout. Equally important, Jews have felt that nearly two millennia of persecution along with the devastation of the Holocaust more than justify excluding Jews from any measures to contain reproduction.

Looking beyond the scope of Jewish history to Jewish values, it would seem that the duty to reproduce might very well be understood as a fulfillment of a larger duty of world building. As we greet a new millennium, world building will require many forms of creativity and nurturing of life on the planet. Reproduction will still be a profound and cherished responsibility, but there will be plenty of room for others to take the time, money, attention, and care that parents shower on their children and use it in other ways—to wisely settle a very crowded world.

11

The Rationale of Social Disruption

The rationale of social disruption emerges from a story about a rabbi and his comedic antics at a high-society rabbinic wedding. The bawdy talmudic tale is told with a set of practical concerns in mind regarding homosexual relations between men. Whether same-sex desire and sexual relations undermine the creation or not, wandering husbands surely undermine families.

In some premodern societies as well as in a number of contemporary cultural settings, homosexual men marry and afterward, when the pressures overwhelm or when opportunities arise, wander. They marry, of course, because no other decent life is socially conceivable or practically available. For Judean men of the third and fourth centuries this sort of homosexual opportunity presented itself most apparently in the larger cities where Romans and Jews lived side by side. The following story suggests some anxiety regarding husbands in Judea who were running after men and neglecting their households.

Rabbinic Wedding Jokes

The context is the wedding of Shimon, the son of the famed Judah the Prince, Rabbi Yehudah HaNasi. The scholar and funny man Bar Kappara is a student of Rabbi Yehudah. Rabbi Yehudah HaNasi (often called simply "Rabbi" in the Talmud) was a rather severe person, not given to easy laughter, and his student Bar Kappara never missed an opportunity to get him to belly laugh. The family thought this scandalous and chose not to invite Bar Kappara to the wedding. Ben Elasah, Rabbi's wealthy (and not so learned) son-in-law, finally

166

invited Bar Kappara to the wedding. Bar Kappara became a comic teacher of Torah at the wedding by giving his playful interpretations of three prohibitions in chapter 18 of Leviticus. Male intercourse, incest, and marrying both a mother and a daughter are each occasioned by a different odd Hebrew term *(toevah, tevel,* and *zimah),* which Bar Kappara explains to great comic effect. Ben Elasah was incensed by the show, exited in a huff, and earned a backhanded compliment about his hairdo.

> Rabbi made a wedding feast for his son Simeon and did not invite Bar Kappara. He [Bar Kappara] wrote above the wedding canopy, "Twenty-four thousand myriad dinars have been spent on this wedding, and they did not even invite Bar Kappara! If those who transgress his will fare so well [are so rich], how much more so with those who do his will!" When he was later invited, he said, "If those who do his will fare so well in this world, how much more so in the world to come!"
>
> When Rabbi laughed, calamity would come to the world, so Rabbi said to Bar Kappara, "Do not make me laugh, and I will give you forty measures of wheat." He [Bar Kappara] replied, "Let the master instead say that I may take whatever measure I desire." So he took a large basket, covered it with pitch, put it on his head, and went to Rabbi and said to him, "Give me my forty measures of wheat!" Rabbi burst into laughter and said to him, "Did I not warn you not to make me laugh?" "I want only to take the wheat that you owe me" [Bar Kappara replied]. Bar Kappara said to Rabbi's daughter, "Tomorrow I will drink to your father's dancing and your mother's singing."
>
> Ben Elasah, the son-in-law of Rabbi, was a very wealthy man, and he invited Bar Kappara to the wedding. At the wedding Bar Kappara asked Rabbi, "What does *toevah* mean?" Every explanation that Rabbi offered he refuted. So Rabbi said to him, "Explain it yourself!" He [Bar Kappara] replied, "Let your wife come and fill up my cup." She did so. Then he said to Rabbi, "Arise and dance for me, and I will tell it to you." This is the meaning of the Torah. *Toevah* means *toeh-attah-bah* = You wander by this [intercourse, leaving your wife to find satisfaction with a male].
>
> At the next cup Bar Kappara said to Rabbi, "What does *tevel* mean?" Rabbi responded as before, and Bar Kappara asked him to dance again, and he did. What does *tevel* mean? *Tavlin yesh ba* = Sex with an animal is a confused mixture. [Some translate *tavlin* not as "mixture" but as "spicy." If so, *tavlin yesh ba* becomes a question: "Is

sex with an animal that spicy?" questioning whether sex of this sort is actually very tasty to begin with.]

[With the same buildup to the punch line he asks:] What does *zimmah* mean? Again Bar Kappara asked him to dance, and he did. *Zimmah* = *zu ma hi?* = Which one is this? [A slapstick line spoken by a man who married both a woman and her daughter or a line spoken in a clan where everyone has sex with everyone, so in regard to the children everyone asks, "So which one is this?"]

Ben Elasah [Rabbi's son-in-law] could not stand this [comedy routine]. He got up, he and his wife, and they left the wedding. What [else do we know about] Ben Elasah? It is taught that Ben Elasah spent a fortune on his hair styling in order to look like the high priest. . . . One sage said that it was a Julian haircut [after the manner of Julianus Ceasar]. What did it look like? Rabbi Yehudah said that it was a very unique haircut. Rava said that curls of one row would end where the next row began—and this was the hair style of the high priest.[1]

The story line is simple. Bar Kappara loves to play court jester and make his teacher laugh. Rabbi's family is not amused, so when the family holds a great wedding for their accomplished son, they don't invite Bar Kappara to the wedding. Bar Kappara does not hesitate to make known his displeasure and gets himself invited by Rabbi's son-in-law, Ben Elasah. To prevent his antics, Rabbi promises Bar Kappara forty baskets of wheat if Bar Kappara does not make him laugh. Bar Kappara agrees and comes the next day for his wheat with a basket lined with pitch, which he turns upside down on his own head. Rabbi, seeing Bar Kappara with a basket on his head, breaks out in laughter.

The story then moves to a scene at the wedding. Bar Kappara asks Rabbi a riddle. What does *toevah* mean? Everyone seems to understand that while the word appears in many places, he means to focus on its use in connection with male intercourse. Rabbi offers answers, and Bar Kappara rejects them all. Finally, just as we might imagine the crowd in stitches, Bar Kappara explains the word as a pun. *Toevah* means *toeh atta bah*—you wander because of it. The punning quip is rather vague. Rashi explains that such a man leaves the permitted sexual haven of his wife and is caught up in lechery. The word *toeh* also has the sense of losing one's way. Isaiah uses the word to convey distortion, confusion, the flailing of a drunkard.[2]

While straying suggests a loss of direction, straying from God conveys error as well.[3] Adding to the wordplay is the fact that the word *toeh* can be spelled in two ways and mean two things. With a *tav*, as it appears in our text, it means "to wander" or "to go astray"; spelled with a *tet* it means "to err" or "to make a mistake."

So Bar Kappara announces at the wedding that men who have sex with men leave their wives, wander from their homes, and err by choosing a prohibited sexual liaison over a permitted one. Whether the wandering leads to the emotional or physical neglect of a wife or whether it means a full-fledged abandonment or divorce is not made clear, but in either case the problem of homosexual desire is located within a marital context.

Bar Kappara's antics continue as he asks Rabbi about two other strange descriptions of sexual violation. Bestiality in Leviticus is called *tevel*, and marrying both mother and daughter is called *zimah*. In both instances Bar Kappara finds explanatory puns that describe social confusion. *Tevel* means "confusions" or "mixtures." *Zimmah* is translated as *zo ma hi*, meaning "which is this one?" All three prohibitions are constructed as social confusions.

Ben Elasah, Bar Kappara's friend and the son-in-law of Rabbi, is infuriated by the embarrassing sexual humor that Bar Kappara has staged at a family wedding. An interesting postscript follows the story. It seems that Ben Elasah spent enormous sums of money to get his hair cut in the fashion of Julian, perhaps a stylish patrician or a Caesar. One can only speculate why Ben Elasah in his high-style hairdo would storm out of the wedding just after Ben Kappara finished making his puns on sexual perversity.

Considerations from a Comedy Routine

The author of this narrative has presented the issue of homosexual philandering in a very comic fashion. Bar Kappara baits the honorable Rabbi into offering answers that he casually rejects and gets Rabbi's wife to play his dancing barmaid, while he offers his bawdy puns.

The idea of racy jokes at a wedding celebration may not surprise some people, but in contemporary Orthodox circles such antics would seem extremely out of place. A wedding banquet is a rather strange place to publicly open up the question of husbands who fool around on the side with men. Why raise the issue of sexually bored men seeking extramarital thrills with other men, who try doing it with barnyard animals to see if it's spicy or not, or who sleep with so many women that they lose track of which woman is which? Is it sex that makes fools of men or marriage? Indeed, toward what end would one focus on faltering marriages at a wedding? Bar Kappara's humor seems to make fun of and honor marriage at the same time, in much the same way that he pokes fun at his teacher's stiffness and honors him as well by the effort to make him laugh.

In one other instance Bar Kappara obliquely criticizes the austerity and moneyed formalism of Rabbi's household and the fear that it inspired. He might very well have been using the bawdy humor as a way to undermine the rabbinic highbrow atmosphere of such an occasion. Another possibility is that the show is directed to a particular person, "YOU have wandered because of it from your marriage bed!" Could it be that Ben Elasah is that person? Might it be that the wealthy and expensively coiffed Ben Elasah is himself a wandering husband? If the joke is on Ben Elasah, then we can well understand why he stormed out.[4]

Lastly, it could be that Bar Kappara was mocking himself for being something of an outsider. There is no mention of Bar Kappara's wife, and while that is no evidence that she didn't exist, the absence might mean that he remained unmarried. This seems like a reasonable option, given that he makes a fool of himself with Rabbi in the initial story when he puts the basket upside down on his head. Perhaps he is making fun of his own unconventional life, by listing the sexual options that he has rejected. Men, animals, even marrying a woman and her mother have all been considered and rejected for reasons of good judgment and taste. Men are a big mistake, animals aren't fun in bed, and two women are confusing.

Bar Kappara as a Teacher

If Bar Kappara is thought of more as teacher than comedian, then the text might be understood to be punning and still quite serious. By seeking sexual fulfillment outside marriage, a man neglects his wife and family. Since early marriage was nearly universal in Jewish circles, it may be that homosexual relationships were nearly always enacted within the contexts of married life. The prohibition against male relations then may come to prevent married men from wandering from their wives to find male company.

When in the late nineties it became an open secret to many in the gay community that there was a gay Orthodox rabbi to speak to, I was contacted by many people in crisis. Among them were many married men and women who were struggling with issues of sexual orientation. Some had actively repressed their homosexuality all their lives and married with the hope things would work out. Some had been promised by rabbis that their aberrant desires would disappear in the context of a permitted sex life with a spouse. A few claimed that they had no inkling of desire for a person of the same sex until, in the midst of marriage, their true sexuality dawned on them.

Some of these men and women had resisted temptation throughout their lives, living as if in constant combat, and they felt utterly exhausted by the fight. A few had begun to explore their desires and decided, after some exploration, to return home and renew ties with their spouses. Many had lived double lives for years and wanted to continue doing so, and others were no longer willing or able to sustain the lie. One ultra-Orthodox woman with many children had constructed a working arrangement with her spouse. Rather than leave the marriage, he had agreed that they should discreetly integrate her girlfriend into the family. Another man had fallen in love with his best friend, and both men were trying to persuade their wives to keep the families together. In a few cases men who discovered their gayness late in their marriages decided in the end that their lives were richer and fuller in the context of their families.

However, the most common outcome has been divorce as most of these people decided that they were not doing their spouses any favors by staying married. No matter what the story, the tension between heterosexual married life and same-sex desire is not to be denied—except in the Orthodox community.

In traditional circles dating and courtship are usually short and to the point. Men in the community marry young and women even younger.[5] While the social pressure to marry is intense, men can hold out by dating superficially and consistently claiming not to have found the "right one." Women cannot so easily avoid marriage. The option of repeatedly rejecting suitors and resisting parental pressure is much more difficult. A much higher degree of initiative is required for a young man to pursue a woman. Orthodox girls need only say yes to end up married and pregnant within a year. By the time a young woman has a clear sense of her emotional and physical needs, she is usually a mother with two or three children in tow. While no study has been done to date, the anecdotal evidence suggests that the vast majority of Orthodox lesbians are or were married at some time.

Even today most gay teens and twenty-somethings in the Orthodox community have at best a vague sense of their sexuality. Those who are aware of their homoerotic desire will often jump into marriage, naively hoping that it will cure them. Very few of these men or women would dream of sharing with a potential marriage partner the fact of their sexual attraction to the same sex, much less the limits (or absence) of their desire for the opposite sex.

Two, five, seven years later, the men are cruising parks, hanging around men's rooms, or attempting to sustain a double life with a lover. Their wives are confused, not understanding their husbands' disinterest and moodiness, and easily blame themselves for the marital problems. Typically couples have children immediately and find their lives dominated by those demands. For a number of years the pleasures and burdens of childcare can distract partners from their own needs enough to bury the growing sense that the marriage is not working. In time, however, the distaste for sex with the spouse rises and causes emotional hurt on both sides. Often the situation leads to deep depression for both the gay and the straight spouses involved. Lesbian women in particular feel trapped, because they have no avenues of contact with other lesbians, given their limited mobility and independence, and no way to explain themselves to their confused, angry, and dejected husbands.

Women married to homosexual husbands are trapped as well. Unaware of the issues, a woman easily blames herself for the husband's lack of interest. Denied elements of intimacy, often both emotional and physical, such women feel confused, angry, and hurt. A woman who is told or discovers the secret is not much better off.

Placing the onus on her husband's essential lack of desire may free a wife from guilt, while making her feel all the more helpless. Whether angry or understanding of their husbands' situation, women will often still feel protective enough of their husbands to avoid sharing their feelings with friends and family. As a result, these women are left utterly isolated and hopeless.

Given these realities, it would appear that the problem of social disruption is not caused by the wandering from one kind of sexual fulfillment to another, but by the forcing of homosexual men and women into marriage in the first place. Unless Orthodox authorities are willing to address the possibility that some of their teens will have homosexual feelings and should not be rushed into marriage, they actively endanger the futures of their own, presumably straight, children. Of course, it is for this reason that teenage homosexuality is a largely unthinkable prospect.

Were parents to admit such a possibility, they would not want their rabbis counseling gay teens to overcome their evil desires and marry. They would try to generate communal circumstances that would serve honesty and not a terrified deception of self and others. If homosexuals exist, and if no decent life trajectory is offered to them other than a deceptive heterosexual marriage, then no one ought to be surprised at the outcome. However, since parents tend to feel not very empowered or even motivated to change the social milieu regarding homosexuality, they avoid worrying by denial. Homosexuals don't exist here.

If the rationale behind the prohibition of same-sex sexual relations is social confusion and family disruption, then the solution is obvious. Don't get married. This rationale, by explicitly marking the danger of familial disruption, directs our attention away from the nature of the sin to the consequences for people who are pushed into marriages that do not suit them. Some rabbis have publicly discouraged gay men and women from marriage, while others still promise young people that if they marry, everything will work out.[6]

In telling us a funny story, the Talmud lays bare the dangers of what Adrienne Rich has called "compulsory heterosexuality."[7] We live in a culture that enforces the expectation of heterosexuality. When young men or women in high school grasp their sexual orientation and want to attend the prom with same-sex partners, all hell breaks loose, not because we think there are no homosexuals in high school, but because the normative presumption of heterosexuality is undermined.

The meaning of "don't ask, don't tell" is just this: Homosexuality is pushed into the shadows to sustain the illusion that everyone is heterosexual. It is a way to delude ourselves into thinking that there are no homosexuals here. However, statistically speaking, in every class of thirty high-school kids, at least two students are gay; in every yeshiva of three hundred boys, nearly two dozen are gay. Whose sons and daughters are put at risk by our denial? Is it worth it? While Bar Kappara's teaching appears limited in its halakhic import, it is actually a very potent challenge to Orthodox communal and familial life.

12

The Rationale of Category Confusion

In examining this next rationale we return again to grand anxieties. While the first rationale addressed the legitimate uses or goals of sex implicit in the creation, this rationale views homosexuality as a threat to the very order of the creation in that it confounds the gender divide. Two discrete sexes were created to unite in intercourse and in doing so to become one flesh.[1] The primary distinctions between maleness and femaleness begin with the processes and motions of reproduction and specifically with the act of sexual intercourse. Men are penetrators and women are penetrated. The problem of homosexual intercourse as an inversion of this simple binary truism is sparsely articulated by the medieval Spanish commentator Abraham Ibn Ezra: "Since the male was created to act and the female to be acted on, the verse [prohibiting male intercourse] reminds us not to overturn the word of God."[2]

Men who have sex with men turn the tables on gender identity, confuse the categories, and thereby overturn the word of God. The rationale of gender confusion marks male-male intercourse as a perversion of the categories of gender embedded in creation and so ordained by the Creator. Men who behave like women by allowing their bodies to be "acted on" violate the design of creation.

The focus of this rationale carries us to body parts, their use, and their meaning. For a man to lie with a man just as he might lie with a woman poses a problem of body parts. How does a man lie with another man in the manner of lying with a woman, given that men don't possess vaginas? It must be that the "the lyings of a woman" means intercourse, modeled after penile-vaginal intercourse but using a different body orifice, one that both men and women possess. It is the anus used as a vagina that reconfigures the male body and "overturns the word of God." Since both men and women have anal orifices, but only men have penises, it is obvious then why women's homoerotic relations are not relevant. Men can subvert the penis on their bodies by turning their anus into a quasi vagina; women cannot (save through modern surgery) invent a penis.

Daniel Boyarin has suggested that the fundamental construct of the prohibition of male intercourse is similar to that of another biblical injunction against gender bending, that of cross-dressing.[3] "A woman may not dress in a man's apparel, nor shall a man wear women's clothing; for doing these things is abhorrent to the Lord your God" (Deut. 22:5). The prohibition against cross-dressing is a direct attempt to keep the boundaries clear. The relationship between these two commandments deserves further inquiry.

Most commentators explain the prohibition of cross-dressing as an attempt to prevent licentious behavior.[4] The cross-dresser enters the closed world of the opposite sex to gain easy access to a desired partner of the opposite sex.[5] In societies that strongly separate male and female social orbits, the cross-dresser is not only a subversive but also an opportunist. There are very few social settings in Western society, outside locker rooms and public bathrooms, where men and women do not commingle freely. In ancient societies, where men's worlds and women's worlds were radically different spaces, cross-dressing was a ticket into the mysterious and usually closed off world of the other sex. While cross-dressing women might have been drawn to the power and access of a man's world, cross-dressing men were understood as voyeurs eager for a sexual adventure. According to this explanation cross-dressing is a form of heterosexual opportunism, having nothing to do with homosexuality.

Still, it is interesting that both male intercourse and cross-dressing are specifically called *toevah*—abomination. *Toevah* is a difficult word to pin down, as we have seen in the chapter on Leviticus. The fact that the word appears associated with both of these prohibitions may point to their relatedness. Both may be deemed hateful because they confound gender-role identity or, perhaps, as some scholars have claimed, because they were both associated with pagan ritual.[6]

Maimonides, famous for his defense of seeking rationales for all 613 commandments, associates cross-dressing with pagan ritual.[7] In his view cross-dressing was prohibited because it was included in certain idolatrous worship rituals. While Maimonides does not make this association in the case of homosexual relations, other traditional and modern commentators have.[8] Whether in the form of orgiastic rites or cult prostitution it has been assumed that sexual rites were common in the world of the Hebrew Bible. The text often used to support the association of homosexuality with cult prostitution is Deuteronomy 23:18: "There is to be no *kadeshah* among the daughters of Israel, nor a *kadesh* among the sons of Israel." The text prohibits the practice of the *kadeshim* but does not tell us who they are or what they did. A few biblical texts taken together have suggested to scholars that the *kadeshim* were prostitutes employed in pagan worship. The Second Book of Kings reports that the righteous King Josiah removed the *kadeshim* from the Temple in Jerusalem along with their houses where women wove coverings for the goddess Asherah (2 Kings 23:7). This text implicates the *kadeshim* with Josiah's antipagan reforms, but it also doesn't tell us what they did. The association of the word *kadeshah* with prostitution appears clearly in the Book of Genesis. Tamar, Judah's daughter-in-law, dresses herself in a veil, stands by the roadside, and is taken by Judah to be a *zonah,* or prostitute. Later when Judah seeks her out to pay her and to retrieve the pledges he left with her, his Canaanite comrade refers to her as the *kedeshah* at the roadside. What Judah calls a *zonah,* his Canaanite friend calls a *kedeshah.* The combination of the 2 Kings and Genesis references encouraged scholars to read Deuteronomy as a prohibition of the sacred prostitution presumed to be part of Canaanite worship.

This interpretation of the verse in Deuteronomy, which combines the sacred and the sexual uses of a word in different biblical books, has been challenged by contemporary scholars. Biblical scholar Tikva Frymer-Kensky has argued that the *kadeshim* were cult officiants and not temple prostitutes.[9] Furthermore, in the view of another biblical scholar, Rabbi Jeffrey Tigay, the pagan religion of the surrounding peoples did not include sex acts.[10] Moreover, in the more distant Mesopotamian cults that employed sacred prostitutes, there is some question as to whether the male prostitutes engaged in intercourse with males or only with females.[11] Given that orgiastic rites in Mesopotamia were usually part of fertility rituals, there is doubt as to whether sex between male prostitutes and male celebrants was involved at all.[12]

Consequently, it seems more likely that the two prohibitions, cross-dressing and male homosexual relations, are both abominated because they both threaten gender-role identity. Support for this can be found in the rabbinic rulings, which expanded the list of gender-confusing behaviors. While putting on a wig and a dress might help a man get into a woman's dressing room, the rabbis added a number of women's grooming and toilet practices because they were thought to be gender-category violations independent of heterosexual opportunism. For example, men were prohibited from dyeing their hair or shaving their pubic or underarm hair.[13] In a similar vein women were not to wear male accessories, such as weapons, even though such minor costume additions would not serve as a full-blown disguise. The concern here is not so much to avert successful cross-gender passing as to ensure categorical purity.

Interestingly, one commentator associates cross-dressing directly with homosexuality. Rabbi Isaac Ben Judah Abrabanel, a fifteenth-century Portuguese biblical commentator, suggests that the prohibition is designed to prevent men from dressing up as women in order to seduce other men. Apparently, Abrabanel knew of a pattern of same-sex cruising in which cross-dressing played a central role. The sages of the Talmud were likewise aware of a cultural formation by which a very subtle cross-dressing gesture was a sign of homosexual availability, the mark of a cruising lad. The rabbis, like their Roman conquerors, associated expressions of male effeminacy with sexual provocation. They warned young students of the academy not to go to the marketplace wearing perfume. In the Mishnah we learn that "It is a disgrace for a scholar (*talmid hakham,* literally, "wise student") to go to the market perfumed."[14] Rabbi Abba, the son of Rabbi Hiyyah bar Abba, said in the name of Rabbi Yohanan that the

Mishnah's statement applies only in places suspected of male homoeroticism. In many cities in Judea, Romans and Jews lived side by side. Obviously, some markets were known to be places where boys and men met for pederastic encounters. Whether the motivation was to ensure that yeshiva boys were beyond reproach or to prevent them from actually cruising for sex in the Roman marketplace, the relationship between gender bending and homoerotic practice was clearly known to the sages.

To think of anal intercourse between men as a form of cross-dressing sheds some interesting light on the prohibition. By lying receptively with a male—as does a woman—a male reconfigures his body into the body of a woman.[15] In fact, anal intercourse between men is a far more radical form of gender bending than cross-dressing. Cross-dressing juxtaposes bodies with costumes that don't categorically match. Cross-dressing is a wrapping error. However, what is inside the wrapper is a whole, unambiguous thing that can be categorized. Take off the drag and you've got a man. With anal intercourse the category violation is a full step further than costume. Anal intercourse between men is a category violation in which the meaning of gender itself is undone by the man who offers his penetrable body to another man, his lover—as does a woman.

If so, then there are two very different destabilizations that male intercourse might accomplish. It can unhinge the maleness of the particular penetrated male or, if taken as a cultural statement, it can debunk the meaning of penetrative intercourse itself as the defining frame of gender. To put it another way, anal intercourse either transforms a particular man into a woman, or in a more radical fashion it transforms the meaning of sex for everyone. In the first example the threat of confusion is local. The particular males who engage in such behavior are punished for their active frustration of their own gender identity. The violation directly affects no one except the perpetrators. However, if the great male-female divide is at stake, if the acting-acted upon dichotomy is debunked, then everyone is affected. Male sexual intercourse then becomes not only a grave personal sin but also a collective threat.

The most immediate source for the collective danger of male intercourse (among other sexual violations) is in the chapter of

Leviticus where the initial prohibition is found. The chapter lists an array of sexual prohibitions, including incest and adultery, continues with male intercourse and bestiality, and then gives a stern warning regarding the consequences of violating these rules. "Do not defile yourselves in any of those ways, for it is by such that the nations that I am casting out before you defiled themselves. Thus the land became defiled; and I called it to account for its iniquity, and the land vomited out its inhabitants. . . . So let not the land vomit you out for defiling it, as it vomited out the nation that came before you" (Lev. 18:24–28).

Vomiting is a powerful image of things out of place, categories violated. The image is physical and psychological, but the threat is supremely political. Individuals who violate these norms threaten the security of the settlement.[16] The collective threat is even more pronounced in the midrashic literature. Sexual-boundary smashing can bring in its wake a catastrophe even more horrifying than military defeat and exile.

The Flood, Bestiality, and Male Intercourse

The sages tell us the great deluge that wiped out life on the earth was the result of sexual corruption. "All flesh had corrupted its way on the earth." The "way of flesh" is understood as copulation and its corruption as perversion. "Rabbi Yohanan said: beasts copulated with animals, animals with beasts, they all had intercourse with human beings, and humans had intercourse with them."[17]

Cross-species intercourse unleashes the waters above and below. It is interesting that Rabbi Yohanan (the same beautiful Rabbi Yohanan we encountered earlier) did not include male intercourse among the sexual confusions that end the world. Later we will have the opportunity to contrast the two sexual violations of bestiality and male intercourse in greater detail, but what may motivate Rabbi Yohanan to exclude male intercourse here is likely a formal problem. The boundaries that keep the world orderly are those that insist on sameness within categories: like mating with like—a horse with a horse. The world is undone by the mating with unlikes—a cow with a horse. Homoerotic sexual relations, however, are a doubling of sameness, like with like twice, two humans, two males.

Rav Huna offers a competing view that specifically does not distinguish between bestiality and homosexual unions. This text is unique in the literature in that it addresses not a sexual act per se, but a ritual of marital union. "Rav Huna in the name of Rabbi said: The generation of the flood was not obliterated from the world until they wrote nuptial songs for [unions between] males and animals."[18]

Rav Huna equates the two prohibitions and adds a new element. It appears that polymorphous sexuality alone could not have brought the deluge. The pandemonium preceding the flood reached its apex with the staging of marital rituals for animal-human unions and male-male unions. Private bestiality and male-male intercourse are not by themselves ultimately ruinous. It was the sanctification of perverse couplings in public wedding celebrations that ultimately brought the world to an end. Social sanction is the last straw, the final violation of order that draws down the watery chaos.

Rav Huna's identification of male couplings with the deluge is a rather grandiose expression of the rationale of confusion. It is also ancient history. It can never happen again specifically because God has promised so with the rainbow as a sign of comfort and safety. God will never again destroy the earth because of human aggression and lust. However, immediately following Rav Huna's statement, we hear from Rav Simlai, who extends the dangers of the flood to the present. Sexual chaos still brings ruination in its wake. "Rav Simlai said: Fornication brings indiscriminate destruction *(androlomusia)* to the world, killing the beautiful and the wicked."[19]

While Rabbi Yohanan and Rav Huna speak of events that in principle cannot occur again, Rav Simlai is not as confident. He describes a continuing element of the flood that, while neither as global or catastrophic, is still terribly destructive. Unrestrained sexual promiscuity brings *androlomusia* to the world. *Androlomusia* is a Greek word referring to the forced seizure of a man regardless of his innocence or guilt. The implication is that sexual chaos is not punished per se. If that were so, then the guilty alone would suffer. Polymorphous sexual expression unleashes terrible forces that take everyone with them. Wild sexual promiscuity, even of a minority, is a force that can bring suffering down on us all.

Even more vivid than Rav Simlai's *androlomusia* is Rav Aha's

claim that earthquakes come to the world because of male intercourse. He puts the following words into God's mouth: "You shake
your organs in a place not fit for you, so I will shake the world."[20]
While hyperbole was common among the rabbis, especially when
there was little biblical material to support their moral sensibilities,
Rav Aha's message is made overwhelmingly clear. Misplacing one's
penis displaces the crust of the earth. The map of the body and the
map of the globe are one when it comes to sex; disorder begets
disorder.

Moral Abominations

The problem of category confusion is also at the heart of a statement
by Rabbi Judah Loew of the sixteenth century, the famous Maharal
of Prague. The Talmud tells us that the children of Noah voluntarily
refrained from two practices: writing a marriage contract for two
men and selling human flesh in the markets.[21] Over and above the
seven laws of Noah, the nations do not publicly legitimate male
homosexual sex or cannibalism.

The Maharal carries this text one step further by suggesting that
cannibalism and homosexuality are, in fact, conceptually related.
"There is nothing more hateful or disgusting than male intercourse,
which the Scripture calls abomination. There is nothing more abominable than someone who eats the flesh of the human dead, because,
in a sense, he eats himself, which is similar to male intercourse because such a man connects to a male like himself."[22] According to
the Maharal, cannibalism and homosexuality are forms of self-
negation. While the body eaten or sexually penetrated is not one's
own, these acts reflexively undo the self in relations to others, removing a person from the social world and thus making him disappear as
a person.

The contemporary moral theorist Jeffrey Stout makes a similar
point.[23] He compares homosexuality and cannibalism (and adds
bestiality) in a way that may help to sharpen our understanding of
the problem of categorical confusion. Inspired in large measure by
the work of Mary Douglas, he begins his analysis by exploring our
natural repulsion to anomalies.[24] Objects or acts that violate categorical boundaries often physically repulse us. He whimsically describes

how revolted he felt when he saw his first cabbit, a creature spawned by the crossbreeding of a cat and a rabbit. He assures us that his two-year-old daughter would hardly have been offended or disgusted by such a creature. But his familiarity with cats and rabbits and the sharp distinctions between them caused his stomach to turn upon seeing a cabbit on the cover of a tabloid. Similar to the bearded woman at the county fair or the famous elephant man, anomalous objects and acts are emotionally charged. They can make us laugh, inspire us with awe, terrorize us, or disgust us.

With this context in mind, Stout then draws our attention to cannibalism, bestiality, and homosexual sex. Why is it, he asks, that cannibalism offends? The cannibal does not kill living people; he just eats dead ones. No one is harmed, and someone benefits. What's the problem? He suggests that cannibalism offends in much the same way that becoming a werewolf does; it threatens our unambiguous status as human beings. Cannibals and werewolves slip in between the categories of animal and human. While both animals and humans eat, the eating of certain things threatens one's status as a human. Nonhuman carnivores have no scruples when it comes to eating human flesh. To eat human flesh is to become like an animal. In societies where the line between the human and the animal is not sharply drawn, cannibalism will be less likely to offend. But societies that sharply demarcate such a boundary will find eating human flesh abominable.

In a similar way sexual intercourse with beasts is abominable. Bestiality, like cannibalism, calls into question one's social identity as a human being. Having sex with beasts is what beasts do. The appetites that we share with animals, eating and copulating, are the sites where we may need to be most careful to mark our humanness and where the categorical violations are most repulsive.

Stout extends this conceptual framework to homosexual sexual relations, which, like bestiality, involves using the sexual organs in ways that violate social boundaries. However, in homosexual sex the boundary crossed is not that between man and beast, but that between male and female. Similar to his insight in regard to cannibalism, Stout posits that the sharper the social boundary, the greater the sense of abomination. In societies where the role divisions between men and women are drawn lightly, homosexuality will be less threatening. Where great importance is attached to belonging in absolute ways to one or the other gender, where the social roles, division of labor, and inheritance laws are sharply divided along gender lines, homosexuality will be abominated.

But does the fact that most people in the past and many still today find homosexuality revolting justify an ongoing moral outrage? Indeed, why should our revulsions have any moral significance at all? One might as easily claim that it is our moral duty to overcome our "disgust with the anomalous." Whites used to be (and some still are) disgusted by interracial marriage. The famous book and movie *To Kill a Mockingbird* is a story about just such ironclad rules belonging to the category of race. The idea of a sexual act between a black man and a white woman generated enough horror and disgust that an innocent man could be condemned to death for the crime of making a small southern town consider such a possibility. The fact that we have emotional difficulty with anomalies might seem to obligate us to overcome it.

Stout responds firmly to this contention by insisting that we should hold our ethical theories accountable to our deepest feelings and hunches, including our sense of revulsion in the face of the abominable. An ethical theory that ignores our emotions loses contact with the data of moral experience. With further scrutiny we will surely discover that not all acts that repulse us are immoral, but it is certain that some will be. What distinguishes the merely repulsive from the morally abominable, according to Stout, is the nature of the categories that are blurred.

The question is "not whether homosexuality is intrinsically abominable, but rather what, all things considered, we should do with the relevant categories of our cosmology and social structure."[25] Cannibalism and bestiality threaten one's membership in the human community; male homosexuality threatens one's membership in the community of men. To hold on to the moral abomination of cannibalism, one must believe that the line between the human and the nonhuman ought to have moral significance. There are certain ways in which human beings and their remains should not be treated. To hold on to the moral abomination of homosexuality, one would have to believe that the line distinguishing between male and female identities has a similar moral valence.

Some people do feel just this way. When men behave like women or when women behave like men—when they violate the gender code by their hairstyle, clothing, gait, mannerism, speech, or sexual activity—the line crossed has moral significance. Rav Moshe's portrayal of homosexuality as an intrinsically revolting subversion of the cosmic order squares well with this social world. Surely for earlier generations defective gender was no less horrifying than defective humanity. Today, however, for most people in the West the gender divide is a fuzzy and rather makeshift line no longer seen as cosmic or even essential but as a morally neutral (or potentially oppressive) social construct. In democratic societies for a man to behave like a beast is still a moral abomination, but for a man to behave like a woman is not.

In my conversations with American Orthodox rabbis, few resonated with Rav Moshe's portrayal of homosexuality. What was disgust for Rav Moshe has become more like discomfort for rabbis living in the United States. For many Modern Orthodox Jews the horror of homosexuality has abated, along with the moral threat once associated with it. While the halakhic rule is sustained in Orthodox communities, its violation inspires more sadness than revulsion. If Stout is correct, the reason for this shift has as much or more to do with gender generally and with the change in the status of women specifically than with attitudes about homosexuality per se. The civil and economic freedoms of women and their access to education, jobs, and political power have simply begun to blur the gender boundaries for everyone, resulting in less abominable abominations.

Stout has helped us to understand what is at stake. The rationale of category confusion depends on an understanding of the differences between men and women that I no longer possess. While gender-bending may be disturbing to many, for most of us the boundary is not longer sharply drawn and its violation no longer morally salient. However, perhaps we should not be too quick to invite the blurring of all boundaries or disregard the dangers of confusion. An egalitarian utopia bleached clean of all masculine-feminine difference would appeal to few people. While I am clearly at odds with those rabbinic voices that still consider the blurring of gender to be a great moral threat, like Stout I am also not ready to jettison the potential moral significance of category violations altogether. In the natural world some boundary blurrings are good, while others are decidedly bad. The body can function only when some tissues are permeable and others are impenetrable. Likewise, in the Torah we discover that some mixtures were considered holy and others profane. A closer look at the tradition will reveal a more nuanced and complex negotiation with category confusions that may offer yet another layer of insight into the prohibition.

Good and Bad Mixtures

The problem of category confusion does not immediately speak to our age. Modernity is the age of mixtures. The juxtaposition of very different media, images, styles, and colors, to play off one another and make something new, is the core of modern art and design. Mixing things together has been a human preoccupation from alchemy to bioengineered corn, practiced by folk healers, master chefs, and scientists. Much of what we eat and wear in America is grafted and hybrid. Given the success of modern chemistry, what can be said of the biblical concern for categorical purity?

We may love to mix up our world, but even in our own contemporary setting there are mixtures that we, too, would think of as morally problematic or at least dangerous. The most obvious of the modern problems regarding the keeping of things in their place is articulated by ecologists. Pollution of the air and water is surely a sort of category confusion that contemporary alchemy engenders on the earth. While few would deny the unimaginable progress of the last hundred years, we have become increasingly alarmed at the dangers of things being in the wrong place. Human creativity has some very destructive side effects for the biosphere, not the least of which are the hole in the ozone layer and global warming. It is no idle threat to suggest that life on our planet might very well be destroyed by the confusions we engender on it. Clearly categorical mixing unleashes great creative powers that can be wondrous or dangerous or both.

Even in the biblical world-view, mixtures of themselves were not necessarily considered sinful. The woven mixture of linen and wool

(shatnez), which may not be worn, might very well have been prohibited not because it was inherently bad, but just the opposite,
because it was too intimately tied to the sacred. While no Jew was
permitted to wear the linen-wool mixture in regular garments, the
special fringes worn by an Israelite containing a thread of royal blue
were expressly made of linen and wool. The linen-wool mixture was
included in the sash of an ordinary priest and the breastplate of the
high priest. It appears that the reason one may not mix certain
things is because mixtures participate in the sacred. The ordinary
Jew is permitted a single mixed thread, a priest a bit more, and the
high priest, who enters the holy of holies, the most. Like alchemy,
mixtures are about the power of transmutation and miraculous
change. They are a divine handiwork.

According to biblical scholar Rabbi Jacob Milgrom the field
planted with mixed seeds was not destroyed, as some have suggested,
but became holy property of the Temple priesthood. The planted
mixtures were instantly sacred and so made out of bounds for ordinary Israelites.[26] For this reason they were warned not to plant a field
with mixed seed because if they did so they would lose the produce
to the Temple.[27] Lastly, the cherubim, the angelic winged figures
with childlike faces above the ark, were mixtures as was the heavenly
chariot in Ezekiel's dream.[28]

It appears that mixtures of things can be wondrous or monstrous
depending on how they are understood. They may violate categorical boundaries or mediate between them. The violators are notably
taboo, the mediators sanctified. In some cultures intersexed people
are considered sacred mediators between the worlds of men and
women. A famous example is the American Indian berdache, a ho-
mosexual/transsexual or mixed-gendered person given a hallowed
role. While neither the Torah nor rabbinic literature offer a sha-
manic role for intersexed people, both include a good deal of discussion about the existence of people who do not fit neatly into either
the male or the female categorical box. The very idea of category violation tends to presume distinct categories with clear boundaries.
While normally people come in two sexes, it is not always the case. If
the prohibition is concerned primarily with gender bending, what
does it do when nature itself confounds the categories?

The Hermaphrodite: Nature's Mixture

The gender order might appear straightforward, but nature itself seems not always to care to keep its boundaries clear. The theology of divine order as the rationale behind the prohibition of male intercourse would sit better if tampering with gender was something only humans do. For those who are concerned about God's desire for men to be men and women to be women, the hermaphrodite poses an interesting dilemma.

What did the sages do when a baby was born whose body exhibited genitalia of both sexes? How did they manage the violations of the order of creation that appeared regularly, if rarely, within the creation itself?

The Mishnah Bikkurim includes two discussions of naturally occurring beings that violate binary categories of organization.[29] The first is an animal called a *koi*, thought to be an antelope of sorts, that is in some ways like a wild animal, in some ways like a domesticated beast, and in some ways like neither.[30] The second case is that of a hermaphrodite, referred to in the Talmud by the Latin term *androgynus*. An *androgynus* is in some respects like men and in others like women, in some ways like both men and women, and in other respects like neither. Chapter 4 of Mishnah Bikkurim is filled with the dizzying categorizations of persons who do not fit into either sex box. At the end of the chapter, almost as an apology, there is an explanation for the Mishnah's confusion in regard to the hermaphrodite.

"Rabbi Jose says, A hermaphrodite is a creature unto itself: But the sages were unable to decide whether it was a man or a woman."[31] The confusion has two forms. For R. Jose the confusion is tactical. R. Jose is attempting to help a three-dimensional being negotiate a two-dimensional social space. No room has been assigned in the male-female order for this "other" sexed person, and thus his task, so to speak, is to help the hermaphrodite, a third-sexed being, know which public bathroom to enter when only two are available.

The rabbis see the confusion differently. For them the confusion is about the essence of the hermaphrodite. They assume that such a being must be either male or female, but they do not know which. There is no possibility of a third sex for them. Their task is to manage their own ignorance of this person's essential sex. For R. Jose the world is less ordered than it is for the sages. He sees the difference of a third sex as a challenge to society. The sages see that difference as a structural impossibility. The hermaphrodite becomes to them a frustration, a challenge not to the binary order per se, but to their certain knowledge of its workings. Functionally, for lack of a better option, except for those bodily functions that were explicitly female such as menstruation, the hermaphrodite was in practice treated as a male.[32]

In a similar vein the sages attempted to determine the status of a firstborn animal born with both male and female genitalia. Only a nonblemished animal can be consecrated as a firstborn. Rabbi Ishmael says that a double-sexed animal is actually a male with a "blemish greater than any" and is consequently disqualified. What could be more blemishing of a male calf than a vaginal orifice? But the sages here seem to agree with R. Jose that a mixed gendered creature is neither male nor female but "a kind of its own."[33] Struggling to map the world, the rabbis again debate whether doubled-sexed beings are a deformity deviating from nature or a natural wonder expanding nature's repertoire.

The Nursing Father

According to at least one sage the mixed-sexed body can be a miraculous blessing. The rabbis address the moral aesthetics of a case of sex/gender confusion in a midrashic tale about a man who grew breasts.

> There once was a man whose wife died and left him with an infant to suckle, and he could not afford to pay a wet nurse. A miracle occurred, and he grew breasts like a woman's two breasts, and he nursed his child. Rabbi Joseph said: Come and see just how great this man must be that such a miracle was performed for him! Abbaye said: On the contrary. How bad this man must be that the order of nature was changed for him.[34]

The disagreement between R. Joseph and Abbaye is about whether this miracle demonstrates the goodness and worthiness of the man to whom it happened. For R. Joseph the miracle was a wondrous and blessed thing bestowed by heaven on a great man. For Abbaye the miracle was a perverse and ugly thing that could only have been sent by heaven to a base person. R. Joseph understands the miracle as a sign of God's love, while Abbaye thinks of it as a divine curse. At the bottom of their disagreement might very well be a difference of visceral reaction, aesthetic opinion, or as Stout has suggested, a difference in the cosmological significance of gender. For Abbaye the sex/gender divide is like gravity, a fundamental structure of the creation with which God does not play. For R. Joseph, God's love for his creatures is more like gravity than is the sex/gender divide. The debate in the Orthodox community surrounding homosexuality may boil down to just this. Is a man with breasts marvelous or monstrous?

A Blessing over Difference

The rabbis innovated a blessing to be recited upon seeing any peculiar-looking creature, animal or human: "Blessed are you, Lord, who makes unusual creatures (literally: who differentiates the creatures)."[35] An ordinary elephant or monkey might require the blessing and so would an albino or a giant. But in relation to people the sages were not certain when a difference was to be blessed and when it was to be mourned. On seeing someone blind or smitten all over his body with boils, they said, "Blessed be the true judge," the same blessing said on the news of a death. This blessing is both an acceptance of divine judgment and a subtle expression of how impossibly painful the world can be.

How does one distinguish between painful and wonderful difference? The solution the rabbis offer applies an objective, if somewhat simplistic, criterion for discerning good and bad difference. Someone who was born whole and then suffers a bodily loss or disfigurement evokes sadness and quiet acceptance of God's judgment—blessed is the true judge *(baruch dayan ha'emet)*. Someone who was born with an unusual bodily difference evokes more wonder than sadness—blessed is the One who makes all sorts of different creatures *(baruch mishaneh ha'briot)*.

In the thirteenth century Rabbi Menahem ben Solomon Meiri explained the blessing as a response to "the experiencing of new things, without necessarily enjoying or being troubled by them."[36] New things, even ones that do not particularly strike us as beautiful, are signs of the fullness of creation. The blessing then is an expression of wonderment at divine creativity, a hallelujah in response to the multiplicity of life forms invented by the Creator. Were R. Jose to have seen with his own eyes the man who miraculously grew breasts, he would have rejoiced in God's creative genius, and he would have said, "Blessed are you, Lord, who makes the creatures different from one another." Abbaye would have quietly intoned the blessing over the dead.

So far in our explorations we have considered three rationales suggested by traditional commentators, none of which have seemed unambiguously compelling or conclusive. The rationale of reproduction was shown to be implausible given the halakhic acceptance of nonreproductive sex. The rationale of social disruption was discovered to be more a result of compulsory heterosexuality than of homosexuality. The rationale of category confusion remains salient only if, like Abayye, we invest the category of gender and the infractions of pure belonging with an overriding moral significance. On this score most of us more readily identify with R. Josef and no longer think of homosexuality as a moral abomination.

We are now ready to address the last rationale, one that returns us to the themes we discovered in the story of Sodom—the rationale of humiliation and violence.

13

The Rationale of Humiliation and Violence

There is another rationale for the prohibition that, while being only indirectly intimated by the sages, has accompanied our inquiry from the beginning. We have seen that homoeroticism in the Book of Genesis never appears outside of violent contexts. Ham rapes his father. The sons of privilege and power take all that they want, starting with the daughters of the poor abducted from their nuptial beds and eventually including young men and animals. The violence of male-to-male sexual expression is continued in the story of Sodom. The men of Sodom were guilty not of sexual perversion, but rather of the humiliation of strangers. The foreigner, who should be invited into the protective care of the tent, is greeted instead with a mob clamoring for his submission to violent, forcible sexual entry.

What Leviticus prohibits, then, may be the humiliation of one's fellow by sexual penetration, and the willingness to humiliate oneself by allowing such a violation of one's male body. This is not to say that the verse prohibits male rape to the exclusion of sex between consenting male adults. It suggests something much more demanding and problematic. Under the sway of this reading, Leviticus seems to claim that all intercourse between men cannot help but be a degrading, abominable humiliation of one male by another. In many ancient cultures being penetrated by another male was the height of disgrace because in being so used, one was cast into the realm of women. Rabbinic culture was no exception to this belief.

Penetrated Like a Woman

The following midrash cites the case of four kings who, according to the author of the text, were justly and fitly punished for their hubris. Their hubris consisted of the simple and common ancient association of royalty with divinity. Their punishment, hinted at in Scripture, and boldly articulated by the midrash, is anal penetration by other men.

> There were four men (kings) who made themselves into gods and [consequently] were penetrated like women . . . Hiram, Nebuchadnezzar, Pharaoh, and Yoash.
>
> 1) From where do we learn of Hiram? As it says, "Say to [Hiram,] the Prince of Tyre, 'So says the Lord God: Because you have been so haughty and have said "I am a god" . . . I will bring against you strangers, the most ruthless of nations. They shall unsheathe their swords against your prized shrewdness and they shall strike down your splendor'" (Ezek. 28:3–7). Since he claimed that he was a god, he was penetrated as a woman, as it says, "Your heart was haughty because of your beauty, you debased your wisdom for the sake of splendor; I have cast you to the ground before kings and given you over to them to make an exhibition of you" (Ezek. 28:17). What does it mean "to make an exhibition of you"—they will have their desire will with you.
>
> 2) From where do we learn of Nebuchadnezzar? [About Nebuchadnezzar] it is written: "Once you thought in your heart, 'I will climb the sky, I will set my throne higher than the stars of God . . . I will match the Most High" (Isa. 14:13–14). God replied to him, "Instead, you are brought down to Sheol, to the bottom of the pit" (Isa. 14:15). [God] exiled him from his kingdom and fed him grass like a beast, as it says [referring to Nebuchadnezzar in the Book of Daniel], "You will be driven away from men and have your habitation with the beasts of the field." [What does this mean?] Beasts will see him in the form of a beast and sexually penetrate him.[1]
>
> 3) From where do we learn of Yoash? After king Yehoiada's death, the princes of Judah came to bow before the king [Yoash] (2 Chron. 24:17). What does it mean that they bowed before the king? They deified him and he accepted it. . . . [Later, in the same chapter we discover the fate of king Yoash.] It is written, "They inflicted punishments on Yoash" (2 Chron. 24:24). Taught Rabbi Ishmael: This teaches that they appointed over him cruel guards who never

knew a woman, and they would abuse him the way one abuses a woman.

4) From where do we learn that Pharaoh deemed himself a god and was penetrated like a woman? From the verse, "I will deal with you, Pharaoh, king of Egypt . . . who says 'The Nile is mine, I made it for myself' (Ezek. 29:3). It is I who created myself"! Pharaoh made himself a god, and [as punishment] he was penetrated like a woman, as it says, "Behold I will deliver Pharaoh Hophra, king of Egypt, into the hands of his enemies" (Jer. 44:30). Why was his name Hophra? Because he spread him open *[phar'a]* from behind. This is Pharaoh who was a male and was made into a female.[2]

God, Men, Women

The midrash provides a map of relations between God, men and women. God is on top and men on bottom; men are on top and women on bottom. In relation to God humans are receptive; in relation to men women are receptive. As God rules men, men rule women. The order is meant to be beneficent, but its potential for violence is implicit. The midrash understands that Pharaoh and his friends have violated the given hierarchy of power. Because they have promoted themselves to a divine status, their punishment is demotion to a female status. It is a typical measure-for-measure punishment—humiliation for arrogance. And how does one humiliate a male? By sexual penetration. And why is this humiliating? Because this is what a man does to a woman.

The rabbis living under Roman domination experienced the humiliation of subjugation as particularly shameful because they associated Rome with men who are penetrated. The midrash tells us that the Jewish people cry out to God, saying, "Master of the Universe, it is not fair that we should be subjugated to the seventy nations, but certainly not this one that is penetrated like a woman!"[3]

Lilith

When men brazenly rise up and claim divinity, they are cast down, literally beneath the station of men. When women rise up to be the equals of men, they, too, are rejected. The most famous cautionary midrashic tale of a woman who wishes to be treated as an equal to her man is the story of Lilith. After creating the *adam,* God saw clearly that "it is not good for the *adam* to be alone." It would seem to make sense that a creature from the earth needed another earth creature for a partner. God made a partner for the *adam* from the earth and called her Lilith. From the beginning they did not get along.

> Lilith said, "I am not lying on the bottom!" And Adam said, "I am not lying on the bottom, but on the top, for it is appropriate for you to be below and me above!" She said to him, "We are equal since we were both created from the earth!" And they wouldn't listen to each other. Since she saw [this], she spoke the holy name and flew away into the sky.[4]

This marital squabble begins simply. She insists that she not be on the bottom, presumably in sexual relations. He is adamant that he, too, will not be on the bottom, but he adds something more. While God has not, to our knowledge, preordained any top/bottom order for this first man-woman dyad, Adam assumes there is one. He must be on top. Lilith's refusal to lie beneath him would not exclude side-by-side intercourse, nor would it seem to exclude a playful switching of top and bottom. From Adam's response it is clear that nothing will work for him but climbing on top.

In both biblical and rabbinic culture above and below are domains assigned especially to God (above) and humans (below). In this midrashic tradition, unlike the one that understands the first *adam* as androgynous, the very beginning of heterosexual partnership is fraught with the power battle of women wanting side-by-side equality and men wanting dominance. She knows what she deserves. She, too, is a creature of the earth. Unlike the moon she does not ask God how he imagines two rulers sharing a single crown. She seems to understand that God will side with Adam, that for her, partnership will mean domination. Lilith gets the message and leaves. In her anger and detachment she roams the earth threatening the lives of newborns.

As a folktale the story both legitimates a feminine desire for gender equality and demonizes the woman who insists on it, who is ready to leave if she doesn't get it. It tells us that what women who feel equal to men want is a man who is not threatened by their desire for side-by-side parity or perhaps even for a shared dominance. It responds to such women with a warning that men will not be willing to cede their dominance so easily. Men experience equality with women as a demotion of status.

The rabbis of late antiquity did not conjure up this discourse of sex and power completely on their own. In their cultural neighborhoods similar conceptions of sex and of gender were widely shared. While among Jews normative behavior was largely shaped by Scripture and its interpretations, the fundamental meanings of maleness and femaleness and of intercourse that were brought to bear upon the text were a common inheritance. Greco-Roman culture was both resisted and adopted by Jews during the three centuries before the Common Era. Later, during the rabbinic period, Jews lived very closely with both pagan and Christian Romans. Rabbis of antiquity had no choice but to deal with sexual relations between men because it was a fact of their social environment. A view of the similarities and differences between the Jewish and Greco-Roman discourses on sex and gender generally and on homosexuality specifically will sharpen our understanding of Jewish sensibilities and shed considerable light on this last rationale.

Power and Sex

In the sexual rhetoric of the Greek and Roman world, sex is a power relation. It occurs legitimately only between parties of unequal power. Men of stature may have sex with women, slaves, boys, and foreigners. Hierarchies within the community of men permit some men to have legitimate penetrative sexual contact with men lower than they. To engage in receptive anal intercourse as an adult in Hellenistic culture was to be demoted to the class of women.

Kenneth James Dover, among others, has demonstrated that in Greek and Roman cultures intercourse was conceived of as an act of domination.[5] A male was to have intercourse only with someone beneath him in rank. A free man in Rome could have intercourse with a slave, a boy, or a woman, but not with a citizen of equal standing. Intercourse between equals was deemed unseemly and was legally actionable. Michel Foucault very clearly describes how sexual relations in the ancient world were structured as power relations. He writes, "[S]exual relations [were] always conceived in terms of the model act of penetration, assuming a polarity that opposed activity and passivity—were seen as being of the same type as the relationship between a superior and a subordinate, an individual who dominates and one who is dominated, one who commands and one who complies, one who vanquishes and one who is vanquished."[6] The classical world was divided, says Daniel Boyarin, into the penetrators, who were all men, and the penetrated, who were both male and female.[7]

According to David Halperin inappropriate sex deprived one of social status.[8] Any male citizen who was found to have been sexually subordinate to his fellow was stripped of his citizenship, of his membership in the community of men, and demoted to the ranks of women, foreigners, and slaves—those whose bodies were formally and legally receptive to the control and pleasure-seeking goals of the men acknowledged as the masters of Athens. The judgment was retroactive as well. If in his youth an adult male citizen had prostituted himself, he had surrendered his future right to speak in the public assembly. Having once become the instrument of another person's pleasure, whether out of poverty, greed, or desire, he ceased to be an autonomous actor in his own right and was forever disfranchised. "To be a prostitute meant, in effect, to surrender one's phallus—to discard the marker of one's social and sexual precedence—and so it was next to enslavement, the worst degradation a citizen could suffer, equivalent to voluntary feminization."[9]

The social hierarchy in rabbinic sources shares some of the features of this Athenian discourse. The Athenian testifying in court had to swear that he was not a slave, not a woman, and not a foreigner. The rabbis introduced three blessings in the morning prayer service that are essentially identical to the Athenian oath and have a similar task of defining the nature of membership before the testimony of prayer begins. To this day traditional Jewish men begin their prayers by praising God for not having made them a gentile, a slave, or a woman. Later, when out of piety women wanted to recite the morning blessings, the following replacement blessing for women was constructed: "Blessed are you, Lord our God, Ruler of the universe, who has made me according to his will."[10] As the fourteenth-century Spanish liturgical commentator David ben Joseph Abudarham explained, women who cannot say "who has not made me a woman" should replace that blessing with "who has made me according to his will"—"like one who justifies an evil decree that has come upon him."[11] Men are grateful not to be women; women are accepting an evil decree.

In the rabbinic understanding of sex and gender it seems that here, too, the Hellenistic sexual hierarchies, while not identical, are structurally quite similar. Sexual intercourse is an act between unequals. Adam is on top and Eve on bottom. Adam rejects the very thought of equality. While the Halakhah actually permits any sexual position, the midrash regards the "missionary position" as normative sex. Each partner, says the midrash, looks toward its source, from whence it comes. He looks down toward the earth; she looks up toward the rib.[12]

Penetration, as we have seen, is equivalent to domination for the rabbis as well. While in Greco-Roman society that form of domination has a number of legitimate recipients—boys, women, slaves, and foreigners—in Jewish society there is only one, women. Intercourse for men is seen as legitimate and positive when conducted with women, holy in the context of marriage, and as utterly illegitimate and violent with men, irrespective of their social standing. Men in Judea are not hierarchically ordered in regard to sexual roles. Powerlessness does not render a man legitimately sexually available to other men. While in both ancient Jewish and rabbinic society there were social distinctions between the freeborn and the slave, the Jew and the gentile, these social hierarchies were already somewhat minimized by Jewish law, and more importantly, were not reinscribed within the gender-role economy.

Even with regard to minors the biblical text appears quite clear. "And with a male you shall not lie the lyings of a woman" distinguishes between male and man. The words *zakhar* and *ish* ("male" and "man") are as distinct in Hebrew as they are in English. It would seem that the biblical verse prohibits intercourse with any person possessing the sign of maleness (i.e., a penis), even a boy.

In Athens prepubescent boys were in a transitional state of boyish feminine beauty that was destined to end. Boys grow up to be men and take their place in the public life of the city as citizens. Thus, the measure of a boy's passage into full adulthood was crucial for determining when he had to begin to reject sexual reception and participate only in penetrative sexual roles. In Sparta a boy's status as such might continue till his late twenties; in Athens, however, by the time a boy began to develop body and facial hair, he was already on his way to the adult status that would make sexually penetrating him an offense.

In just this instance of prepubescence one halakhic detail demonstrates the limits of the rabbis' resistance to Hellenistic discourse. Working interpretively from the Leviticus text, the rabbis determine that the "male" in question that one must not penetrate must be above the age of nine. Below that age the prohibition is in force, but the crime is no longer capital. An adult is flogged for the act of anally penetrating an eight-year-old, while the same act with a ten-year-old would be formally punishable by death.[13]

The rule is shocking to our sensibilities in no small measure because our notion of childhood is very different from that of the ancients. It is barely thinkable that sex between consenting adults receives the death penalty, but sex between a thirty-year-old man and an eight-year-old boy is a misdemeanor. But if we put the horror aside, what is at work in this rule is the same principle of masculinity = power that we have seen in Athens. While legal majority begins at thirteen years and a day, at the age of nine years and a day a boy was considered to have begun puberty. From then on his sexual acts were considered effective if not punishable. In a sense, then, male identity does not wait till legal majority. It begins four years earlier at the age of nine and a day.

The nineteenth-century scholar Rabbi Joseph Hayyim ben Elijah al-Hakham explains this strange halakhic ruling in the following way. Quoting kabbalistic sources, he says that when a man mounts a male, he injures him in the *zeir anpin* (lit., the "small face"), which is the source of maleness. However, in a lad under the age of nine there is no formation of the *zeir anpin* in him yet. Since his male identity is incomplete, the one who penetrates him is like one who is wasting his seed. But when the boy is nine years and a day old, then his maleness in the body below becomes parallel to the maleness in the divine above.[14] Consequently, even though he is not yet able to rise up completely from elements of the feminine still in him (not until he is thirteen and a day), he has the necessary vital fluids and in theory can reproduce. Consequently, from nine years and a day the prohibition is in full force but not before.[15]

While the rabbis succeeded in separating power from masculinity, they reveal here that the separation is not complete. A boy under the age of nine is simply "not a male" in this system in a parallel fashion to the way an adolescent is "not a male" in Athenian culture. This rabbinic exclusion, which is codified in all normative halakhic works, would seem to demonstrate that the prohibition for the rabbis is not about the order of creation, but about the clarity of gender roles. Only a true male can be unmanned by being penetrated anally. The anal penetration of an eight-year-old boy is a horrifying crime to our sensibilities, but it does not threaten the gender economy. It is, says Rabbi al-Hakham, "like spilling seed on rocks and stones." While the differences in the definitions of a man in each culture should not be minimized, the horror for the sages was the unmanning of a man, just as it was for their Greco-Roman neighbors.

It appears, then, that penile penetration in intercourse is understood in both cultures as an act of domination injurious to true men and appropriate to others. Sexual penetration of one man by another is by definition a humiliation and feminization of the penetrated partner. The differences should not be overlooked. In Athens if the partner was a boy, a woman, a foreigner, or a slave, then no wrong had been committed because the penetration had subordinated (feminized) a person already subordinate (effeminate). Because male identity in Jewish culture was not fused with power, the only permissibly penetrable parties were those made to be penetrated (i.e., women). The sexual penetration of any male in Judea above the age of nine is then similar to the penetration of an Athenian citizen. Both are considered acts of abject humiliation. God punished arrogant men with anal rape because such is the measure for measure. Enjoying the experience does not matter. Pharaoh allegedly enjoyed the experience. Regardless of one's will or desire, being sexually penetrated demotes one to the status of a woman.

One last important difference between Jewish and Greco-Roman views of adult male-male sexual relations bears discussion. In Athens the crime is one against the individual and the state since the body of a male citizen has been violated. However, in Judea it is God who prohibits such humiliation and who prescribes punishment for both the aggressor and the one who willingly submits himself to humiliation. The maker of men in Athens is the polis; in Judea it is God. The polis guards the honor of its citizens but instantiates the legitimate sexual penetration/humiliation of slaves, foreigners, underage boys, and, of course, women. In Judea all men are men. The stranger and the slave were men with full rights as men. Underage boys were also covered by the prohibition (despite the disturbing discrepancy regarding the full force of the punishment when the boy in question was under the age of nine). In Athens masculinity was fully dependent on power; in Judea the mere possession of a penis was essentially enough.

Homophobia and Misogyny

Sacred narratives are not philosophies or mathematical formulas. In the first chapter of Genesis, we learn that all people are made in the image of God and in the second chapter that all women are under the control of men. The equality of men is not unrelated to the subordination of women. From the verse in Leviticus that prohibits sex between men, we have learned that men, all men, even those at the bottom of the social hierarchy, have the sexual status of the Athenian citizen. None may be penetrated. However, we have learned this rule of the equality of men at the expense of women, for the way we know that all men are equal is that one cannot treat any of them as one treats a woman. In Judea only a woman can be treated like a woman.

According to this rationale, male-male intercourse is prohibited because it is inevitably an act of aggression and degradation. The Mishnah lists only three cases where a pursuer may be killed before he commits a crime: that of a pursuer intending to murder, that of one intending to rape a betrothed or married woman, or that of one intending to rape a male. Rashi explains that in the case of the male, since it is not "his ways" to be penetrated by a male, one may kill the pursuer to prevent shame and embarrassment.[16] A male who penetrates another male catapults his neighbor into the category of a woman. No humiliation is more apt for the arrogant than being abused like a woman. No deterrent to open doors and receptivity is more apt than that of raping passing travelers. Leviticus 20:13 censures both parties of a male sexual encounter because the willingness to be turned into a woman, to be mounted by another man, is parallel to self-castration. To be like Jacob—to dwell in tents; to be pale, soft skinned, and hairless; to study Torah and spurn physical aggression like Rabbi Yohanan—are not inconsistent with manhood in Judea. To be physically receptive to another man is surely a way to lose oneself as a man.

The system of hierarchy is responsible both for the meaning of gender and for the meaning of intercourse. Intercourse humiliates only because women are already despised, only because the social milieu confirms the hatred formally in a myriad of ways, only because men are on top, women on bottom. Were men and women to live together, side by side, intercourse would not need to be domination. While Lilith is ready for side-by-side sex, Adam demands to be on top. Intercourse, then, is a communication shaped by the male-female hierarchy, and then that same hierarchy is reinscribed by the very act of intercourse, in circular fashion. Sexual intercourse becomes an act of domination because of the already "bottom" status of the women in the picture.

It is important to note that none of this cultural formation excludes a mutual and loving emotional relationship between husbands and wives. Still, the formal and legal relationship was defined by the power differentials between men and woman. The chicken-and-egg connection between intercourse as domination and the debasement of women should be obvious. In Hellenistic culture to be a woman was to be culturally marked already as weak, hysterical, and dull; to be a man was to be strong, in control, and intelligent. This rigid hierarchical construction of gender leads to an experience of intercourse that confirms the hierarchy and reifies the difference between men and women. If being the recipient in intercourse makes a woman into a woman, then it makes a man into a woman, and to be cast down from maleness to femaleness was the epitome of humiliation.

A common retort in traditional circles is that women are considered the spiritual superiors of men, that the husband must put his wife on a pedestal. In fact, while certain feminine qualities associated with loyalty and perseverance were held in high regard, generally speaking these qualities did not give women any formal power over men. Women were to be subservient to men by natural design and certainly by the formal demands of marriage. Rabbi David ben Shlomo ibn Abi Zimra (RaDbaZ) said that since the wife was intended by nature and temperament to be subservient to her husband, a man should not dress like a woman, because this would indicate degradation.[17] It was wholly understood that to be like a woman in any way was degrading for a man.

Rereading Leviticus

This understanding of the prohibition against male-male intercourse is derived from both biblical and rabbinic textual sources. It is the most demanding of the rationales because it asks us to reread Leviticus in its light. The results are both troubling and amazing.

First, the trouble. Faced squarely, this rationale seems to endorse and even to legislate the hatred of women. If a man may not do to his fellow man what he ordinarily does to women because it "feminizes" him, then femininity is itself the worst of humiliations. Given this rationale for the prohibition, intercourse itself cannot be understood except as an act of domination, a marking of superiority, an act of mastery over someone. Reading the verse in this fashion might seem to demand that traditional Jews work to protect masculine power by ensuring the hatred of femininity wherever it appears, especially among men.

However, and this is the amazing part, it is possible to read the verse using this very rationale in a way that turns the verse directly against the fusions of sex and power and the misogyny described in this discussion. Such a rereading will become clear over the next several sections of this chapter. It begins by resisting the presumption that the demotion and hatred of women are fixed in the text.

Let us return again to Leviticus 18:22.

Ve'et zakhar	And a male
lo tishkav	you shall not bed (sexually penetrate)
mishkeve ishah	(engulfing one's penis) as in the lyings of a woman
toevah hi	it is abhorrent

Given our rationale, the verse might read something like this: "You shall not humiliate a fellow male by the kind of penetrations men do with women; it is abhorrent." Let us assume for a moment that the Torah deplores the idea of sexual intercourse as an act of domination and humiliation. If so, one would wonder why the unusual case of male-male intercourse is addressed while the more common sexual domination of women is not mentioned. The answer is, of course, obvious. Until very recently the domination of women was ordinary and invisible. Women in the ancient world were so vulnerable to male aggression that without the protection of a father, a husband, or at the very least brothers, they were utterly defenseless.

Rape

Our contemporary notion of rape of women is surprisingly a rather modern category according to Kathryn Gravdal.[18] Indeed, there was no word for rape in Old French. In medieval French literature rape was commonly a romantic trope. Male violence against women was depicted as a frustrated expression of love, and male aggression and female suffering were coded as erotically appealing. Young couples who could not secure parental agreement for marriage would arrange a rape that would force the father to marry off his daughter to the lover/rapist.

In the Bible the rape of a single woman, as in the case of Dina, was an act of tribal violence to be avenged by brothers. As strange as it sounds to contemporary ears, the rape of a woman was a crime between men. In biblical tort law the rape of a single woman demanded that the rapist pay a fine to the father for the lost bride price. If she were physically harmed, the attacker would have to pay for damages, but the rape of a woman with no male protectors is ordinary assault and battery. Not so out of sync with the medieval association of rape with romance, the law in Deuteronomy required the rapist to marry the violated woman and to be forever deprived of his power to divorce her.[19] While the women needed to agree to such a bargain, to refuse could easily have doomed a woman to spinsterhood. Having been deflowered, she would find few if any men who would be willing to marry her.

The absence of an accounting of rape from the vantage point of women screams out of these texts but is sadly not surprising. Male aggression is considered so normative that the sages find Dina at fault for wandering out into the fields where Shekhem rapes her.[20] There is simply no way to speak about the sexual penetration of women in intercourse as potentially humiliating and demeaning in cultures where women are beneath men in the hierarchy and where, by their station in society and in the creation itself, they are made to be mounted and penetrated. In a male-dominated society sex cannot help but become part of this invisible violence.

Mishkeve Ishah

The only way to speak about something outside the box of cultural intelligibility is to do so by allusion, to point in a direction without specification, to provide a paradigm that might later be more widely applied. With this in mind I returned to the verse in Leviticus and pondered once again the kind of sex that was prohibited between men. It was called the "lyings of a woman" or in Hebrew, *mishkeve ishah*. The term is odd because it appears in no other place in all of Scripture. In fact, even the first word of the phrase, *mishkeve*, "lyings of—," is found in only one other place in all of Scripture.

The word appears in the account of the rape of Jacob's concubine by his eldest son, Reuven. After the death of his beloved Rachel, Jacob moved his bed from Rachel's tent to the tent of Rachel's hand-maiden, Bilha, and not to the tent of Leah, Reuven's mother. Reuven was infuriated by this added humiliation of Leah, and in defense of his mother, he raped Bilha. At the instance of the rape in the story, there is no record of Jacob's response, but on his deathbed, Jacob cursed Reuven for this rape. The language is poetic: "You went up upon the lyings (or beds) of your father; then you defiled—He mounted my bed!" The Hebrew for "your father's bed(s)" is *mishkeve avikha*. Here, in a context that is fully heterosexual, the language is clear. *Mishkeve* is the word for intercourse used when the motive is not love but a demonstration of virile power, not connection but disconnection, not tenderness but humiliation and violence.

That violence is the point of the prohibition should not surprise anyone. Leviticus 18 focuses almost exclusively on sexual violations, none of which are about promiscuity per se, but rather about the de-structive power of sexual expression. Most of the rules in the chapter concern incest. When familial intimacy and trust are exploited for sex, the resulting damage is deep, often crippling, and irreversible. Marital commitments ground the stability of families. Adultery violates the sworn promises of partners, unravels trust, and splits families apart.

The chapter includes the law of *niddah,* which forbids sexual intercourse during menstruation. Even this rule might fit the general frame of sex and violence if we imagine that sex during menstruation has the visual effect of wounding, of spilling blood by penetrating the body of another. During menstruation sexual intercourse looks like violence. The chapter ends with the prohibition of giving one's seed, meaning one's children, over to the sacrificial cult of Molech. There is great debate as to the exact nature of Molech worship, but most authorities concur that child sacrifice was part of the cult worship of the Canaanite deity. This law seems out of place unless, as we have suggested, the whole chapter revolves around the problem of violence inside sexual and familial relationships.[21]

According to this rationale the verse prohibits the kind of sex between men that is designed to effect the power and mastery of the penetrator. Sex for the conquest, for shoring up the ego, for self-aggrandizement, or worse, for the perverse pleasure of demeaning another man is prohibited. This is an abomination.

The verse now reads as follows:

Ve'et zakhar	And a male
lo tishkav	you shall not sexually penetrate
mishkeve ishah	to humiliate
toevah hi	it is abhorrent

This reading of Leviticus 18:22 as a law against sexual domination and appropriation is a rather radical approach to the biblical verse. It is a reading that offers gay people a way to reconnect to God, Torah, and the Jewish people. While the sources that undergird this interpretation are traditional, talmudic, and biblical, they have never before been used together in concert toward this end. The implications of this new reading of Leviticus will follow in the next chapter, but there is yet one further interpretive possibility, another rabbinic insight, that provides an even more sweeping and satisfying rereading of the verse.

Interpreting *et*

The sages of the Talmud believed that every letter of the Torah was filled with meaning. Nothing was accidental. For this reason there was great competition among sages to find ways to read everything as important, nothing as inessential.

The Hebrew word *et* is a grammatical word that often has no translatable meaning but simply marks a transfer of action, usually after a verb and before a direct object. Since its use is sporadic, sometimes appearing before objects and sometimes not, the rabbis decided that when it appears, it must mean something. The standard reading was that *et* adds something to the general class of things mentioned, to include hidden elements, to speak the unspoken.

An extra *et* in a sentence could at times not only expand the meaning of a text but also innovate and authorize additional halakhic responsibilities. The fifth of the Ten Commandments is the duty to respect one's parents. The text in Exodus reads: "Honor your father and your mother, so that you may long endure on the land that the Lord your God is assigning to you" (Exodus 20:12). The standard English translation of the verse does not mark the presence of *et,* which in the Hebrew appears before both father and mother in the verse (kaved *et* avikha v'*et* imekha). The sages interpreted the two appearances of *et* to include the duty to honor one's stepmother and stepfather. "Honor *et* your father and *et* your mother: *et* your father comes to include your father's wife, and *et* your mother comes to include your mother's husband.[22] The interpretative expansion was incorporated directly into the Halakhah and generated an array of formal obligations upon stepchildren in regard to their stepparents.[23]

A celebrated incident of this rabbinic penchant for finding added meaning in every letter of the Torah appears in the command to fear the Lord.

> Nehemia Haimsoni was expounding on all the *et'im* in the Torah, explaining how each *et* was there to add something. As soon as he reached the verse, "You shall revere (et) the Lord your God" (Deut. 10:20), he stopped. [For there is nothing to revere other than God.]

His pupils asked him, "Rabbi, what will be with all the other *et'im* that you already expounded on?" He answered them, "Just as my attempt to interpret them all was worthy, my withdrawal from the project is equally worthy." Until Rabbi Akiva came and expounded: "You shall revere *(et)* the Lord your God," the *et* comes to include the students of the wise.[24]

For Rabbi Akiva *talmidei hakchamim,* the sages of every age, deserved a portion of reverence as well, because without them God's Torah would remain inert. Without the living embodiment of the Torah in the lives of great teachers, few of us would have the resources to revere God. In this fashion the presence of *et* in a verse offered the rabbis an opportunity to open up verses to say what was left unsaid.

There is only one sexual prohibition in Leviticus 18 that begins with the word *et.*

Ve'et zakhar	And *(et)* a male
lo tishkav	you shall not sexually penetrate
mishkeve ishah	to humiliate
toevah hi	it is abhorrent

In less poetic Hebrew the sentence would read, "You shall not penetrate *et* a male to humiliate, it is abhorrent." If *et* adds a missing element, then the verse should read, "You shall not penetrate either an [?] or a male, to humiliate, it is abhorrent."

Given that *et* adds an unspoken element to a text, there is an obvious candidate to suggest—a woman!

V'(nekeva o) zakhar	And (either a female or) a male
lo tishkav	you shall not sexually penetrate
mishkeve ishah	to humiliate
toevah hi	it is abhorrent.

Until very recently only the sexual humiliation of men could be understood as abhorrent. However, as women become their own agents, as they approach equality with men, the verse cries out to apply to women too. It could be argued that this superfluous word was ready and waiting for the moment when human equality would be fully extended to women, when as a culture we would be ready to interpret the verse to mean that the fusion of sex and power into a single act is abhorrent between any two people.

208

In an amazing and paradoxical fashion the very verse that was for centuries read as requiring the ongoing demotion of women through the marking of intercourse as humiliation and thus femininity as degraded could be read as a full-fledged critique of the male-dominated social hierarchy! The only way to redeem intercourse from its inevitable dominations is to press for gender equality on the deepest of emotional planes, to work formally toward ending the gender hierarchy, and to heal the ugly misogyny at its foundation.

This rationale explains the prohibition in a way that potentially marks loving sexual intercourse between men as active resistance to the normative meanings of intercourse. What was thought of as the primary prohibition, penile-anal intercourse, is transformed by this interpretation. This is not to say that all sexual relationships between men are automatically free from the kind of domination and violence that the verse abhors. It simply says that given the ugliness of both the demotion of women and the use of sex to affirm it, any act that demonstrates the opposite, that employs intercourse for connection and union and actively rejects the hatred of women by a celebration of receptivity, is good.

The Halakhic Import of Rationales

For a law generally, and for a divine law all the more so, reasons are not the source of authority. Our inability to come up with a rationale in regard to a biblical commandment does not compromise our duty to fulfill the law. For a traditional Jew whether or not any convincing rationale can be offered to justify the prohibition of eating pork or kindling a fire on the Sabbath is irrelevant. One obeys the law as a Jew because one has been born into a covenantal duty to God; we trust God's law because we trust God.[25] We keep the law essentially because it is the "decree of the King."[26]

While these traditional sensibilities are well grounded in the Talmudic literature, they are a fig leaf covering the actual enterprise of lawmaking, which despite the dangers cannot help but constantly employ rationales. Reasons and rationales are ubiquitous in the talmudic literature in all phases of its task of translating scriptural verse and received tradition into legal constitution and code. Reading is always an act of interpretation. Whether engaged in debate over the meaning of words, sentences, or whole chapters, whether generating interpretations or choosing between different interpretations, the rabbis employ values. At times those values are present beneath the surface of the discourse, functioning as the implicit assumptions, and other times they are employed consciously and explicitly.

In short, while the self-conscious inquiry into the possible underlying reasons or aims of the commandments may be presumptuous and incomplete, and while the entire enterprise cannot begin without a fundamental trust in the law, reasons aside—still, there is no other way to make sense of and implement God's word in the world. The audaciousness of the rabbis on this score, their trust that their good sense of the law's purposes would guide them well, led them to produce a vast work of jurisprudence and wisdom. It is just this record of rabbinic boldness that has nourished Jews and Jewish communities for over two millennia.

Indeed, the raucous debates of the Talmud often hinge on whether one or another value was to be predominant, or which value in a conflict of values should properly override others. In this way readings were seen not to reveal a single divine intent but to open up multiple possible divine intents. The refusal to assume that the text held one true reading, that it was instead a matrix upon which to pile up possibilities, was thought of as the core of its divinity.

The Torah is black fire on white fire, eternal and holy. It is also lovingly, brilliantly, divinely not clear. Its openness to successive interpretations is its assurance of eternity. The Torah is divine not because it finishes all discussion about right and wrong, but because it inaugurates and legitimates those very discussions, shapes their ongoing development, and empowers leaders in different times and places to make difficult decisions about its meaning. An eternal work needs to be a beacon for all moments of human history. It needs to press toward deeper values while not prematurely attempting to force paradise on us. It says what it can, and then it points, sometimes overtly and sometimes obliquely, toward Eden.

In chapter 1 of Genesis, both men and women are created in the image of God. In principle women and men are equal. This visionary commitment to human equality has always been there, despite the historic limits of human understanding and readiness. In practice it is not unlike the U.S. Constitution, which speaks in grand ways about human freedom and equality but did not extend these rights to black Americans or to women until generations after its inception.

The sages of the Talmud were of a time and place where the mere thought of gender equality would have been absurd. Still, they were able to fault God for the unfair diminishment of the moon, a sin for which God brings a monthly sacrifice of atonement on his own behalf. Mystics of the sixteenth century were able to establish a monthly prayer for the moon's restoration to her former glory. It would be hard to say who among the scholars of these periods or even among Orthodox scholars today would have been or is now ready to acknowledge this coded future vision of gender equality. Sacred texts can only say what we are ready to hear. The reading of Leviticus 18:22 I have suggested has always been there. Whether future Jewish communities will judge it as a legitimate reading of the Torah cannot yet be known. It is only now becoming audible as a possibility.

For gay Orthodox Jews, and especially for gay men, the discovery of a faithful way of making sense of Leviticus in light of our experience is like manna from heaven. Arguments for our inclusion from within the tradition are a tremendous spiritual armor and a profound comfort. Many of us feel in our hearts that God has not rejected us. To be able to see that it is so from inside the Torah is a salvation beyond words.

In some ways, my aim is similar to that of Daniel the Tailor, who comforts a spurned minority with a midrash of his own making. Daniel the Tailor was cursorily mentioned in the introduction, but now the specifics will be worth our efforts. An ordinary tailor named Daniel happened to join the rabbis in their study of the Book of Ecclesiastes in the talmudic academy of Pumbedita. Daniel reads a concern of his into the text. He is bothered by the seeming unfairness of the law of the bastard *(mamzer),* which dooms the child of an adulterous couple to a marginal existence. He or she is cut off from the clan by a law prohibiting the marriage of the *mamzer* to any Jew. Here is the verse from Ecclesiastes, along with Daniel's midrash.

> I further observed all the oppressions that goes on under the sun. Behold, the tears of the oppressed. There is no one to comfort

them. In the hands of their oppressors there is power, and there is no one to comfort them. (Eccles. 4:1)

Daniel the Tailor explained that the text was speaking about *mamzerim*.

Behold the tears of the oppressed—Their fathers sinned, but what has it to do with these insulted ones! The father of this one went to a woman forbidden to him, but how did this child sin, and how does it concern him?

There is no one to comfort them . . . but in the hands of their oppressors there is power—These are the hands of the Great Sanhedrin [Court] of Israel, which moves against them with the authority of the Torah and removes them from the community because it is written: "A *mamzer* shall not enter into the congregation of the Lord" (Deut. 23:3).

And there is no one to comfort them—Therefore, says the Holy One, blessed be he: "It is upon me to comfort them." In this world there are unworthy ones among them, but regarding the times of the Messiah, Zechariah prophesied: "Behold I see them all like pure gold." For this is symbolized by his vision: "I saw, and behold, it was an oil lamp of pure gold" (Zech. 4:2).[27]

This text is an amazing expression of the rabbis' willingness to engage ethical questions that challenged not only their power base and authority but also their fundamental assumptions about God and Torah. Criticism is laid at the feet of the Sanhedrin, who, armed with an unambiguous verse of the Torah, oppress the innocent. Why should the court be guilty for doing its job, the charge of every court, the implementation of the law? God is blameless and the Sanhedrin guilty, Deuteronomy notwithstanding, because the decisive power is not only or even primarily in the text, but in the hands of its appointed interpreters. Daniel the Tailor faults neither the law nor God. The law of the *mamzer* might well be taken as a useful protection of the family. However, the Sanhedrin failed to balance this value against the general biblical concern for justice and fairness. Even worse, the Sanhedrin, it would appear, rests easy with the sacrifice of the happiness of the bastard to a greater good. Whatever they decide to do about the problem, Daniel cannot bear their resting easy. He wants the rabbis to experience the human implications of their power.

Daniel conveys his message in a midrashic morality play in which he casts himself as the prophet Amos and the rabbis as the Temple priests of Bethel, whose pious fulfillment of the sacrificial order becomes an abuse of the poor. The oppressors are those religious authorities who, having a verse to cite, feel fully justified in causing great harm to innocent people. Moreover, the "clarity" of the text in Deuteronomy offers no refuge from the potential of becoming an oppressor. Acting with blind certainty on a single verse, as if no other verses existed and with no concern for the human costs, leads to the oppression of the stranger, the hatred of a brother and a sister.

In time the rabbis actually heard Daniel. Later authorities became unwilling to fully implement the law of bastards. Rabbi Yitzhak bar Aha ruled that if a family appears in which a *mamzer* has been submerged, he should remain submerged. No investigations should be made to discover who is and who is not a bastard. Rashi explained, that in the end, all families will be declared pure anyway. On the basis of R. Yitzhak's ruling, R. Yohanan (the same R. Yohanan we encountered in chapter 6) swore that he could prove the presence of bastards in some of the families in the Land of Israel. "But, what can I do!" R. Yohanan said. "Some of the great ones of this generation are intermixed with them." This language of "what can I do" is rare in rabbinic literature. It is used to express the impossibility of fulfilling a law of the Torah because of weighty contravening considerations. While the law remains on the books, the authorities refuse to fully implement it. Is R. Yohanan fearful of the powerful Jews whom he would destroy with his information, or is he making a principled refusal to act on a law that would accomplish none of its purposes and be disastrous for the community? In the end it was forbidden for anyone to reveal that someone is a *mamzer*.[28]

Daniel understood the rabbis well. Get them to fantasize about a messianic future law, and the desire for that future justice will be too much for them to contain. They will be hard pressed not to move ahead incrementally toward the messianic age in anticipation. While only the messiah could restore all the *mamzerim*, declaring them all worthy, the rabbis could urge an active inattention to facts and even a suppression of the truth.

We do not know how much of a role in this process Daniel's radical interpretation played. He did not wholly reframe the law in his own time, but perhaps he did make a difference. He surely must have stirred the rabbis to feel less easy, and equally important, he offered a profound consolation to the *mamzerim* of his time. For us this work is no different. To demonstrate that God does not hate us for innocently being who we are is fundamental if we are to continue to trust in the goodness of God and in the truth of the Torah.

However valuable it might be to prod some people and to comfort others with a creative rereading of Leviticus, it does not finish our task. Most Orthodox rabbis will not be open to the reinterpretations of this chapter for jurisprudential reasons. The interpretive tools available to the sages of antiquity have been significantly narrowed over the centuries. For better or for worse, Orthodox halakhic methodology today is much less fluid than it was for its founding sages. Leaving aside the question of whether and how these interpretive methodologies might indeed be revived for the sake of renewing halakhic creativity and responsiveness, we must engage in a different sort of conversation if we are to achieve any tangible improvement in the circumstances of lesbian and gay Orthodox Jews. Such an inquiry would turn less on the intent of the law and more on the law's own formal considerations, less on hermeneutics and more on communal authority, less on the genesis of a law and more on its legitimate application. Even those Orthodox Jews who may now be convinced that the text in Leviticus associated with homosexuality actually abominates sex fused with power and violence should understand that if we wish to engage the majority of the community and its leadership, we must provide a more prosaic treatment of the issue as well.

If you are a gay person who has the patience to enter into a halakhic dialogue with the hope of finding a pragmatic, if imperfect, solution, you are invited to join in the conversation. If you are a religious leader feeling caught between your desire to take care of people and your responsibility to the canons of a sacred tradition, the next chapter may help you to navigate. While this sort of conversation violates a kind of purity of conviction, perhaps sometimes it is best not to propound opposing arguments and walk away but instead to find a way to live together, admitting difference.

Conversations

14

Admitting Difference

From the ordinary familial contexts of mommies and daddies, to the fairy-tale princes and princesses of our bedtime stories, we are all schooled in heterosexuality. We are taught that when it comes to gender, the structure of our bodies is both identity and destiny. We must belong to one or the other of these categories, and as we grow older, in increasingly perfect ways. Infractions of the gender order are disciplined first by adults and later by peers so that by the onset of puberty we are fully indoctrinated in the ironclad rules of gender dimorphism and compulsory heterosexuality.

When you don't fit the boxes, you learn the first rule of survival: don't get found out. Despite the limits of awareness gay kids know that their feelings are not safe to share. The art of passing is learned as we repeatedly discover that if we don't monitor our natural responses, we will be humiliated and rejected. Gender expectations split us into the desiring, feeling, expressing self and the censoring self.

Eventually we come into contact with adults who communicate their disgust with homos, dykes, fairies, faggots, and queers. We read verses, hear sermons, and are taught in school that women who love women are disgusting, that men who love men are sick, and that God hates fags. What begins as a defense mechanism becomes an internal accuser supported by everything we have been taught about the world. Given that we have no other cultural frames for understanding our inner life, we come to despise ourselves, or at very least the part of us that has such perverse feelings. Like the self-hating Jews of the European Diaspora who came to believe the worst of the

217

anti-Semitic lies told about them, we become disgusted with our-selves. The most destructive effect of prejudice is often not what is actively done to minorities, but how they are seduced into a suicidal collusion with the oppressor to destroy themselves from the inside.

During my twenties and thirties I had countless dreams of dis-covering myself naked in public places. The dream would begin with some sort of social situation in which I would come to find my-self suddenly totally exposed. I would panic, looking for some way of covering up or explaining myself, of hiding or escaping un-noticed. On occasion I would find myself naked before a tribunal of rabbis. This dream image of rabbis as the agents of shame has been true enough for many of us. But it is not the whole story. In unex-pected ways many of us have discovered in our rabbis and teachers angels of comfort.

Rabbis

In the process of coming out many of us turn to religious leaders for help. The first person with whom I shared my attraction to men was an ultra-Orthodox rabbi in a secluded neighborhood of Jerusalem. Coming out to a religious leader from another social and religious universe has the advantage of deniability, of keeping one's world in-tact. People will often travel far distances to find a safely unfamiliar rabbi who nonetheless has a reputation for being tolerant and understanding.

Others choose instead to seek counsel with a familiar rabbi, someone whom they know and trust. Sharing with a rabbi who knows one's family saves time and offers the potential for rabbinic support for the whole family when (and if) the circle is widened. No matter the scenario, that of anonymity or of familiarity, we go to rabbis hoping that somehow, in the privacy of the rabbi's study, we will be comforted, understood, and helped.

We confide with both hope and enormous fear. Instead of offer-ing comfort and support, religious leaders can confirm our worst fears of ugliness and despair. Even when they attempt kindness, they can unwittingly say things that strike up the chorus of demons in our head, the split-off pieces of our own selves that are ready at a moment's notice to abhor, humiliate, and condemn. And in the breach, when we feel utterly alone and hopeless, they can say the most amazing things to revive and restore us.

Rabbis desperately need help. Most of my colleagues admit that they have no idea what to do or say when a young man or woman comes out to them and asks for their understanding and direction. While the risks of coming out are so much more personal for the gay person, the risks of empathetic listening on the part of rabbis should not be minimized.

Rabbis are trained to help and comfort. Rabbi Joseph Dov Soloveitchik, the late and highly revered dean of modern American Orthodoxy, taught that rabbis are, first and foremost, defenders of the downtrodden and healers of broken spirits. Rabbi Neil Turk tells a story of Rabbi Soloveitchik receiving a phone call from a prominent English rabbi with a halakhic question about a man who felt he needed a sex-change operation. Rabbi Soloveitchik was very upset by the conversation, and Rabbi Turk asked him why this halakhic question was troubling him so much? Rabbi Soloveitchik explained, "Do you realize how tortured this man is feeling? Can you conceive what he is going through in his life? Can you imagine what it's like? He feels like a woman, but he is a man. I don't know if I can help him out, but I must understand the suffering that he is feeling."[1]

Empathy is the first response to any halakhic question. While rabbis are accustomed to this holy work, they often are not prepared for the depth of the personal and religious challenge they face by fully grasping our predicament. When we share our secret with them, we pull them with us into our closet, and they find themselves feeling a measure of our powerlessness and alienation.

A man or woman comes into the rabbi's study and says, "Rabbi, I'm gay." What should the rabbi say next? How can he help without undermining the tradition? And yet how can he repeat the tradition's well-worn judgment without inflicting further pain on an obviously tortured soul? If he speaks first with his heart, will some version of acceptance be broadcast afterward to others? Will his empathy end up threatening his standing in the Orthodox rabbinic community? Does he admit that he, too, cannot understand why a compassionate and loving God would make someone gay and then doom him or her to such torture?

I once heard that an esteemed colleague of mine had, in a public setting, said remarkably open and human things in regard to the issue. When I later reported his statements to a gathering of Orthodox psychologists, the word got back to him, and he called me and asked me never to quote him on the matter again. The exposure was more than he could take. Although he did not retract his words, he was unready or unwilling to take the heat. He was afraid of having his compassion employed in a way that appeared to undermine his halakhic resolve on the matter.

While this sort of cowardice is saddening, on an issue as fraught as this one rabbis understandably find themselves stuck between a rock and a hard place. Often they see the suffering of the gay person who turns to them and feel moved and responsible to help but feel equally duty bound in their role to protect the tradition as they know it. Rabbis cannot help but feel torn between these profound responsibilities.

These scenarios are becoming increasingly common. Rabbis in the field regularly have gay people and their families come to them with questions laced with confusion, anguish, and fear. Knowing what the law says is not the most important expertise demanded of rabbis in such situations. At least in the short run they need something other than a conclusive halakhic responsum. They need models of conversation, ways to begin rather than to finish the human encounter with the gay person.

For this reason I have chosen to write this chapter with two subjectivities in mind. While not in the form of a conversation, the positions offered will shift back and forth, as in ordinary conversation, alternating between the subjective voice of an Orthodox rabbi and that of an Orthodox gay man.

I have chosen a man because I feel more confident of a man's experience and because it is somewhat more common for men to seek Orthodox rabbinic counsel on this issue than for women to do so. In addition the halakhic issues regarding male homosexuality provide the most demanding sort of rabbinic negotiation because of the greater weight of the biblical prohibition. As noted in the introduction, far fewer Orthodox lesbians than gay men are "out." It is also crucial to note that rabbis only rarely acknowledge lesbians in their responses to homosexuality. Since male homosexuality is far more halakhically and socially challenging, this focus offers a more convincing platform for rejection. Still, the fact that women are virtually ignored or, worse, clumsily and erroneously appended to halakhic discussions about men would suggest that rabbis are avoiding the topic for other reasons. It may be that attention to lesbians demonstrates the difficulty of shaping any general Jewish response to homosexuality because it shows how different the Jewish discourse on the issue is from the contemporary categories. It may be that rabbis are afraid to reveal the leniencies in regard to lesbian relations for fear their revelations would be heard as a support for homosexuality generally. It may also be that lesbians are even more threatening than gay men in some way that translates into rabbinic blindness to their existence. And lastly it may be that Orthodox rabbis, as men, are familiar with male sexuality and so may feel more comfortable discussing it, whereas lesbian sexuality is doubly foreign.

I have chosen to structure this chapter in a dialogic fashion, similar to what the Talmud calls *shakleh v'taryeh,* which means literally "take and give," similar to the English locution "give and take." *Shakleh v'taryeh* admits that truth seeking is never a monologue. It is what happens when people who are different attempt to understand anything deeply. It is not like a debate that sets its hope on winning. Rather than winning or even reaching agreement, the explicit goal of *shakleh v'taryeh* is the expansion of knowledge by multiplying possibilities.

The danger of this method is that those on each side will feel slighted, unable to speak as freely as they otherwise might. Conversation is much less ideologically coherent than are speeches or legal briefs. Each side is apt to feel that the range of what can be said has been narrowed by the demands of responsiveness. This is how conversation works. People who talk to themselves can say anything they want. They do not need to aim their thoughts to the subjectivity of another or to address themselves to what another has said. They do not have to work hard to be understood. Real conversation is empathy in action.

As a caveat, I must admit that this inquiry will surely be uncomfortable for gay people, particularly those who have fought hard to achieve a sense of self-worth. Rabbis must begin to imagine what it is like for us to enter with them into a halakhic inquiry that so contradicts our experience and so demeans our hearts. Those gay people who are willing to accompany rabbis in their halakhic exploration do so in an act of amazing empathy. They understand that rabbis are profoundly responsible to fairly represent and defend the sacred tradition. They also understand that their very presence alongside their rabbis and the emotional risks that such accompaniment entails are what ensures the fullest rabbinic empathy to our predicament. Moreover, accompaniment does not mean agreement. When each side understands better the subjective frame of the other, the demand for theoretical agreement can be put aside in favor of a working relationship. The environment of such a relationship makes possible new creative responses to the complex intersection of sexuality, community, and faith.

In this chapter I try to represent both perspectives and mark the concerns of both rabbis and gay people. I take on this task while recognizing that my being both a rabbi and a gay man is a resource and a liability. The chapter moves between the subjectivities already in me as both a gay man and an Orthodox rabbi. For this reason it should be made clear that this chapter is not intended to limit the possibilities of real conversations but just the opposite. It is offered as a bridge toward the many possible dialogues between gay people and their rabbis based on mutual respect, empathy, and understanding.

Especially for issues as complex and as emotionally charged as this one, there is a great need for models of listening. The colleague I mentioned who did not want to be quoted said that when homosexuals came to him for counsel, he would tell them that he used to know what to say, how to represent the tradition. He now felt humbled by the life journeys of the people who had come out to him. He no longer really knew what to say. He began to admit to gay people who came to him that he did not know enough about the phenomenon or the experience to answer the question responsibly. In short, he admitted uncertainty on an issue that has appeared clear to his forbears for thousands of years. Just as conversation cannot proceed without empathy, real listening requires a measure of humility.

Humility demands that we admit the limits of our certainty. We are in the midst of profound social changes, the futures of which are unknown. The very meanings of gender, sexuality, marriage, family, and love are in flux. Perhaps we could imagine a number of policy directions, both communal and halakhic, formulated to respond to these social changes, but even on this score we could not predict the consequences or implications of such policies. Given the fluidity and uncertainty of the moment, any hard and fast conclusions seem premature. In such a situation it makes good sense to move from convention to conversation. Instead of rehearsing the citations from law books, we ought to return to the kinds of discussion common among the sages of the Talmud.

The sages of antiquity promulgated a method of weighing opinions, sharing interpretations, and hearing testimonies. The Talmud leaves most of its raucous debates unsolved and many explicitly so with *teku!* literally meaning "the question stands!"[2] In the same spirit today's rabbis will need to share ideas with one another without insisting on an immediate and conclusive answer *(psak halakhah)* to the questions posed by gay people in their communities.

I have kept our rabbi in the following discussion anonymous, but I have named our young gay man Joshua. While I was still in the closet and struggling mightily with my own homosexuality, a young man came out to me and asked for my help. He had been to a class of mine two years before, and while passing through New York he decided to approach me. For some reason he felt that he could confide in me. In retrospect I don't think I was much help to him. He was actually ahead of me. He couldn't imagine what world he might be able to live in. I was still unable to imagine a self to be. His name was Joshua; he did not give me his last name. I do not know what became of him.

Halakhic Frameworks

Were Joshua to turn to a liberal rabbi for counsel, the ground rules would be very different. A liberal rabbi would be comfortable saying either that the law is changeable or that as modern Jews we need not follow ancient laws. Our Orthodox rabbi would claim that the law is both binding and unchangeable. He legitimately affirms at the outset of the conversation that his commitment to the Halakhah is nonnegotiable. How exactly this commitment will play out is best left unclear at this point. What is clear is that he cannot be expected to debate his fundamental commitments. This position is no different from a gay person's refusal to accept even the smallest bit of guilt or shame as a condition of entering into conversation. A gay person's self-esteem is no more negotiable than the halakhic commitment of a rabbi. Both parties simply agree to be as honest and as responsive to each other as possible.

Our rabbi does not want to deceive Joshua. He affirms his position that sexual relations between men are prohibited. If Joshua acts on these sexual impulses, he will be sinning.

If he is condemned to being a sinner, Joshua wants more information. There are sins and then there are sins. What is the import of this sin? The rabbi hesitates. Joshua assures him that he is prepared to be a study partner of the rabbi, no matter where it takes him. He urges the rabbi on. Formally speaking, there are two kinds of sinners, the willful and the indulgent. This distinction, difficult as it may be for Joshua, will help to begin the conversation.

1. The Willful Transgressor. The willful transgressor *(mumar le-hakhis)* violates the law, not for the sake of pleasure per se, but as a rebellion.
2. The Indulgent Transgressor. The indulgent transgressor *(mumar le-te'avon)* does not resist temptation and so violates the law for the sake of pleasure.

Le-hakhis: Willful Transgression

As we have seen earlier, Rabbi Moshe Feinstein puts sexually active homosexuals into the first category of wanton and rebellious transgressors. While this is a minority opinion among halakhic authorities today, Rav Moshe's responsa are widely read and universally respected among Orthodox Jews.[3] The tone of shock and horror in his responsa well represents the emotional response of many Hasidic and ultra-Orthodox Jews. For some Jews the very preservation of shock and disgust are what *toevah,* abomination, is about. When homosexuals are treated as wanton violators, they are actively shunned in their communities. Religious leaders portray them as a scourge and blight. They are seen as proponents of a contemporary moral relativism that has adopted every perversion as an expression of freedom. The sense given to gay Orthodox young people when they come out to rabbis with this view of homosexuality is that they are under a corrupt spell, body snatched, as it were, by a promiscuous hedonistic society out to destroy decency and morality itself. The remedy is to recognize the extent to which one has succumbed to the depraved acceptance of perversion and turn to God for help in conquering the evil in one's heart.

Therapeutic options for the wanton sinner are not totally excluded, but in practice they are more like deprogramming than therapy. In spring of 2000, *Tradition,* the journal of the largest Orthodox rabbinic council, the Rabbinic Council of America, published an article titled "Homosexuality: A Political Mask for Promiscuity: A Psychiatrist Reviews the Data."[4] The title says it all. According to the author homosexuality is an excuse for promiscuity born of choice and habit, not "orientation." Given that rebellious violators by definition have succumbed to a bad ideology of rampant sexual depravity and relativism, the therapeutic methodology could be little more than counterindoctrination.

Le-te'avon: Indulgent Transgression

The most common Orthodox viewpoint is that homosexuals are indulgent transgressors, who, with effort could resist temptation, one way or another. Transgressors of this sort violate the law for reasons of appetite. A *mumar le-te'avon* knows that pork and shellfish are not kosher but eats them anyway for the pleasure of it. The homosexual as a *mumar le-te'avon* is hardly applauded, but sins of desire are ordinary. Even if the particular transgression is somewhat uncommon, its source is universally shared.

In the previous category of willful transgression, Rabbi Feinstein presents homosexual desire not as desire at all but as a destructive intent to corrupt the creation. The religious authorities who understand the homosexual as a *mumar le-te'avon* reject this demonic characterization of the homosexual. Also most do not interpret the reference to "abomination" as a demand that we confront homosexual desire with a sense of innate disgust. Homosexual desire, for them, is as normal as any other prohibited desire.[5]

While one might be able to tolerate missing the mark and being less than a perfect Jew, to think of oneself as being taken over by a depraved and malicious spirit of the age, as a battlefield between demonic and divine forces, is quite another matter. An indulgent transgressor's acting out sexually is regrettable, but it need not unravel the person's attachment to God nor his or her membership in the community. Homosexual expression under the framework of indulgent transgression does not generate horror. A sexual sin, especially one that shares billing with adultery and incest, is nothing to take lightly. But if it falls into the category of indulgent sin, it belongs to a very familiar universe of human failings.[6]

In fact, where homosexuals are understood as indulgent transgressors, religious leaders in the community are apt to treat sexually active gay Jews no differently from those Jews who are not Sabbath observant. While the lack of self-restraint is not condoned, such people are also not portrayed as succumbing to the forces of pernicious evil. Rabbis who deal with homosexuality as ordinary sin are in effect saying that if nobody is perfect, why pick on this sin instead of that one? Rabbi Meir Fund in *Trembling before G-d* put it this way: "If the rule was that sinners weren't allowed in shul, I doubt there would ever be a minyan." In some environments totally nonobservant Jews are welcomed into the Orthodox community without hesitation. This contemporary tolerance of the explicit nonobservance of unaffiliated or liberal Jews has been largely supported by Orthodox outreach movements.

Nonobservant Jews are considered indulgent transgressors with special consideration. Unlike a Jew who violates for pleasure in spite of his or her experience and knowledge of Jewish life, nonobservant Jews are considered "captured as children among the gentiles."[7] The category was once used for Jewish children who had actually been kidnapped and raised among gentiles. Such "captured Jews" were not to be derided for their failure to observe the commandments since they had been deprived of the primary experiences, relationships, and learning necessary for commitment. They were to be loved and welcomed into the Jewish community and slowly integrated into its practices. Some have considered gay Jews the epitome of those "captured among the gentiles." Gay Jews, they claim, have been captured by the gay subculture or at very least the libertine sexual ethics of the open society. They, too, should not be attacked or derided but welcomed slowly back into the Jewish community, where they will be able to reclaim their connection to the Torah.

Rabbis who conceive of homosexuality as indulgent transgression strongly discourage gay people from coming out in public ways. Flaunting transgression transforms a sin of lust into a brazen rejection of the Torah. Coming out may threaten to turn a *mumar le-te'avon* into a *mumar le-hakhis*. Indeed, gay people who have come out publicly in the community have been told that their publicity is worse than their sin. By coming out they undermine the authority of the law and in doing so cause irreparable harm to public order. Gay persons quietly struggling in private to overcome their inner nature, whether they succeed or fail, are seen as heroic. The rabbis who conceive of homosexuality in this way encourage the homosexual to attempt to minimize violations, if possible. Commonly men are encouraged, at the very least, to avoid the biblical violation of anal intercourse. Both gay men and lesbians are strongly discouraged from publicly formalizing and celebrating their relationships in commitment ceremonies of any kind.

Central to this approach is the belief that homosexual desire is conquerable. We are promised the power to overcome the evil inclination, if we so choose. It may be difficult, but with commitment to change, prayer, and study a homosexual, like any sinner, should be able to change his or her behavior.[8] This is the very essence of repentance. While this advice is still commonly given to both gay men and lesbians, increasingly, as rabbis enter into conversation with gay Jews, they begin to doubt whether prayer and will power are enough.

Our rabbi has been persuaded that Joshua is no rebellious transgressor. He is an ordinary Jew with a sinful desire, and our rabbi would like to help him. In order to do so he begins to educate himself. He has heard that there is help available for men like Joshua.

From Indulgent Sin to Curable Illness

Conservative religious leaders have long attempted to claim that homosexuality is changeable. They have been helped by the emergence of what has come to be called "reparative therapy" or "conversion therapy." Our rabbi would love to offer Joshua a way out of his predicament. If homosexuality is indeed pathology, then recommending that he seek therapy would be the most caring advice a rabbi might give. Moreover, our rabbi's theological, moral, and halakhic conundrums are solved if homosexuality is a curable illness. Conversely, if sexual orientation is either innate or fixed at a very early age and unchangeable for the overwhelming majority of gay people, then the Torah itself becomes highly problematic. How does God create a person as homosexual and then doom him to alienation and loneliness? How can the rabbis ask the impossible of a person? Because so much hinges on the nature of homosexuality and its susceptibility to conscious attempts to change it, our rabbi decides to delve a bit deeper into reparative therapy.

Reparative Therapy

In the early 1980s a British theologian and self-proclaimed psychologist, Elizabeth Moberly, wrote a book titled *Homosexuality: A New Christian Ethic*. Her "research" involved no subjects. She had treated no one and had conducted no formal research. She simply did an extensive literature review of the works of Irving Bieber, Lawrence Hatterer, and Sigmund Freud and came up with a reinterpretation of their findings. Her theory was that homosexual men were suffering from what she termed "defensive detachment" and "same sex ambivalence." The theory presumes that the homosexual as a young boy, for any of a variety of reasons, did not bond with his father in a meaningful way. Moberly saw homosexuality as a "reparative drive" to meet the heretofore unmet needs of the child for love and bonding and thus "identification" with males. Moberly was invited to speak at "ex-gay" conferences and soon became the darling of the "ex-gay" movement.

Evangelical Christian groups, conservative Catholic groups, and an Orthodox Jewish group (JONAH) sell the near inevitability of "change"—given appropriate effort and commitment—to young men and women desperate to be anything but homosexual. Some groups have modeled their programs on the twelve-step process of Alcoholics Anonymous, defining homosexuality as a powerful addiction. While each group uses different theological and therapeutic resources, the message is largely the same. If the homosexual is motivated by a great desire for change, he or she, according to these rabbis, priests, ministers, and therapists, will be able to change. The same-sex desires will subside, and the person will uncover or create in himself or herself sufficient desire for the opposite sex to marry, have a family, and conduct a fulfilling life.

Eventually secular professionals as well joined the ranks. In 1992 Joseph Nicolosi and Charles Socarides started NARTH, which has claimed to have a success rate with two-thirds of its clients. In the 1990s the explosion of "ex-gay" organizations offering various forms of "reparative therapy" led to a flurry of official public statements from organizations of healthcare professionals. The American Academy of Pediatrics, the American Psychiatric Association, the American Psychological Association, and the National Association of Social Workers all publicly announced their opposition to reparative therapy, raising serious doubts about its efficacy and expressing concern that it might indeed be harmful.[9]

Dr. Robert Spitzer, a therapist who was instrumental in removing homosexuality from the American Psychiatric Association's list of mental illnesses in 1973, conducted a study in 2001 that suggested some people do change in therapy. The theraputic community was largely unconvinced by the study and took Spitzer to task for weak if not faulty methodology. While he was touted by NARTH and "ex-gay" activists as having proven their claims, Spitzer later said in interviews that only "a small minority" might be successful in reparative therapy, when success is defined as "functioning heterosexually at least once a month without fantasizing about a same-sex partner more than 20% of the time."[10] "There's no doubt that many homosexuals have been unsuccessful and, attempting to change, become depressed and their life becomes worse."[11] Many people have been profoundly harmed by these therapies, and the therapists offering them do not usually inform their patients of the dangers.[12] There are many anecdotal accounts of patients who did not convert and who, believing themselves to be at fault for the failure, were left feeling anxious, depressed, worthless, hopeless, and even suicidal.[13]

Our rabbi is now convinced that sexual orientation is not ordinarily changeable either by repentance or by therapy. Backed into this corner, having no "cure" to offer, no mystical remedy or prayer that heals, and no therapy that works, he reads that many of his colleagues advise celibacy.

Rabbi Aharon Feldman suggests that a Jewish homosexual must make a commitment to embark on a course through which he will ultimately rid himself of homosexual activity. It is necessary not that he change his sexual orientation (if this is at all possible) but that he cease all sexual activity. A Jewish homosexual can live as a celibate "if he decides that the Jewish people are his 'wife and children.'"[14]

A story is told of the Brisker Rav, a renowned talmudist and halakhic authority of Brisk, Lithuania, in the late nineteenth century. A gay man came to him and explained that he could not find in himself the desire to marry a woman. The rabbi said that since he did not have the necessary drives, he was free from the duty to marry and have children. Consequently, he must make the Jewish people his family and so "be fruitful and multiply" in other ways. The man lived as a celibate bachelor in a very religious quarter in Israel and, since he was not tied down to family, traveled all over the world as a fundraiser. His efforts helped to build a school (yeshiva) and an orphanage in Israel.[15]

Our rabbi asks Joshua if celibacy might be an option. Joshua thinks for a moment and then asks the rabbi what he would have done had Judaism required lifelong celibacy of him. Our rabbi admits that he does not know. Joshua responds that he could not commit to lifelong celibacy. A life without the possibility of love, intimacy, and companionship is just not conceivable to him.

Up to this point Joshua has been on the defensive for the most part, struggling to understand the rabbi's limits. He feels he has earned the right to press the rabbi further. He wants to know, given the significant changes in our understanding of human sexuality, why the law can't change.

Halakhah and Change

Our Orthodox rabbi has claimed that the law is both binding and unchangeable. This tenet has been the central organizing principle of contemporary Orthodoxy. However, Joshua is knowledgeable enough to know that, despite protestations to the contrary, the law has surely changed. The standard Orthodox insistence on the immutability of the Halakhah is largely a defensive posture vis-à-vis liberal Judaism, but it is not a historical fact.

Various examples of halakhic reformulation in response to shifting circumstances can be found throughout the history of the Halakhah.[16] Exactly how much latitude for creativity and responsiveness to new circumstances should be given to contemporary authorities is hotly debated among scholars. Since the issue of homosexuality is bound up with this question of the changeability of the law—if and how law changes and under what circumstances—it will be helpful to explore an example of such a change in the history of the Halakhah.

Usury

One of the most impressive examples of profound halakhic change occurred in antiquity, transforming the application of the biblical laws of lending and borrowing money. Exodus, Leviticus, and Deuteronomy contain similar versions of a rule that prohibits the exacting or paying of interest on loans.[17] According to Maimonides a usurious creditor violates six biblical prohibitions.

By the last half of the third century C.E. Babylonia had become the center of Jewish cultural and religious life, surpassing the Jewish community still living in the Land of Israel. During this period changing economic conditions in Babylonia made the laws against taking interest incompatible with the growing economic needs of the community. The process of change occurred in stages. The demands of the situation pressed the sages to consider different solutions. The initial solutions were a mix of very specific exceptions and leniencies. Over time the various exceptions and leniencies joined, gathered strength, and gave birth to a more general category of leniency. Finally, as the new halakhic category was employed, the accepted social valence became a new social norm justifying even greater legal flexibility. The end result was the creation of a legal fiction, the *shtar iska*.[18] Formally speaking, the *shtar iska* (translated simply as "business contract") turned a business loan into a limited partnership. The lender would supply the capital, and the borrower the services. The borrower would manage the business, guarantee the lender's investment against loss, and promise the lender a fixed amount of minimum profit. The lender would receive a fixed sum (the minimum profit stipulated) equal to the interest on payment of the loan.[19]

In the initial phase of the legislation the contractual demands on lenders and borrowers were detailed. Today the legalization of interest has become so well established that transactions in compliance with Jewish law are carried out freely by simply adding to the note or contract the words *al pi hetter iska* (according to the business permission). What was once a morally weighted prohibition became a formal matter. In this fashion a biblical command appearing three times in the Torah was effectively eliminated from business relations and relegated only to the sphere of friendly and charitable loans.

The rules of lending were once strict and categorical. Even when goods were sold, the seller could not offer a discount on early payment because the benefit of the early availability of the money was considered a loan and the discount its interest. Any benefit gained for money use was considered a form of interest and prohibited. The sages might have continued to hold the laws of interest taking as absolute and considered any legal fiction circumventing them as wicked deception. There were traditions that would have supported such a commitment to the fullest application of the prohibition of usury. "All who lend on interest," say the rabbis, "deny the existence of God," are like shedders of blood, and have no share in the world to come.[20]

But had the sages refused to reframe the law, business between Jews would have come to a virtual standstill. We might have poured all our effort into a religious fight against the use of money lending for profit, or we might have been scattered sparsely in communities where our business transactions with Jews would have been minimal. Perhaps we would have been able to establish a usury-free economic zone, an Amish-like enclave in regard to the use of capital.

One can only surmise that the result of such measures would have been disastrous for rabbinic leadership as well as for faithful Jewish communities.

Under the convincing force of the new economic reality, the rabbis came to understand the law differently. It became clear to them that the original law was not applicable to the new economic forms that were emerging. Loans had been about providing a means for the destitute to restore their footing. They were originally a form of charity. However, as the economy developed, new kinds of loans became necessary if the well-being of the community was to be assured. Distinctions between different kinds of loans slowly emerged that helped to justify a reapplication of the law. Eventually the sages invented a way to circumvent the law on the books in regard to business loans while leaving it otherwise intact. In effect the commandment in the Torah was split into two applications. The rule's full force and moral imperative was narrowed to friendly and charitable loans; in regard to business loans the rule became a formal ritual with no moral force whatsoever. This rather bold reframing of a biblical prohibition was inaugurated by new social meanings of business, money, and lending.

The question is obvious. Joshua wants to know why the rabbis could accomplish such a dramatic legal reframing of the law of interest taking, while in regard to homosexual relations all attempts at legal reframing are sharply rejected. Why can't the Orthodox halakhic establishment find some manner of rereading or reframing or reapplying the law in Leviticus in order to permit homosexual life partnerships?

This challenge to the Orthodox establishment is hardly new. The battlegrounds between the denominations, and especially between the Conservative and the Orthodox movement, have been largely shaped by the question of halakhic authority and change. Exactly what is allowed to impinge on the tradition has been debated since the middle of the eighteenth century and is still the central question debated in and between the various denominations.

Our Orthodox rabbi will have a number of ready responses. While admitting that the Halakhah has indeed changed, he tends to mistrust the modern pressures urging change. When in 1960 the

Conservative movement's law committee unanimously permitted driving cars to synagogue on the Sabbath, the social and economic justifications were compelling.[21] After World War II a burgeoning suburban empire offered comfortable and affordable housing, and Jews were among the first to take advantage of the opportunities. Automotive transportation made possible the development of new communities spread out over many miles. People simply lived too far from one another to build synagogues accessible by foot. The decision to allow driving to the synagogue on the Sabbath was considered a "compromise" with the law for the sake of communal cohesion and synagogue attendance.

Orthodoxy protested loudly at the time and has insisted that the Sabbath prohibition of kindling fire, a central element of the combustion engine, is inviolable. This Sabbath rigor has led, in unexpected ways, to some of Orthodoxy's most impressive achievements of the last fifty years. Orthodox communities are by definition walkable. The social proximity necessary for Sabbath observance produces more cohesive, face-to-face communities where families spontaneously join together for Shabbat and holiday meals. On long Shabbat afternoons passersby are invited in for tea and cake and a debate on the quality of the rabbi's sermon. On Purim revelers walk from house to house singing, drinking, dancing, collecting charitable contributions, and delivering treats. In such communities nuclear families are less isolated, and interfamilial relationships thrive in more natural ways. Liberal Judaism's disregard of the Sabbath travel laws has, in effect, kept Judaism sequestered inside the synagogue. The Sabbath walk constructs a Judaism that lives much more expansively in a whole neighborhood.

Orthodox authorities extended the prohibition to kindle fire to the operation of electrical appliances. This means no TV, no computer, and no telephone, and since commerce is also not allowed, no mall. Once a week a set of uncommon prohibitions and duties make room for a day of technology-free, shopping-free leisure focused instead on good food and wine, walks in the park, reading, napping, praying, schmoozing, singing, studying, and love making. In a workaholic consumer society the Jewish Sabbath is an unmitigated cultural success. This and other cultural successes of the community have engendered a certain triumphalism. Orthodox Jews feel that adherence to the law has and will vindicate itself in time and that the call to change the law to fit the times is a siren's song.

So, if tampering with the Halakhah is tricky business and should rarely be considered, when it is considered, the effort requires the weightiest of authorities and the most brilliant of minds. While the great lawmakers of the past transformed the law of usury, contemporary Orthodox rabbis feel inadequate to the task. It is assumed that the *gedolim,* the great ones of the past, had a much greater spiritual clarity than do we. "If the first ones [earlier authorities] were like angels, then we are human beings. If the first ones were like human beings, then we are like donkeys, and not even like the donkeys of Hanina ben Dosa and Rabbi Pinhas ben Yair (unusually smart donkeys), but like ordinary donkeys."[22] The humor of this passage conveys some tongue-in-cheek hyperbole, but its point is taken quite seriously by contemporary Orthodox authorities. The *gedolim* had the power to enact halakhic innovation, but we do not.

This humility in face of the past is central to all tradition-centered worlds, but in fact, no social world can exist without it. Memory of the past is the glue of the self, and socially it secures the continuity of peoples. Honoring the past is what gives authority to legal precedent and what constitutes the canons of education. But of course, this is not the whole story.

Our rabbi admits that there is a tension between honoring the past and living in the present. The Jewish tradition articulates not only a sense of diminishing spiritual greatness over time but also a counterforce of ongoing debate and legal development. Initially when authorities differed, a teacher took precedent over his student. However, eventually the rule turned around, and decisive trust was placed in the most contemporary rabbinic opinion. Since the fourth century, "the law follows the last authority."[23] It was understood that current authorities will know best how the law should be understood and applied in their moment.

Joshua insists that deference to the past should not trump a rabbi's responsibility to the present. Moreover, he knows the difference between changing the law for convenience sake and responding to human suffering. He insists that the rabbi explain to him why, given the torment that he and other homosexuals have experienced, can't the law be reformulated as it was in regard to usury. While remaining respectful Joshua is asking our rabbi whether it is simply a matter of rabbinic courage or whether the rabbi is not sharing all his concerns.

The laws of usury took hundreds of years to evolve. Since law is meant to ensure stability, it is not easily given to change. This static quality is the very nature of law. Susan B. Anthony began her fight for women's vote in America sixty years before Congress voted to enfranchise women.[24] She spent fifty-four years changing the hearts and minds of Americans. Our rabbi reminds his friend that the law is the last step in social transformation. If halakhic change is to happen, it will take time.

More recent and to the point is the landmark 2003 U.S. Supreme Court case *Lawrence v. Texas,* which held that a Texas state law banning sexual intercourse between men in the privacy of their home was unconstitutional. The six to three decision, swept aside sodomy laws in thirteen states. Justice Anthony Kennedy, writing for the majority, argued that "the state cannot demean their [homosexuals'] existence or control their destiny by making their private sexual conduct a crime." This ruling overturned *Bower v. Hardwick,* a 1986 Supreme Court decision that upheld an antisodomy law in the State of Georgia. The Bower Court expressly grounded its ruling on religious history and tradition, holding that "proscriptions against that conduct [male-male sodomy] have ancient roots." In a dramatic rejection of the 1986 decision, Kennedy argued that just as tradition and history were not sufficient reasons for upholding the law against miscegenation, they could not be sufficient in regard to homosexual conduct. During the seventeen years between these decisions, the social mores in regard to homosexuality had shifted. The Lawrence decision simply responded to the increased social acceptance of homosexuals in the society and applied to them standards of privacy and civil rights that had been ignored earlier.[25]

While there are exceptions, legal systems do not usually lead the way toward social revolution.[26] To expect them to do so is to misunderstand them. As society-building enterprises they maintain the social order along with their own internal coherence and plausibility by resisting change and reorganizing themselves in response to new social realities only when the social transformation is well underway. The Halakhah similarly is reformulated only when the shift in social realities is clearly established, widely acknowledged, and deemed largely positive. Only then can previously unrecognized competing values challenge the existing norm. When such a reformulation takes place, the change is experienced as the proper commitment to the Torah's original purposes.

Joshua believes this is a compelling argument. He understands that social change cannot be imposed on people. While the acceptance of gays and lesbians has grown remarkably over the last decade, the kind of shift in social consciousness that would legitimate a universal acceptance of homosexual partnership is still a long way off for many Americans and surely for Orthodox Jews. There is not nearly enough grassroots understanding of homosexuality, not enough evidence of its pervasiveness in Orthodox communities, and not enough appreciation of the distress caused by the present halakhic ruling for Orthodox halakhists to attempt a bold reframing of the law any time soon.[27]

Even in the face of overwhelming social change our rabbi would have misgivings. By instinct and training he is wary. As human beings we are apt to deceive ourselves into a permissiveness that will lead to bad ends. This is especially true when sexual desire and gratification are at stake. Even though homosexual identity and desire are (presumably) alien to the contemporary rabbis responding to the questions of gay Orthodox Jews, they nonetheless seem to feel that their personal knowledge of the power of sexual desire is sufficient to justify their extreme caution when people clamor for an expansion of their sexual freedoms.

For these reasons our rabbi, understanding that he disappoints our gay man, shares with him his belief that the law cannot change. While the rabbi remains open to continuing the conversation, the question is whether our gay man has anything more to say to him. Is the conversation over? Given that in Orthodox communities the Halakhah will not change in the foreseeable future, what are Joshua's options?

Ortho-Gay Options

In the Ortho-gay community the response varies. Many believe there is no choice but to submit to the Halakhah as it stands. Assuming this to be the only choice, some gay people force themselves or are forced by families into marriages. Others, striving to do what they believe God wants of them, lead celibate lives. Those who are not prepared to embrace celibacy or to deceive a prospective spouse are left with only two options—to live a sinful and closeted life or to abandon the Halakhah altogether.

A Hasidic couple of more than twenty years lives in New York City, formally in two separate apartments. They have an intensely religious household, full of learning and joy, and are fiercely closeted. They do not legitimate their sexual life and disagree with others' attempts to do so. Many other people faced with the choice of rejecting themselves or the tradition have opted to reject the tradition. Sometimes the tradition is jettisoned in anger and sometimes in despair and resignation. In Sandi DuBowski's film, one of his subjects, a man named Israel, rejects Orthodoxy as the source of his pain and suffering. Having been shunned by his family and subjected to emotional abuse growing up in the ultra-Orthodox community of Williamsburg, Israel walks away for more than ideological reasons alone. While he loves the values he gained from his upbringing, he is a passionate critic of what he sees as ingrained cruelty.

Shmuel, a young Satmar Hasid I met during my coming-out process, left traditional Hasidic Jewish life with surprisingly little rancor. When he could no longer manage the double life he was leading, he divorced his wife, cut off his beard, put in an earring, and moved in with his boyfriend. He had to learn a new trade, having been black-balled from the diamond district, and would dress up a bit to visit his children in Williamsburg. In his new life he no longer keeps kosher or observes the Sabbath. When I asked him if he believed that God had given the Torah at Sinai and that all Jews were duty bound to fulfill it, he responded without hesitation, "Yes! I simply cannot do it." Shmuel's inability to keep it all unraveled the whole thing for him.

For Israel the tradition was so wrong that he wanted no part of it; for Shmuel the tradition so was right that his inability to keep one commandment put the whole system out of reach. People like Israel and Shmuel opt out of Orthodox Jewish life because they believe what was repeated to them over and over: The law is clear, and it will never change.

If the first option is to lie and the second to leave, the third option is to stay and tell the truth. To stay and tell the truth means to remain committed to the fulfillment and the study of the Torah while accepting and even celebrating one's gayness. It means being generally honest about who one is, patient with those who do not yet understand, and ready to get on with the business of finding a life partner and building a Jewish home. This is surely a religious path, and despite its apparent disobedience to certain religious norms, it is in my view the most faithful.

Surprising as it may seem, some traditional resources appear to support a limited form of sacred "disobedience" on both the personal and the communal level. Two mystical thinkers spoke of a divergent will of God, a frequency beyond the law that sometimes guides the destiny of individuals and communities.

Rabbi Mordechai of Izbica

Among students of Hasidut (Hasidic thought) the Izhbitzer is well known. He was among the most audacious and imaginative of the Hasidic rebbes. Rabbi Mordechai of Izbica writes in his Torah commentary about a story in the Book of Numbers, the story of Pinhas the Zealot.

According to this story, while the people of Israel were traveling in the desert toward the Holy Land, they camped for a while near Moab. The men went after Moabite women, who seduced them to attend sacrifices for their god. "Thus Israel attached itself to Baalpeor, and the Lord was incensed with Israel" (Num. 25:3). Just as things were getting out of hand, "one of the Israelite chiefs took a Midianite woman into his tent in the sight of Moses and of the whole Israelite community and began engaging in sexual intercourse" (Num. 25:6).

> When Pinhas, son of Eleazar, son of Aaron the priest, saw this, he left the assembly and, taking a spear in his hand, he followed the Israelite into the chamber and stabbed both of them, the Israelite and

the woman, through the belly, and the plague against the Israelites was checked. . . . The name of the Israelite who was killed, the one who was killed with the Midianite woman, was Zimri son of Salu, chieftain of a Simeonite ancestral house. The name of the Midianite woman who was killed was Cozbi daughter of Zur. (Num. 25:7–8a; 14–15)

This text applauds well-timed violent zealotry. Pinhas embodies divine wrath at a key moment in the story and stops a plague in the camp. In rabbinic tradition the story was read ambivalently. One finds praise of Pinhas alongside a deep suspicion of vigilante justice.[28]

Rabbi Mordechai of Izbica read the story in a way that marks not Pinhas but Zimri as the unlikely hero of the episode. His defense of Zimri begins with a depiction of how sexual passion accords with God's will. These are his words:

Behold there are ten levels of sexual passion. The first is one who adorns himself and goes out intentionally after a sinful liaison, that is, he himself pulls toward him the evil inclination *(yetzer hara)*. After that there are another nine levels, and at each level another aspect of freedom is taken from him so that increasingly he cannot escape from sin until the tenth level. At that [level] if he distances himself from the evil inclination *(yetzer hara)* and guards himself from sin with all his power until he has no capacity to protect himself further and still his inclination overpowers him and he does the act, then it is surely the will of God. . . . For Zimri in truth guarded himself from all wicked desires, and when he understood that she was his soul mate, it was not in his power to release himself from doing this deed. . . . The essence of the matter is that Pinhas thought Zimri was an ordinary adulterer . . . and the depth of the matter eluded him regarding Zimri that she (Cozbi) was his soul mate from the six days of creation.[29]

Of course, the key to this interpretation is that Zimri's subjective experience, fought and denied, guarded against and so purified ten times, is in the end God's will. This is likely the most antinomian religious text anywhere in the Hasidic tradition. Rabbi Mordechai was not widely supported in his understanding of the conflict between powerful personal emotional experience and the law. Still, the text is there, and it invites us to explore how the fullness of subjective experience might, in surprising ways, reveal the will of God.

For Rabbi Mordechai, when it comes to sexual prohibitions, strong desire, desire that cannot be overcome with great effort, introduces us to another frequency of divine will. What Zimri did with Cozbi violated no prior contracts or marital vows, took no advantage of familial closeness, and forced no unwanted intimacies. It was the act of uniting with a passionately desired but formally unacceptable soul mate who was beyond Zimri's ability to refuse and so beyond the law.

One is required to wage a great spiritual battle in order to arrive at such a conclusion. One must fight to resist temptation through ten levels of struggle before accepting a prohibited sexual urge as divine will. Zimri did the hard work of *birurim* (clarification), but Pinhas could not fathom these workings of the soul. He was a typical "true believer," spiritually unsophisticated and dangerously sure of himself. Like other zealous defenders of public morality, Pinhas poured his wrath onto a man whom he did not understand. Zimri's proof of innocence, the story of his ten-fold resistance and final surrender to God, was never shared.

While God may have willed this match made in heaven between star-crossed lovers from different sides of the track, no protection is offered them in the story from brutish zealots like Pinhas, who rise up in righteous indignation ready to punish those who defy the rule. Even worse, God's later promise to Pinhas of a covenant of peace (Num. 25:12) is hard to reconcile with Rabbi Mordechai's interpretation of the story. God seems forced to live with simplistic religious leaders who think of every difference as a danger. For Rabbi Mordechai, God emerges as torn between the great structures of nation building defended by Pinhas and the lives of those individuals whose unconventional love is also God's will.

Rabbi Kook

Rabbi Abraham Isaac Kook was the chief rabbi of Israel before it was declared a state. A man of unusual poetic talent, Rabbi Kook honed his deep knowledge of traditional and mystical Jewish thought on both the nationalist aspirations of the Jewish people and on the family of man. The very nearness of the unification of all humankind, the evolution of the human spirit toward the good and the holy, was an invitation to Jews everywhere to return to their ancestral land and restore their ancient spirit. His writings are still popular today among religious Israelis.

His sensitivity to the demands of a new age made him unusually tolerant of those who had returned to Zion without religious faith. He was able to give secular thought an honored place in his religious world-view, something that angered his colleagues. The following text is an excerpt from *Arpelei Tohar*, which translates roughly as "mists of purity."

> There are times when there is a need to violate the words of the Torah since there is no one in the generation who can show the way [to do it permissibly] and so it comes as a breach. It would be much better if such [violations of the law] came about as unintentional transgressions, as the saying goes, "Better they be accidental sinners rather than intentional sinners." However, only when a prophetic spirit rests on the people of Israel is it possible to fix such matters legally by a decree of the sages. Then the matter is addressed legitimately and openly as a straightforward mitzvah. But by the obstruction of the light of prophecy, the matter is fixed by a breaking [of the law], the external manifestation of which saddens the heart and yet gladdens the heart by its inner essence.[30]

These words were written by Rabbi Kook in the 1920s and have been censored out of his recently republished works. They mark the legal bind of an age. Sometimes the necessary halakhic innovations must come as violations, as determined revolts breaching the fabric. What Rabbi Kook suggests here is that religious leadership cannot always show the way. It can happen, even if rarely, that those who break the law are closer to the inward essence of things. In doing what must be done, they make us sad for the necessity and happy for the outcome.

Rabbi Kook may indeed be speaking from his own experience. He was among the first Orthodox rabbis to support the Zionist cause. The Orthodox establishment initially rejected Zionism. Because Zionism's original political message shaped a Jewish national identity decidedly unconnected to faith or religious observance, most all the Torah giants of Rabbi Kook's day strongly disapproved of the nascent movement, and many condemned it outright as rebellion against God. His own adoption of the Zionist cause before there was a full-fledged religious justification was itself a kind of "breaking."

The position Rabbi Kook takes is indeed a bold one. It marks the halakhic system as no longer self-contained. In effect he has admitted there are leaps of judgment that the Halakhah cannot make by its own internal mechanisms. It is a system that must at times depend on those who breach it in order to play out its fullest possibilities. Sometimes it takes the audacious rebellion of breachers to get the machinery moving, to challenge the system to do the work of building bridges toward new horizons.

There is no prejustification of such a breach by a moral or religious argument. Indeed, the language Rabbi Kook uses is one of explosiveness and not deliberation. Actions are taken because the leaders cannot see what must be done and others can. Whether the revolution is in the end a cause for joy always remains to be seen. Such are the insecurities of an age that, perhaps more than any in history, has been overwhelmed with revolutionary changes whose sad or joyous outcomes could not be told in advance and in too many instances still cannot.

This violating of the law for the sake of its own moral expansion is a kind of "civil disobedience" that the halakhic community must learn to tolerate. It is similar to what Gandhi called *satyagraha*. *Satyagraha* is not just a political tool but a form of prayer, an avenue of spiritual renewal. The point of *satyagraha*, or "truth force," was never to defeat the opponent, but to engage his heart and soul. For this reason the *satyagrahi* is a devotee of truth who gravitates toward, rather than away from, the centers of conflict and who accepts upon himself or herself all the consequences of action.[31]

Rabbi Mordechai of Izbica and Rabbi Abraham Isaac Kook in different ways offer halakhically committed gay and lesbian Jews a way to make sense of the decision to get on with their lives, to find a life partner, and to create a Jewish home.[32] Many of us have spent years going through clarification after clarification to discover that our desire is neither changeable nor debased. Are we not now ready to say the truth about our hearts and bodies so that future generations of gay youth will not need to suffer our degradations, will not have to fight for every shred of self-acceptance and integrity?

Orthodox rabbis should know that most of us will not wait for the halakhic ruling that permits us to be who we are, that authorizes our love and sanctifies our relationships. Moreover, they should know that many of us will not leave because no formal room has been made for us in Orthodoxy. We are ready to do what few have done till now—to tell the truth about ourselves and to stay in our communities. In doing so, we will become a truth force that cannot be ignored.

This is the course that Joshua decides to take. And since we will be out in our synagogues, coming to shul with our partners, and pushing our strollers into shul alongside the rest, rabbis will need to come up with a policy. Should the rabbi not want to publicly fight Joshua's desire to belong to his synagogue community, he will have to devise a way to navigate between the given halakhic prohibitions and a policy of inclusion. Given this desire, what frameworks might be available for our Orthodox rabbi that, while not revising the law altogether, might help him to formulate a policy? Our rabbi, pressed by Joshua's insistence on belonging, considers his options. He wonders if, after all, the example of usury might provide him with a limited solution to his dilemma.

The Narrowing Option

Our rabbi returns to Leviticus and reads: "And with a male you shall not lie the lyings of a woman: it is an abomination." He wonders if perhaps he could sustain the verse in its original meaning and still offer a way for Joshua to live. Much of the last half of this book has been dedicated to exploring the possible rationales for the prohibition in Leviticus of male homosexual intercourse. We explored these rationales because we believed that understanding the "intent" of the prohibition would help us to apply it to a new set of social circumstances.

In each of these rationales we have shifted the authority of the law from the statute to its conjectured purposes. While this approach is not unprecedented, it is important to take a step back and think about the prohibition for a moment on its own terms. Might it be that God has God's reasons that are not ours to know? Might the verse prohibit intercourse between men, period, no reason needed?

One might be justifiably suspicious of a process of rationalization when it comes to sexual desire. Why not say the law is simply "a decree of the King" to which we must submit as we do in other religious matters?[33] Surprisingly, in light of the history of usury, this rather traditional approach to the prohibition may offer us an interesting, if imperfect, "solution" to the problem.

A Decree of the King

We have already seen in the chapter on Leviticus that the biblical law prohibits anal intercourse between men specifically. Were we to be thoroughgoing in presuming no particular rational aim to the law, then the law could be sustained narrowly on this single sexual behavior rather than on a relationship of one kind or another. In this way the Halakhah, while remaining in force, would not prevent the acceptance of same-sex coupling. Men would be permitted to engage in committed sexual relationships so long as they did not engage in anal intercourse. Since lesbian sexual relations are not specifically prohibited by the Torah, they too would be acceptable. Promiscuity would be disdained, as it is for heterosexuals, but no one would be expected to live a life of celibacy. In fact, such a choice would be discouraged, given the Jewish commitment to human companionship: "It is not good for the human to be alone" (Gen. 2:18).

While this limitation of gay male relations might seem unreasonable to some, Orthodox tradition has always seen the bedroom as a holy place requiring both expression and restraint. Married heterosexual couples are obliged to enjoy and share the pleasures of sexual congress, but they are also required to abstain from physical intimacy of any kind during the woman's menstruation *(niddah)* and for a week following its termination. Given that physical separation is required of straight couples for what is commonly twelve days a month, it might not seem like undue hardship to demand that gay men refrain from a single sexual relation throughout their sexual lives. There would be a significant difference, however. For straight couples the prohibition of intimate relations during the *niddah* period gives way to a full sexual expression at other times. For gay male couples, sex in the form of oral sex, mutual masturbation, and so on would be permissible at all times, but intercourse would be prohibited at all times.

For lesbian couples, neither abstention would be necessary. Since the *niddah* prohibition is directly linked to penile-vaginal penetration, there would be no particular reason to prohibit sexual relations between lesbian partners. It might be claimed that the movement between separation and reunion is so central to the ethos of Jewish sexual ethics that the Halakhah should be expanded creatively in such a direction. Women could choose to commit to such a practice of periodic separation as a spiritual practice or, given the absence of any formal prohibition, enjoy a sexual freedom not available to heterosexual women.

Just as heterosexual couples in the Orthodox community are presumed to keep the laws of *niddah* (whether they do or don't), gay men would likewise be expected to refrain from intercourse, and we would presume no less. Rabbis do not check to see which couples do or do not observe the *niddah* laws. It is seen as the height of immodesty and impropriety to ask such a question. The level of observance of *niddah* in Orthodox synagogues varies from community to community. While there are no studies documenting Orthodox observance in detail, it is clear that the use of the ritual bath marking such a monthly observance is much lower than it would be were *niddah* universally observed. Observance of *niddah* is higher in ultra-Orthodox communities than it is in Modern Orthodox communities, but because the fulfillment of this commandment is left to couples, and because it touches on private matters, no one knows for sure. Even in circumstances where a couple's noncompliance with the law might be shared with the rabbi, no one is ever expelled from the shul for the violation of *niddah*. It is deemed a private matter between couples and between individuals and God. Orthodox rabbis commonly conduct marriages between men and women whom they know or at least strongly suspect will not keep the laws of *niddah*.

The significance of the comparison between the two prohibitions, that of *niddah* and of homosexual intercourse, comes home best in an anecdote. I was living in Riverdale, New York, in 1993 when the controversy erupted over the desire of Congregation Bet Simchat Torah, New York's GLBT synagogue, to march in the Salute to Israel Parade. Headlines of the *New York Post* read: "Oy Gay! Now

Homosexuals Want to March in Salute to Israel Parade!" On the Shabbat morning preceding the Sunday march I was running late, so I decided to attend the Riverdale Jewish Center's young couples minyan, which began later in the morning.

The assistant rabbi of the synagogue who ran the minyan said that he wished to speak about the issue, but first he wanted to get a sense of the community's feeling on the matter. People were asked to voice their opinions, and individuals said all sorts of things. Some were angry, others were understanding, and most were not in favor of the gay synagogue's presence at the march. At the end I decided to add my own perspective. I shared with the group that recently in my travels as a community educator, a young single man approached me and asked if he could speak with me in private. He told me that he was Orthodox and gay and was looking for an understanding rabbi to help him sort things out. I was totally in the closet at the time, so neither this young man nor the shul was aware of my connection to the issue. I told the assembled minyan what I had told him then: "I have no unambiguous way to deal with the verse in Leviticus at this point, but I can tell you that if you find a committed monogamous partner and avoid anal intercourse, you are better off halakhically speaking than all the Orthodox Jews you know who do not keep the *niddah* laws." The minyan went berserk. "Rabbi, that's not right! Is that correct, Rabbi? That can't be the law!" The assistant rabbi decided it was best for him not to respond to this challenge, knowing that plenty of Jews associated with the synagogue, likely some of the young couples present and surely some of their parents, did not keep the laws of *niddah*.

The reason this comparison elicited such a strong response is that it seemed impossible to the congregation that a less than perfectly pious Orthodox couple who, for their own reasons, do not keep *niddah* are sinning more gravely than a gay male couple that abstains from intercourse. However, it is absolutely true.[34] Since the laws of *niddah* have been completely relegated to the personal piety of couples, it would seem very simple to do the same for lesbians and gay men. If we were to sustain the prohibition but relegate it to a ritual obligation between partners, a personal piety, then the whole issue would disappear from the public sphere completely. Rabbis would be able to conduct commitment ceremonies, and people could get on with their lives.

The movement of *niddah* from a serious religious and moral prohibition with dire consequences to a ritual prohibition managed privately by individuals is very similar to the movement that we noted in the transformation of usury. What this proposal suggests is that while the law remains in force on the books, it is no longer a public policy issue. It is a matter of personal piety.

This halakhic solution poses a number of problems both for rabbis and for gay men. First, our rabbi may not find it comfortable to transform a prohibition that many people associate with values into a ritual law. Instead of a law with clear purposes, such as the law against adultery, it would become a more formal ritual concern very similar to the laws of *niddah*.[35] Rabbis seeking to keep the rule firm while finding a way to include gay people in the community might welcome this solution. But this solution tends to leap over the values questions instead of addressing them head on. For many rabbis too much is at stake for them to consider the prohibition unrelated to moral concerns.

Rabbis also could claim that while this approach would take care of the biblical-level halakhic issues, it would not take care of the rabbinic-level concerns. The rabbinic rulings against wasting semen for men and against lesbian relations generally cannot be summarily ignored. Rabbis actively seeking to include gay and lesbian couples would need to claim that the level of human suffering entailed by denying people the opportunity for companionship, intimacy, and love would be sufficient to trump the rabbinic concerns. It is a standard halakhic rule that for human dignity *(kavod habriot)* rabbinic-level laws can be abrogated.[36] Few Orthodox rabbis will be bold enough to take both these steps unless they and their congregants actively want to open their community to gay and lesbian Jews.

While lesbians would have no reason whatsoever to reject such an offer, it is questionable how this proposition of narrowing the prohibition to anal intercourse would be received among gay men. For many gay men giving up sexual intercourse would not be a simple matter. Intercourse is not mutual masturbation. It is a highly emotionally charged experience that for many people, both straight and gay, is the most powerful expression of the interpenetrative desires of love. Wanting bodies to intersect, to become one, is for many people part of the essential desire of sexual union. Genital stimulation and orgasm can happen in many ways, but it is especially in intercourse that people can feel not only great physical pleasure but great emotional fulfillment as well.

Also prohibiting sexual union sometimes (as in *niddah*) is not the same as prohibiting it all the time. *Niddah* does not withhold the prospect of a full sexual union; it only delays it. For some men the restriction of their sexual practice to forms of mutual masturbation would be an emotionally damaging demand while for others it might be within a reasonable frame of religious discipline.[37] For many gay men this will not be a realistic choice. However, if the Orthodox community offered total acceptance for gay and lesbian couples on the basis of this halakhic framework, many people would likely take up the challenge.

The proposition is problematic for rabbis in one other very significant way. It would be very counterintuitive for rabbis to relegate homosexuality to the privacy of the bedroom, as they have with *niddah*. Gay sex life, unlike straight sex life, is never a private matter. When a man and woman walk hand in hand, it is their love that they make public. When two men walk hand in hand, it is their sex life that they make public. To admit that one is gay in the United States Army today is tantamount to having been caught having sex with a man in the barracks. Our words are acts; our privacy is public. This reality stems from the nature of homophobia. Were this proposal to be accepted, the difference between gay and straight couples would largely disappear, because it would relegate sex to the bedroom and out of the minds and concerns of others. Such a move might meet halakhic requirements, but it would boldly violate Western homophobic sensibilities. Most Orthodox rabbis are not yet ready for such a daring social policy.

Joshua is unsure how to respond to the rabbi's exploration. He is willing to contemplate the proposed limitation on his intimate life but wonders if indeed the rabbi will be willing to fulfill his side of the bargain and fully accept gay and lesbian relationships.

Our rabbi admits that while he would prefer Joshua avoid anal intercourse, he cannot actually transmute a biblical sexual violation into a ritual infraction. Even though, formally speaking, adulterers and incest violators could not be charged with a capital crime without sexual intercourse, surely no one would want to openly permit, much less celebrate, sexual play that stopped short of intercourse in these circumstances. Joshua reminds the rabbi that the comparison is invidious. Incest and adultery directly violate the family in various ways; same-sex relations between consenting adult partners harm no one. Nonetheless, our rabbi, after consideration, is not very open to this proposal either.

O'ness—Duress

However, our rabbi is aware of another legal category that has been creatively employed by a few religious thinkers in order to address the question of homosexuality. These rabbis have suggested that the legal principle of *o'ness rahmana patrei* (literally: the Merciful One absolves anyone who acts under duress) ought to be used to mitigate the strength of the prohibition. Individuals under duress are not considered culpable for their actions. According to the law, no person can be held responsible for an act over which she or he has no control. Deprived of free will by a psychological condition, gay people could be supported to do the best that was in their power to do.

The classic source of *o'ness* describes a Jew being physically forced by pagans—presumably under mortal threat—to bow down to an animal.[38] Should individuals acquiesce under such circumstances, they would not be deemed responsible for their actions. Freedom of will was understood as a prerequisite for legal and moral culpability. From other textual sources it appears that an internal force, a psychological compulsion to act in a particular way, could also be seen as a form of *o'ness*.[39]

Rabbi Norman Lamm, the former president of Yeshiva University, wrote an article on homosexuality in 1974 for the *Encyclopedia Judaica Year Book* in which he proposed the idea that at least some homosexuals might be considered "under duress."[40] According to Lamm, those homosexuals who have repeatedly failed to overcome their same-sex desire would be considered under the "duress" of a psychological condition. The act would remain an abomination, but individuals afflicted with homosexual desire would garner extraordinary pastoral compassion, tolerance, and sympathy. Rabbi Lamm's use of *o'ness* was obviously intended to ease the circumstances of homosexuals while keeping the religious and communal norms intact.

Lamm excluded what he termed "ideological" homosexuals from his ruling. Gay people "who assert the legitimacy and validity of homosexuality as an alternative to heterosexuality" would not be deemed "under duress" according to Lamm. Only those homosexuals who had attempted to overcome their desires and failed and who "readily admit its pathology could be considered under the duress of a psychological condition." For Lamm, the defense of *o'ness* requires an acknowledgment of both the negativity of the sexual behavior and the pathology of the compulsion.

In 1993, in an article in the *Jerusalem Post,* Rabbi Shlomo Riskin, a prominent Modern Orthodox rabbi, educator, and community leader, suggested that an even broader application of the principle of *o'ness* might be possible. While homosexuals are portrayed in a rather negative light in the beginning and end of the essay, in the middle of the piece Rabbi Riskin waxes passionate in their defense: "But how can we deny a human being the expression of his physical and psychic being? If there's a problem with the kettle, blame the manufacturer. Is it not cruel to condemn an individual from doing that which his biological and genetic makeup demand that he do? The traditional Jewish response would be that if indeed the individual is acting out of compulsion, he would not be held culpable for his act."[41] Rabbi Riskin was obviously troubled by the cruel theological conundrum of denying a person the expression of an inborn (read Divinely created) nature. He implies that, if homosexual desire is like heterosexual desire, an innate feature of a person's physical and psychological makeup, then the category of *o'ness* should be applied widely to all homosexuals.

Our rabbi finds this reading of homosexuality to be compelling, but has misgivings. While one does not choose a sexual orientation, acting upon a sexual desire is generally understood to be free willed.

The characterization of sexual passion as beyond freedom of choice would seem to be counter-intuitive. Were *o'ness* to be widely applied to sexual violations it would undermine the culpability of any sexual offender. "I was out of control" would serve as a universal excuse for all sorts of sexual crimes.[42] While overwhelming sexual desire hardly seems sufficient to justify a court's leniency in judging a sexual offense, the rabbi reminds himself that, at least in certain circumstances, uncontrolled sexual passions are considered a halakhically legitimate form of duress.

The Talmud uses the defense of *o'ness* for a married woman who was raped, and who in the process "consented" due to the arousal of her passions.[43] In this case the woman was to be considered as having refused the liaison despite her change of mind. Her later "consent" was to be deemed "under duress" and would not have the power to transform her rape into an act of adultery.[44] Ordinarily, a male claiming to be a victim of coercive sex with a female, could not be easily exonerated in a comparable situation because an erection was taken as proof of willingness.[45] For parity's sake, the rabbis conjure up a bizarre theoretical frame by which a man could be considered under duress. If he was aroused in a permissible fashion, for example, with his wife, but then forced to conclude coitus with a prohibited woman, then a man would, according to most authorities, not be liable.[46] These discussions reveal, among other things, that sexual passion can, in certain circumstances, be halakhically understood as a force beyond the control of ordinary individuals.

This approach to homosexuality as a unique condition of duress has not received resounding support among Orthodox halakhic authorities. However, a growing number of rabbis have been willing to use the category of *o'ness* as a hook for a policy of "special consideration." While not suffering from a full-fledged mental illness, the homosexual transgressor should be spared the full consequences of his sin on the grounds of a basic innate desire that is fundamentally not chosen.[47]

O'ness provides Orthodox rabbis with a platform for distinguishing between toleration and social transformation, between sexual orientation and sexual liberation. Those physically and emotionally capable of functioning heterosexually would be duty-bound to marry and to fight temptation. Those who have no desire at all for the opposite sex and who are powerfully sexually attracted to members of the same sex would be considered "under duress" and given the opportunity to make the best of the situation.

The category of *o'ness* used in this way may contain within it a claim about celibacy. While limits on sexual expression are part of the fundamental framework of human civilization, the lifelong closing of all avenues of sexual expression would be understood as unrealistic. Rabbi Dr. Nathan Lopez-Cardozo, an Orthodox rabbi interviewed in DuBowski's film puts it this way. "It is not possible for the Torah to come and ask a person to do something which he is not able to do. Theoretically speaking it would be better for the homosexual to live a life of celibacy. I just would argue one thing—it's completely impossible. It doesn't work. The human force of sexuality is so big it can't be done." *O'ness* is the halakhic category that best portrays the unrealistic demand of lifelong celibacy. Rabbis surely understand that were their heterosexual congregants offered membership in the community on the condition that they remain celibate all their lives, the overwhelming majority would not agree to the bargain.

O'ness provides the halakhic grounding for Hillel's common sense adage, "Judge not your neighbor until you stand in his place."[48] Homophobic remarks are painfully common in traditional synagogues. Understanding homosexuality as *o'ness* helps rabbis to become public advocates of the protection of homosexuals from persecution and abuse, in the synagogue, in the local community and in the larger political arena as well.

Rabbis who are persuaded by the sincerity of the gay people who come to them for counsel can use the category of *o'ness* to ground policies that formally accept out gay people as full-fledged synagogue members. Gay and lesbian people, it can be argued, should formally be given the opportunity to fulfill what they can. While falling short of the ideal, monogamous gay partnering could be seen as the most holy life choice available to gay and lesbian people. The halakhic category of *o'ness* is perhaps the most creative frame presently available to Orthodox rabbis by which they can open their doors to gay couples without changing the fundamental rule on homosexual relations.

Captured Children

A parallel argument for toleration based indirectly on the principle of *o'ness* has been proffered by Rabbi Chaim Rapoport, an Orthodox congregational rabbi and a member of the cabinet of the chief rabbi of Great Britain and the Commonwealth. Rabbi Rapoport rejects the notion that practicing homosexuals are formally under the duress of a psychological condition. Instead, he relieves homosexuals from full agency and culpability by portraying them as victims of cultural miseducation. Rapoport describes the sexually active gay Jew as falling under the category of a *tinok shenishbah ben ha-akum*, a Jew captured and raised from infancy by gentiles.[49]

The halakhic category was created in Talmudic times in response to real abductions of children who later needed to be integrated into Jewish communal observance. Such individuals, it was taught, could not be held accountable for their lack of belief or observance. The unruly behavior of people not reared in a Jewish environment or instructed in Jewish observance should be taken in stride. They should be embraced and moved gradually from ignorance to knowledge, and from disregard of the law to respect for it.

The Talmudic category was expanded by Maimonides as a broadly applied leniency when dealing with the children and grandchildren of heretics. The original Karaites, a sectarian group rejecting the rabbinic oral tradition, were to be harshly rebuked for having actively broken away from normative Jewish belief and practice. However, "their descendants are like children who have been taken captive among them. The status of this second generation is comparable to that of an individual who has been coerced. Even if such a person later learns that he is a Jew and becomes acquainted with Jews and their religion, he is nevertheless to be regarded as a victim of compulsion *(o'ness)*, for he was reared in their erroneous ways. The same is true for those who follow in the footsteps of their misguided ancestors. Therefore it is proper to influence them to return in repentance and draw them near with words of peace until they return to the ever-flowing Torah."[50]

In 1849, Rabbi Zvi Hirsh Chajes, an Eastern European Orthodox rabbi of immense Jewish and secular erudition, denounced the burgeoning Reform movement but limited his condemnation to the leaders of the movement. Rank and file Reform Jews were to be considered like "captured children."[51] Writing over a century later in the aftermath of the Holocaust, Rabbi Shimon Shwab, a leader of German Orthodoxy maintained that even "those who have been brought up in a Torah-true atmosphere" but have become disillusioned as a result of despair and nihilism ought to be treated as "captured children." The lack of faith and observance due to the "total eclipse of Divine Providence" during the Holocaust was not to be considered a willful choice. Such rejection of traditional religious life, no matter how angry and insistent an individual might be, was to be a consequence of religious trauma rather than rebellion.[52]

The contemporary Orthodox community has generally adopted this approach to non-observant Jews, considering them to be like "captured children" rather than blatant heretics. Rabbi Simcha Wasserman, a pioneer in Orthodox outreach initiatives directed to non-Orthodox Jews applied the category to "all those who had not been raised with Torah who should not be criticized for not living up to its standards."[53]

Rabbi Rapoport derives from these sources that even when a person has free will to choose right from wrong, he can only be considered guilty for choosing the latter if he was in a position to *know* right from wrong. Given this framework, sexually active homosexuals who have been seduced by the permissive strains of Western cultural values might very well be considered captured children. He writes, "A careful appraisal of the 'conditioning' of an individual sexually active homosexual may well lead to the conclusion that the person in question ought to be granted the status of *tinok shenishbah,* with its attendant ramifications." Rabbi Rapoport argues that we ought to apply to him the verdict of Maimonides, who declares that "he is to be regarded as victim of compulsion" to whom we must reach out with "words of peace" and "thick bonds of love."[54]

Rabbi Rapoport describes gay Jews in this way in order to work against the standard Orthodox assessment that gay people are hedonistic renegades. In a sense, the category of *tinok shenishbah* is a sociological application of a psychological principle. *O'ness* refers to a physical or psychological condition of individuals that diminishes their agency and so their culpability. *Tinok shenishbah* refers to a social condition that miseducates people and so likewise diminishes agency and culpability. *O'ness* treats gay people as psychologically deficient, while *tinok shenishbah* treats gay people as uniquely vulnerable to a morally deficient society.

Both Lamm and Rapoport have attempted to exonerate the individual homosexual while retaining the tradition's normative stance on homosexual sexual relations. A person can be pardoned for sins for which he cannot be deemed fully culpable; however, the behavior itself remains sinful, with all the attendant negativities. Both approaches might be seen as sophisticated versions of the oft quoted principle "hate the sin, love the sinner" used so extensively by contemporary Christian religious leaders dealing with the issue. The attempt to balance the ideal with the real, the divine with the human is similar, but these Jewish formulations above have little to do with either hate or love.[55] Lamm and Rapoport are suggesting something one might hear in a court of law as an argument for the defense: "admit that the law has been broken, but comprehend the context." The sin is formally a violation of the law, but it has been cleared of rebellion, detoxified by psychological or social explanations.

Despite the fact that Joshua prefers *o'ness* and *tinok shenishbah* to other halakhic conceptualizations of homosexuality, they still fall short of providing an adequate solution to his dilemma. These characterizations of his experience do not ring true to him. He feels neither under any duress nor captured by a gentile consciousness. He does not experience his sexual orientation as either a psychological illness or the result of libertine social values. Joshua wants to push the rabbi go further. "Why," he asks, "should a loving relationship between two same-sex adults be characterized in this way?"

Rav Noah

Joshua's frustration is of course, my own. I am both moved by these rabbinic attempts at compassion and deeply troubled by them. My first encounter with a similar sort of conditional tolerance happened when I was in the last few months of my closeted existence. A gay friend asked a favor of me. He wanted to know how his Rav would respond to the issue of homosexuality. His Rav was no ordinary Rav or Rosh Yeshiva. He was Rav Noah Weinberg, the founder and director of *Aish HaTorah,* which was founded in 1974 as a modest *ba'al teshuva yeshiva,* a religious academy for returnees to Orthodox Judaism. It now counts thirty branches worldwide, with teachers conducting classes for business people and seminars for young seekers. From Aish International in Jerusalem, Rav Noah continues to run his local yeshiva along with his expanding franchises.

He is a rough-and-tumble man from Baltimore, Maryland, where his father and then his brother once headed the *Ner Yisrael Yeshiva.* Rav Noah's American ease, his football coach manner, and his sense for the spiritual and psychological troubles of the baby boomers and their children have made him one of the most successful religious renewal efforts in North America and Israel.

Before I went to the meeting with Rav Noah, I sent ahead the article I published under a pseudonym in *Tikkun Magazine,* "Gayness and God," so that we would save time. I wanted him to know that my desire for an audience with him was not due to uncertainties regarding my gayness or my Judaism, just their interrelationship. The meeting was arranged as a conversation and not a counseling session. Self-protectively, I introduced myself as Rabbi Yaakov Levado.

The meeting began with Rav Noah's warm assurance that there was no way to know the weight of God's judgments. I asked him if he had had time to read the article. He said that he had read the article but that instead of responding directly to what I wrote he preferred to make a claim. "We all sin. You, like everyone else, struggle with the *Yetzer Hara* [evil inclination]. You win some, you lose some. You try to do the right thing, you fight it. That's all you can do. Do your best to fulfill the *mitzvot* [commandments]. That's all God asks of you."

He did not attack or condemn. He compared a Jew who has gay sex to a Jew who violates the Sabbath. Both sins call for the death penalty biblically, but people are encouraged to fulfill what they can and to do their best to always improve. He had no taste for the vilification of either sinner. In comparison to the demonization that one finds in Rav Feinstein's writings and in practice in some communities, this was indeed a remarkable achievement of empathy and understanding. In the beginning of my journey I would have been very comforted and encouraged by Rav Noah. He was surely among the most understanding of the rabbis with whom I had spoken. However, for where I was in my journey I was no longer so impressed.

"Rav Noah, if you read the article you understand that I do not fight it anymore, I embrace it. Gay desire surely demands similar kinds of controls that heterosexual desire demands, but the desire and even the fulfillment is no longer fundamentally sinful for me."

"Well, it's understandable," he replied. "Once you have accustomed yourself to live with a sinful behavior that you cannot overcome, it no longer feels like sin. Ok, so if you must sin, then do so. I just insist that you keep it to yourself, that you not turn sin into pride."

He was trying very hard to be as generous as he felt he could be. Still unsatisfied, I told him that I wanted a life of love and of sexual fulfillment that would somehow fit into a Jewish framework. He appeared agitated at my refusal of his kindness. "I want a community where I can have a partner, not a private obsession." No longer suppressing his frustration, Rav Noah insisted. "Look, you can't openly come into the Shul [synagogue] with a lover. No, no! Let's say a single man masturbates to pornography—hardly an attractive quality, but he's single and he can't help himself. Ok. So, that's where he is. But would you think it appropriate for him to announce it, to wear an 'I masturbate to pornography' button in Shul? Would you claim publicly to be a proud masturbator?"

I sighed. How could I explain to Rav Noah how his example so utterly misrepresented my life. I was angry at the reflection of my desire for a shared intimate life with a partner as shameful or pornographic. I wanted to ask him why my partnered presence at a synagogue dinner would be any more sexually explicit then his presence with his wife? I calmed myself and thought for a moment about how to communicate to him on this point. I asked him if I might speak a bit personally, and he told me that I should speak my mind.

I asked him to imagine a circumstance. Suppose your wife goes to bed exhausted one night and the following morning she will have to wake up unusually early. When you get up she is still fast asleep, so you go to the kitchen and prepare her a cup of coffee just as she likes it. You set the cup down on the night table and then you wake her gently with kisses. Imagine how you might feel when she opens her eyes, when she reaches for your hand, when she sees the cup of coffee on the night table and smiles at you tenderly.

Without waiting for his response, I said to him, "Imagine now being told that these ordinary expressions of love, intimacy, and affection were pornographic, sinful, and abominable. Could you live with such a representation of the most tender and loving center of your life?" By this point Rav Noah had become agitated and upset. I, too, lost it, not in anger, but in humiliation and tears. The meeting concluded badly soon afterward.

Rav Noah did not explicitly talk about *o'ness* or *tinok shenishbah*, but his approach was intuitively grounded in both of them. He could understand how one might succumb to powerful sexual pressures, but the possibility of an alternative sexuality was simply unimaginable for him. What especially he could not abide was the possibility of integrating gay love into a coupled life, a familial life, a communal life, and ultimately, a holy life . . . and of course this is just what Joshua most genuinely needs and desires.

O'ness as Difference

Joshua feels confident that contemporary authorities have not fully mined the halakhic creativity available in the category of *o'ness*. Instead of an ugly pathology, he wonders, might gay people be "compelled" by their very difference? Rather than narrowing the text to a single act, could the text be narrowed to apply to only certain kinds of men and not to others?[56] Perhaps when heterosexual men have intercourse with men, such sexual excess is abhorrent. When homosexual men do so, it is not.[57]

This reading marks gay people not as demonic, immoral, or sick, but as different, so different that they could not possibly be the ones about whom Leviticus is speaking. While people attracted only to their own sex do not appear in the traditional literature as a defined group, why should a "different sexuality" be so difficult to consider?

The Torah assumes only two sexes. However, we have seen that some rabbis were bold enough to imagine three sexes: male, female, and hermaphrodite. Was it not audacious of them to theorize a sex that appears nowhere in the sacred text? The answer is, of course, simple. Reality and experience are part of divine revelation, too. The rabbis' real-life encounters with hermaphrodites challenged them to help third-sexed persons navigate a two-sexed social world. So if a third sex can be invented on the basis of real-world experience, why not a second sexuality?

It is true that the double-sexed difference of a hermaphrodite is visible in ways that homosexuality is not. In order to theorize a different kind of man or woman one might need more reliable criteria than self-report. But it would not be very difficult to construct a test by which homosexual difference could be measured. Galvanic skin responses, perspiration, certain kinds of brain activity, and heartbeat are all associated with sexual arousal. Were two men, or two women, one ostensibly straight and the other gay, hooked up to sensors to detect arousal and if an array of visual stimuli were displayed before them, we would undoubtedly be able to discover which was gay and which was straight. If same-sex desire is an embodied fact for most homosexual people, then *o'ness* might be the imposing duress of a different sexuality, a compelling force, but not an illness, a difference rather than a flaw.

This reading of Leviticus might very well employ the sensibilities of our initial rereading in chapter 13. Heterosexual men who use other men for sexual release would be committing an abomination. Where the ultimate motive is love and intimacy, sex would be permissible; where the motive is sexual predation, it would not be. People who cannot find intimacy, companionship, and love with a person of the opposite sex would simply not be the ones addressed by the verse. Such a reading would be most problematic for bisexuals. People who could reasonably entertain an emotionally and sexually satisfying relationship with a person of the opposite sex would be halakhically required to do so. Religiously speaking, heterosexual union and reproduction would remain ideal. The moral and religious achievements of the heterosexual family would be affirmed but not reified. All sorts of differences would be understood as potential resources in the service of God. Gay people would be offered a set of life trajectories that would inspire them to find love and celebrate life in a community where they are embraced as they are.

Our rabbi listens with rapt attention, takes in Joshua's words, sighs, and wonders.

This ambiguously drawn set of negotiated and incremental movements of heart and mind may yet offer the most dramatic potential for a working solution. The trust and respect that has been built between our rabbi and Joshua and the tenaciousness of their search has paid off. Despite the loose ends and the partialness of their endeavor, they have discovered in their back and forth *shakleh v'taryeh* that perhaps they might be able to shape a shared policy.

15

Welcoming Synagogues

Joshua has decided for himself that the text in Leviticus is either speaking about sexual violence, or if it is speaking about same-sex male relations, it is not speaking to homosexuals like himself. He has decided that he cannot accept the Halakhah as it is presently framed, but he remains committed in every other way to traditional observance. He would like to stay in the community and hopes as well that when he finds a partner, he can bring him to the synagogue.

Our rabbi had decided that he can go only as far as *o'ness rahmanah patrei,* "the Merciful One absolves anyone who acts under duress." Our rabbi would like to provide religiously motivated gay people like Joshua with a spiritual home while not undermining the halakhic system or violating his community's sensibilities. He is not interested in changing Joshua anymore. He realizes that gay and lesbian people very much need a supportive religious community that embraces them as they are.

Joshua and the rabbi are both eager to find a pragmatic solution to the halakhic and communal dilemma. The rabbi and Joshua understand that they do not agree, that they have each come to different conclusions in regard to the meaning of homosexuality. Joshua understands that while he has found deeper, more thoroughgoing ways to understand homosexuality in light of the tradition, his rabbi and much of the congregation will not share his perspective. The rabbi understands that Joshua will not be able to accept the representation of homosexuality as illness, which formally grounds the rabbi's most accommodating position. Even so, a shared policy of welcome seems possible.

Over the past few years I have had the opportunity to speak to young gay and lesbian people. I often ask them to dream with me about their futures. What sort of Jewish lives were sufficiently possible to hope for or to make happen? What did they need in order to make a traditional Jewish life possible for themselves?

They all agreed that in order to remain involved in traditional Jewish life they needed a synagogue community. Because Sabbath and holiday observance is so communal in nature, it is absolutely necessary to shape Orthodox communities that welcome gay people. Were Orthodox rabbis to go as far as they thought possible, and were gay and lesbian congregants to be fairly patient and understanding of the halakhic limitations, a practical way to address the problem might just be available. Many concrete realities are born of a shared policy constructed on the basis of divergent reasoning.

The framework of "welcoming synagogues" was envisioned primarily from a scant few congregations that, without any halakhic responsum on the matter, have integrated gay and lesbian congregants into the life of their communities. The principles of a welcoming synagogue are designed for those communities that wish to provide a safe and honest environment for gay and lesbian people, given the present halakhic situation. To do so, a welcoming synagogue would accept three principles that bind together the rabbi, gay and lesbian congregants, and the community as a whole in a covenant of honest inclusion.

1. For rabbis: *No humiliation.* Rabbis will agree not to humiliate or intimidate gay and lesbian people from the pulpit and work to prevent such humiliation in their congregations.
2. For gay and lesbian congregants: *No public advocacy.* Gay and lesbian members will acknowledge the limits of the halakhic process and not presume the Orthodox synagogue will adopt the social agenda of the gay and lesbian community.
3. For communities: *No lying.* Gay and lesbian members will be able to tell the truth about their relationships and their families.

The first stipulation is a given. A rabbi who feels that he must deliver polemical jeremiads in regard to homosexuality will not provide a welcoming home for gay people. Such diatribes help no one and do a good deal of harm. In every community there are closeted gay Jews, parents of lesbian daughters, sisters of gay brothers, and young people terrified of a nameless secret.

The second stipulation is harder. Orthodox synagogues cannot provide a platform for gay liberation because the issue of homosexuality is simply not yet adjudicated. For those gay and lesbian people who want full acceptance immediately, this sort of lukewarm welcome will not be comfortable. To struggle for years against shame and rejection in order to be partially accepted and mostly tolerated will be too painful for some. Nonetheless, many people, I hope, will want the unique vibrancy and intensity of traditional Jewish communities enough to be patient with the process. As we have seen, the halakhic debate is just beginning.

The last stipulation is the most important for gay Jews and the most difficult for rabbis and congregations. Welcoming synagogues would not require us to lie. This stipulation is really the crux of the matter. Communities must understand that above all else we cannot tolerate the lies that were daily required of us in order to pass. Our self-hatred and shame were products of those lies, and an amazing redemption was made possible by the truth. Our honesty is surely the most unsettling demand for rabbis. How can our rabbi allow Joshua to calmly and publicly introduce his partner and by doing so sanguinely admit to being a sinner? The reason is that our rabbi no longer believes that Joshua's sin is willful, and for the moment, that is enough for Joshua.

What will happen over time no one can tell. But it is likely that we will all become less frightened of one another and more willing to live together when we come to enjoy one another's company. The solutions lie, not in imposing ideologies from one side or another, but in nourishing our curiosity about one another and then living with the ambiguities. It is my fervent hope that in time congregations will find cobbled ways to set aside their fears and that gay and lesbian people will find the courage to risk their hearts for the sake of coming home. Many of us are ready to be woven back into the life of the community, to share its joys and sorrows, its burdens and delights, if only a door is left open and a light is left on.

My partner and I were actively encouraged to join the Orthodox synagogue we now attend. We met the rabbi at a screening of *Trembling before G-d,* and he immediately insisted that we start attending his synagogue. He called the next day to make sure we understood that he meant for us to join. Later that week we joined and have been active members ever since.

Notes

Introduction

1. Rabbis have given this sort of advice on the basis of BT Kiddushin 40a. "Rabbi Ilai the Elder said: If a man sees that his inclination is overpowering him, let him go to a place where they do not know him, dress in black, and cover himself in a black cloak and do as his heart desires, but let him not profane the name of heaven in public."

2. This article can be found in Bawer, *Beyond Queer,* 194; Lowenthal, *Gay Men at the Millennium;* and Lerner, *Best Contemporary Jewish Writing,* 42.

3. Orthodox Jews do not eat milk and meat together (Ex. 23:19, 34:26; Deut. 14:21), and on Yom Kippur, the Day of Atonement, the whole day is spent in fasting. So, eating cheeseburgers on Yom Kippur is as an image of blatant nonobservance of the commandments.

4. Rabbi Emanuel Rackman articulates a vision of an Orthodoxy that includes the intellectual freedom necessary for vitality. Proposals proffered by scholars and agitation for legal revision should not constitute heresy. He writes, "In family law we encounter a more circumscribed area. Yet here, too, as a devotee of halakhah one can propose and agitate for changes that will nullify almost every rule of the past. It might be the sheerest folly to do so. But the question under consideration is not whether one should write a new code for Jewish domestic relations but rather whether the power resides in the duly constituted authorities to do so. And it does. Therefore, he who thinks that changes are in order and proposes them for promulgation by the bet din or Sanhedrin cannot be regarded as a heretic when he agrees with the most liberal views heretofore entertained. . . . There are some limitations; but for any Orthodox group to brand as a heretic one who feels keenly that changes should be made—within the Halachic frame and by its own methodology—is to define heresy as it was never defined in the past. One can argue with the proponents of change because of policy considerations, but one may not challenge their loyalty to the faith. Indeed, they may be its most passionate champions as they try to relieve human distress" (*One Man's Judaism,* 270).

5. Leibowitz, *Emunah, historiah ve'arachim,* 71. Leibowitz was speaking of the problems of the status of women in Halakhah. However, the relationship between the two issues of misogyny and homophobia overlap

considerably, as I hope to demonstrate. Moreover, Leibowitz marks the danger to the system not in succumbing to the feminist critique but in not responding to it seriously. In much the same way the resistance to responsibly addressing the issue of homosexuality will weaken and undermine the Torah community by portraying it as unresponsive to new human realities never before confronted, as utterly frozen, fearful, and oppressive.

6. The first such minyan (prayer group), Shirah Hadashah, began in Jerusalem in 2002. Every Shabbat women lead Kabbalat Shabbat on Friday evening, *pesuke d'zimrah* on Shabbat morning, the service for taking out the Torah, and are among those who read the Torah and are given aliyot. In the United States a number of similar groups have recently begun to hold monthly or bimonthly services.

7. See chapter 14 for a detailed discussion of the laws on taking interest.

8. The Pittsburgh Platform was first published as part of the proceedings of the 1885 Pittsburgh conference of reform Rabbis convened by Kaufman Kohler of New York and presided over by Isaac Mayer Wise of Cincinnati The platform can be found in the appendix of Michael A. Myer *Response to Modernity: A History of the Reform Movement in Judaism* (New York: Oxford University Press, 1990).

9. Responsa *Hatam Sofer, Orah Hayyim* 1:28.

10. On the Sabbath all forms of creative work are prohibited. On the holidays most of the same prohibitions are in force to the exclusion of food preparation and transporting goods in the public domain, which are permitted.

11. That feminism and Orthodoxy can occupy the same space is one of the great Modern Orthodox achievements of the last ten years. Today an organization, the Jewish Orthodox Feminists Alliance, gathers Jews in the thousands to conferences. This group of men and women, scholars and lay people seeks to honestly address texts and traditions with an eye toward female subjective experience and equal value. The organization is clearly an attempt to respond to new intellectual commitments and social circumstances and to contemplate the possible halakhic innovations that these social and intellectual changes might inspire. If there can be such a thing as an Orthodox Jewish feminist, then perhaps we are not far from the possibility of the presently considered oxymoron of an Orthodox gay person.

12. BT Eruvin 13b.

13. Levinas, *L'au dela du verset,* 164.

14. Levinas, *Nine Talmudic Readings,* 46.

15. Levinas, *L'au dela du verset,* 136.

16. Religions that are grounded on divine revelation cannot help but suffer the dangers of false prophecy. Following the destruction of the Temple in Jerusalem, the rabbis concluded that prophecy went

underground. "Since the destruction prophecy was taken from prophets and given to children and fools" (Bava Batra 12b). In place of a singular divine message delivered by a prophet, the sages of the Talmud found the ongoing divine word better mediated by discourse and debate, by multiplying possible interpretations and group decision making.

17. On a regulation belt buckle of the German Luftwaffe were engraved the words "Gott mit uns," (God is with us!).

18. Tefillin are leather boxes with scriptural verses inside that are bound with straps to the upper arm and over the crown of the head. They are physical expressions of the commandment to love God. "You shall love the Lord your God with all your heart, with all your soul and with all your might. And these words which I command you this day shall you take to heart, speaking of them when you walk by the way when you lie down, and when you rise up. And you shall bind them as sign upon your hand and as an emblem between your eyes. And you shall write them upon the doorposts of your house and upon your gates" (Deut. 6:5–9).

19. For *b'nei haneviim,* see 2 Kings 2:5, 2:14, 4:1, 6:1. For prophetic ecstasy, see 1 Sam. 10:5–7.

20. *Leviticus Rabbah* 32:8.

21. Shlomo is not this person's real name.

22. By the summer of 2003, *Trembling's* director, Sandi Simcha DuBowski, and I had traveled to over one hundred of cities and conducted over five hundred postscreening dialogues with audiences of all kinds. In 2002 we launched an outreach project to actively bring the film to traditional Jewish communities and schools. In Israel alone over two thousand religious school superintendents, principals, teachers, and counselors have seen the film and participated in facilitated postscreening dialogues with their peers. The film has had an enormous effect on the Orthodox community. It has broken the silence on homosexuality and engendered unprecedented empathy for the plight of gay and lesbian Orthodox Jews.

23. DuBowski has established a Web site (www.tremblingbeforeg-d.com) for open discussion on the issues that the film raises and for helping people organize around the film.

24. While this book was undergoing its final editing, the Conservative movement was focusing renewed attention on this very question. It is only a matter of time before the law committee changes its stand on this issue and agrees to ordain openly homosexual rabbinical students.

25. For example, the prohibition against having intercourse with a woman during her menses, while in the same chapter of Leviticus that addresses homosexuality, was not considered among the "moral" commandments for which Christians were responsible.

26. BT Hagigah 3b.

27. BT Sanhedrin 17a.

28. JT Sanhedrin 4:22a.

29. Based on the work of Mendel Shapiro, two Orthodox minyanim (prayer groups) have begun, one in Jerusalem (Shira Hadasha) and the other in New York City (Darchei Noam), in which women are called up to the Torah for aliyot, read from the Torah, and lead selected parts of the service. The responsum of Rabbi Shapiro was published by Eidah, a Modern Orthodox think-tank organization.

1. The Birth of Gender and Desire

1. Douglas Knight states that a "cosmology designates a group's comprehensive view of reality and represents the effort to grasp the nature of the whole and thereby place all the parts within it" ("Ancient Israelite Cosmology," 30).

2. Mishnah Avot 3:1.

3. I have chosen to translate the pronouns referring to God as they are in the Hebrew, which is nearly always male. I have also chosen not to capitalize the male-gendered pronouns referring to God in order to work subtly against the ingrained male references to God that have limited our understanding of God.

4. Regarding the belief that homosexuality is unnatural, there is great debate as to whether biblical and/or rabbinic tradition thinks of "nature" as a binding normative force. Maimonides scholars are split on whether the *Guide for the Perplexed* supports the idea of a natural law or rejects it. See chapter 10, pp. 158–60.

5. *Genesis Rabbah* 5:3.

6. BT Hullin 60b.

7. While God's learning is an audacious idea for a God who is presumed to know all, the rabbis are comfortable saying such things, given that they remind us that the text itself is crossing the line. "Were it not written I would not dare say" is one such introduction. Another way to mark an audacious expression is with the Hebrew word *kev'yachol,* which means "so to speak" or literally "as if this were possible."

8. This idea is original to my teacher, mentor, and friend, Rabbi Yitz Greenberg.

9. Mishnah Sanhedrin 4:5.

10. See Trible, *God and the Rhetoric of Sexuality,* 145–62.

11. The similarity of this rabbinic legend with the one found in Plato *Symposium* 189d, 190d, suggests some general cultural sharing of this story in antiquity.

12. *Genesis Rabbah* 8:1, s.v. *vayomer elohim.*

13. It is true that the Hebrew Bible addresses God in the masculine. However, there are only two genders and no neuter form for nouns in Hebrew. Unlike most gods in the ancient world, the God of Israel has no female

consort. For a discussion of the problem of God's gender in the Hebrew Bible, see Eilberg-Schwartz, *God's Phallus.*

14. *Genesis Rabbah* 8:1, s.v. *vayomer elohim.*

15. The principle appears in the Talmud and is employed extensively by the medieval commentators. See BT Pesahim 6b; Rashi on Gen. 6:3; 35:29; Exod. 4:20; 31:18.

16. Rashi immediately sees this as God's problem. The fuller midrash that Rashi quotes reads as follows: "Said the Holy One: I am single in my world, and this one is single in its world. I have no reproduction and this one has no reproduction. The creatures will soon say that since it does not reproduce, it must be that this one created us" (*Pirkei de-Rabbi Eliezer* 12). The "not good" *(lo tov)* in the creation for which God did not plan was, as Rashi simplifies, that it will be said that there are two powers, one in heaven and one on earth. Of course, such a mistake could be made in any case. "Why was the *adam* created single? . . . So no one would say that there are two authorities in heaven" (Mishnah Sanhedrin 4:5). Had the first human been created in a pair, then another analogy challenging divine singularity would have been possible. Creation, no matter how it proceeds, threatens divine unity or sovereignty, at least on the level of perception.

17. BT Yevamot 63a.

18. That the rabbis permitted themselves such a wild fantasy, given the prohibition against bestiality, is remarkable. Moreover, how an androgynous creature might go about such an exploration is not spelled out. Perhaps the *adam* had relations with both male and female members of each species. Since midrashic writers weren't working together on a single story line, this writer might very well have imagined a male *adam* having relations with female animals.

19. BT Sanhedrin 42a.

20. In *Siddur Abodat Israel* (338) Yehuda Baer suggests that this addition to the Kiddush Levanah is a tradition from the medieval German pietist Rabbi Yehudah HeHasid. However, in the five-volume commentary on Jewish liturgy, *Netiv Binah,* the author, Issachar Jacobson, admits not being able to find the origins of this prayer but believes that it derives from a mystical source (*Netiv Binah,* 3:343).

21. Rashi on Megillah 22b, s.v. *roshei hodashim.* I thank Rabbi Pinchas Klein for bringing this source to my attention.

2. The Sons of God, Ham, and the Sodomites

1. The word *elohim* in the Book of Exodus is used to describe a person of authority and power. See verses 4:16 and 7:1.

2. BT Sanhedrin 70a.

3. See *Pirkei de-Rabbi Eliezer* 24.

4. BT Sanhedrin 109a.

5. The *Midrash Rabbah* on Leviticus 23:9 says that Sodom was finally and irrevocably condemned in heaven the moment when the crowd outside Lot's tent said to him, "[Bring out your guests] that we may know them."

6. Tosefta Sotah 3:11–12.

7. "I will go down and see whether they have acted altogether according to the cry that has reached me" (Gen. 18:21). What cry? The cry of this young girl. See *Genesis Rabbah* 42, 49; *Numbers Rabbah* 9; *Leviticus Rabbah* 5; BT Sanhedrin 109a–b.

8. BT Sanhedrin 109b.

9. Dover, *Greek Homosexuality,* 105.

10. Boswell, "Revolutions, Universals, Categories," 98.

11. *Homilia Vin Genesim* (PG 12:188–89).

12. Josephus Flavius, *Antiquities of the Jews,* 1:11; see as well Philo, *On Abraham,* 133–41. Hellenistic Jews of the first century B.C.E and the first century C.E. were part of the larger Hellenistic discourse in regard to sexuality and homosexuality specifically. While this material was never included in the canon of sacred and legitimated tradition and so cannot be considered halakhically relevant Jewish source material, it sheds light on some early Christian views that borrowed heavily from this period's ethos. Philo and Josephus are among the only Jewish writers who associated Sodom with homosexuality. They, like the church fathers who followed them, became part of the longstanding Hellenistic discourse around same-sex love. For example, the Theodosian Code, written in 342, includes an outright prohibition of same-sex marriage: "When a man marries [a man] as if he were a woman, what can he be seeking, where gender has lost its place? Where the sin is something that is unseemly [even] to know? Where Venus is transformed into a different form? Where love is sought, but does not appear? We order the laws to arise, justice to be armed with an avenging sword, so that those shameless persons guilty of this either now or in the future should be subject to exquisite punishment" (9.7.3). While the Roman culture is often viewed as accepting of homosexual love, historians have painted a more complex picture. Attitudes about homosexual love and even the laws regulating such sexual expression ranged widely from one decade to another. There were periods of great social latitude and then, in reaction to the sexual excesses of a particular emperor's court, a period of harsh moral criticism and general legislation against same-sex love. In short, there was a full-blown cultural debate on the issue of same-sex love; for some it was the purest and most spiritual of loves, for others is was no better or no worse than heterosexual love, and for others its was a crude violation of nature. Philo and Josephus were fully inside this Roman cultural debate and so read Sodom in its light.

13. Tosefta Sanhedrin 13:8.

14. The same three sins are attributed to the generation of the flood and to Ishmael before he was sent out of Abraham's home. Formally, these were the only sins for which a Jew was expected to die rather than transgress. See *Genesis Rabbah* 31; Rashi on Gen. 21:9; and BT Sanhedrin 74a.

15. The *Tanhuma* was first published in 1522 in Constantinople. Historians place its origins as no earlier than 800 C.E.with new material generated and added to it through the tenth century.

16. *Tanhuma, Va'yera* 12.

17. *Avot de-Rabbi Nathan* [B] 30.

18. Becoming one flesh in sexual union can be taken to mean a number of very different things. It can mean that their flesh literally becomes one in the body of their offspring or more impressionistically that they are joined in sexual intercourse like one body. During sexual intercourse, a heterosexual couple comes close to the original mythic union of male and female in the two-faced *adam* creature (Ibn Ezra, Gen. 2:23–24). According to Nahmanides, the thirteenth-century Spanish commentator, sexual union results in "one flesh" only in humans who "cleave" to their wives and see their committed monogamous relationship "as if" they were one flesh. Flesh in a number of sources has the meaning of close family or kin (Gen. 37:27 and Lev. 18:6). A man leaves his father and mother and cleaves to his wife, discovering in the union with her a kinship even closer than that with his parents. The statement of the *Sekhel Tov* that two men cannot become one flesh can be taken to mean that they cannot produce a child together, that their sexual union neither appears like a single body nor imitates the original double-sexed body of the *adam,* or that two men cannot form a kinship family bond of flesh. It is important to add that the statement in Genesis that bids a man leave his parent's home and cleave to his wife is understood by *Sekhel Tov* as a normative obligation rather than as an explanation of the common way of the world. However, the author of this midrash did not invent this idea; he merely borrowed a discussion among the sages as to whether or not the sons of Noah are prohibited to engage in homosexual relations. The question is a live one in Jewish thought since Leviticus only obligates Jews. However, since the language of "one flesh" is taken from the creation story, the legislation deriving from it would apply to all men.

19. Isaiah 42:6. The one exception to this mission is the forced conversion of the Idumeans (inhabitants of Edom) by John Hyrcanus during his reign in Judea at the end of the second century B.C.E. (Flavius Josephus, *Antiquities* 12: 9.2).

20. BT Sanhedrin 56.

21. The Midrash (*Yalkut Shimoni,* Ezekiel, 373) discovers it in the Book of Ezekiel. There the prophet entertains an argument put forth by the nations that conquered Israel that they now are the land's legitimate inheritors. This is how Ezekiel responds to them: "The word of the Lord

came to me: O moral, those who dwell on these ruins in the Land of Israel, argue: 'Abraham was but one man, yet he was granted possession of the land. We are many; surely, the land has been given as a possession to us.' Say to them: Thus said the Lord God: You eat with the blood, you raise your eyes to your idols, and you shed blood—yet you expect to possess the land?! You have relied on your sword, you have committed abominations, you have all defiled other men's wives—yet you expect to possess the land?!" (Ezek. 33:23–26). The *Yalkut Shimoni* makes the reference to abomination clear. "What does it mean 'and you have committed abominations'? This refers to male-male sexual intercourse *(mishkav zakhar)*." The midrash ends by expressing the point of the passage in Ezekiel. "The laws of Noah you have not kept and you expect to inherit the land?" (*Yalkut Shimoni,* Ezekiel, 373). While this list is different than the rabbinic one, from this source it appears that the prohibition of same-sex male intercourse was understood as one of the laws of Noah.

22. Ramban on the verse "Let us know them" (Gen. 19:5).

23. Rashi on BT Ketubbot 103a, *Kofin al Midat Sedom.*

24. Bailey, *Homosexuality and the Western Christian Tradition* 1–8; McNeill, *Church and the Homosexual,* 42–50.

25. Gen. 19:9, literally "the one who came here as a stranger already presumes to judge us!"

26. Ezekiel 16 and see Lam. 4:6.

3. Leviticus

1. *Midrash Leviticus Rabbah* 7:2.

2. Nahmanides, *Introduction to Leviticus.*

3. In the Articles of Religion of the Church of England drawn up in 1571, the distinction between laws that do and do not bind Christians is articulated as follows: "Although the Law given from God to Moses, as touching Ceremonies and Rites, does not bind Christian men, nor the Civil precepts thereof ought of necessity to be received in any commonwealth; yet notwithstanding, no Christian man whatsoever is free from the obedience of the Commandments which are called Moral."

4. BT Eruvin 13b.

5. Note Num. 31:18; 31:35; and Judg. 21:11.

6. Saul Olyan's invaluable contribution to the understanding of these verses can be found in "And with a Male You Shall Not Lie the Lying Down of a Woman."

7. I gained this insight from a conversation with Professor Jacob Milgrom.

8. JT Kiddushin 58c and BT Yevamot 54b; the one source that may suggest otherwise is BT Shabbat 17b, where *mishkav zakhar* might refer to

sexual play between children. However, Maimonides understands even this reference as intercourse (*Hilkhot Mishkav u'Moshav* 2:10).

9. Gen. 43:32.

10. Exod. 8:22.

11. See Deut. 12:31; 13:15; 14:3; 25:14–16; Lev. 18:22–30; Prov. 6:16–19.

12. Milgrom, "Abomination."

13. See Deut. 18:12 on idolatry; 22:5 on cross-dressing; and 25:16 on honest weights and measures.

14. JT Sanhedrin 6:23.

15. BT Sanhedrin 54b.

16. *Sifra Kedoshim* 9:14 (92b). Nissinen suggests that *kadeshim* were men who had assumed an unusual gender role in expression of a lifelong dedication to a deity. In Near Eastern worship "third-gender" devotion to a goddess was common, often in the form of male castration and cross-dressing. However, Nissinen claims there is scant evidence that homosexual activity was part of Canaanite worship (*Homoeroticism in the Biblical World*, 37–44).

17. See *Sifrei Devarim* 260; *Mavo LeTalmud;* and S. E. Loewenstramm, *Qadesh,* in *Encyclopedia Biblica* (New York: MacMillan, 1899–1903), 7:35–36.

18. BT Sanhedrin 54b.

19. See 1 Cor. 6:9–11 and 1 Tim. 1:8–11.

20. According to BT Sanhedrin 54b, a receptive partner violates two prohibitions, the penetrative partner just one. According to Satlow, this position is put forth by Palestinian rabbis who were likely disturbed by the Torah's focus on the active partner. It was they who struggled to wrest from the text a more onerous indictment of the receptive partner than the penetrative partner, even though they found the opposite in Scripture. The Babylonians, it appears, didn't find the missing reference to receptive intercourse in chapter 18 particularly problematic. See Satlow, *Tasting the Dish*, 197.

4. Lesbian Omissions

1. Lev. 18:23.

2. BT Yevamot 61b. The sages ultimately decided in accordance with neither of these opinions and defined the *zonah* as a woman who had previously violated one of the biblical sexual prohibitions or was a woman not of Israelite birth. See Rambam *Yad, Issurei Biah* 18:2.

3. Rashi, BT Yevamot 76a, s.v. *Nashim mesolelot zo bazo*, "In the manner of intercourse between male and female, rubbing their vaginas against each other."

4. BT Shabbat 65a–b.

5. Rashi suggests that the Talmud is affirming that lesbian relations would surely disqualify a woman from marrying a high priest. While a priest need not marry a virgin (for example, he may marry a widow), a high priest must marry only a virgin. Rashi's assumption is that sex between women has the possibility, if not the probability, of breaking the hymen.

6. *Sifra* 9:8.

7. While the sexual relations between men and those between women are evaluated so differently on the biblical level, one receiving capital punishment and the other not even mentioned, on the level of the social legitimation of such relations in marriage, the rabbis appear to perceive a problem in homosexuality, i.e., the sameness of potential marital partners.

8. See *Tur Pirya u-Rivya* 20:9; *Bet Yosef; Perisha;* and *Shulhan Arukh, Even HaEzer* 20:2.

9. Rambam, *Hilkhot Issurei Biah* 21:8.

10. Maimonides, *Commentary to Sanhedrin* 7.54a. Later halakhic opinions differed as to whether Maimonides considered lesbian relations a violation of biblical or rabbinic law. Among the more lenient views are those of Rabbi Joshua Falk (1555–1614) and Rabbi Eliezer Kolin (1728–1801), who maintained that lesbian relations are a rabbinic enactment on the basis of the biblical law of regarding copying the Egyptians. Rabbi Mordechai ben Abraham Jaffe (1535–1612) and Rabbi Joseph Rosen (1858–1936) considered lesbian relations to be a direct violation of the biblical rule. See *Perisha* to *Tur Even HaEzer* 20; and *Heker HaHalakhah* 14:53.2. However, according to the *Levush* cited in *Aztei Arazim* 21:1 and Rabbi Joseph Rosen in *Tzafenat Paneakh* 3:164, the prohibition is biblical.

11. This view appears in *tosafot* s.v. *mesolelot* and is quoted notably in the Magid Mishnah.

12. The opinion is on shaky ground because a second use of the term in BT Shabbat 65a would seem to imply that the majority view, that it is sexual play rather than actual seed exchange, is correct. Still, the reading helps to make sense of the rabbis' problem with sex between women.

13. It is also possible that Maimonides was concerned more with sexual expression outside marriage. The prohibition of physical contact between the sexes is for him an independent biblical command. See *Yad, Issurei Biah* 21:1.

14. Maharik, *Siman* 88.

15. This is the opinion of the *Otzar HaPoskim,* the edited collection of commentators on the *Shulhan Arukh.* The *Otzar HaPoskim* says outright that "marriage to a woman, in the definitive way that a man marries a woman is 'like the deeds of Egypt.' However, if it is not the way of marriage but is merely occasional, then it is not forbidden by the Torah but is prohibited by the rabbis" (*Otzar HaPoskim* to *Even HaEzer* 20:2).

16. Hildesheimer was closed by the Nazis in 1938.

17. *Seridei Esh* 3:93. Rabbi Weinberg bases his position on the Maharik, *Siman* 88.

18. BT Yoma 18b.

19. I thank Angela Riccetti for alerting me to this source in her very thoughtful unpublished paper, "A Break in the Path: Lesbian Relationships and Jewish Law."

20. *Tzitz Eliezer,* 13:97.

21. BT Yevamot 65b. Maimonides appears to contradict himself, freeing women to choose to remain unmarried (*Yad, Issurei Biah* 21:26) and requiring women to seek marriage in order to avoid suspicion (*Yad, Ishut* 15:16).

22. The verse including "be fruitful and multiply" continues directly with "fill the earth and conquer it." Since conquest is the way of males and not of females, the command of producing progeny is also directed only to men. For a woman to help her husband produce a child was considered an act of generosity and righteousness, but not an obligation. The ruling may be grounded on the sense that women cannot be obligated where they are not actually empowered. Women still, in the main, are not expected to ask men to marry them. Moreover, the idea of obligating women in the arena of progeny might very well have caused husbands anxiety, particularly in situations where male fertility was unclear. Would wives, pressured and perhaps even emboldened by religious duty, seek out fertile lovers to help them produce their children? *Genesis Rabbah* 8:14 seems to suggest such an anxiety when it explains that a woman is not obligated to reproduce so that "she not go seeking in the marketplace." The rule might also have been justified on the basis of the dangers of pregnancy and childbirth. Women died regularly in childbirth until modern medicine. The Torah did not obligate women to bear children, it is claimed, because no person can be commanded to take on such a grave risk; it must be freely chosen. Also, it may be that the natural inclination of women to bear children was deemed forceful enough that no formal duty was thought necessary. See *Shulhan Arukh, Even HaEzer* 1:2 for the suggestion that God instilled in women a greater desire for marriage and procreation. *Tosafot* to BT Gittin 41b seems to suggest that women are obligated in regard to this secondary and related duty, that is, to "settle the world." "Settling the world" is to generally contribute to the ongoing vitality of human civilization, which can be accomplished through various means other than (though not excluding) producing and rearing children.

5. Princely Love

1. *Pirkei Avot* 5:19.

2. *Avot de-Rabbi Nathan* [A] 8. See Maimonides' Commentary on the

Mishna, Avot 1:6, s.v. *aseh lekha rav.* Maimonides describes three sorts of friendship: Utilitarian friendship, Pleasure friendship, and Sublime friendship. Utilitarian friendship is the friendship between business partners. Pleasure friendship includes both the friendship between spouses—dominated by physical pleasures—and Safety friendship, which is the closest to our contemporary notion of friendship. This latter includes someone who is trustworthy, who can keep a secret, with whom one can share anything, even embarrassing things, and upon whom one depends emotionally. Finally, there is the friendship of shared longing of two for the achievement of a single goal, the doing of some good. Each sublime friend helps the other in order that they might reach their goal together.

3. Some scholars have suggested that 1 Sam. 20:41, "They kissed each other and wept together, until David exceeded," if translated "until David was enlarged" implies that David achieved an erection in their embrace. This is a very unlikely translation. The phrase probably means that David wept longer. However, the context of Jonathan's arrow-shooting practice during which the hidden David understands the secret message certainly marks the encounter as strongly homoerotic, if not sexual.

4. Mihal, Saul's daughter and David's wife, is enraged to see David dancing wildly before the ark of the covenant as it is brought into Jerusalem in 2 Sam. 6:16. She too fell in love with David earlier in the story in 1 Sam. 18:20. Might it be that her anger was incited by seeing her husband showing more energy and excitement for God than for her?

6. Rabbinic Heroes

1. BT Bava Metsi'a 84a.
2. Ibid.
3. Ibid.
4. See Boyarin, *Unheroic Conduct,* 127–50.
5. While it was unlawful for R. Yohanan to promise such a marriage without the consent of his sister, in practice the older male family members arrange the marriages of underage girls without their consent.
6. BT Bava Metsi'a 84a–b.
7. If our earlier identification of the lance with an erect phallus is correct, this halakhic disagreement evokes the extremely erotic images of forging in heat and rubbing in water.

7. The Queer Middle Ages

1. There are a few Hebrew war poems from the pen of Shmuel Ha-Nagid, but he was a military man.
2. The last two lines of a strophic poem of this period are called a *kharja.* Typically it finishes a Hebrew poem with a couplet not in Hebrew,

but in a mixture of Romance and Arabic languages. The translation of these two lines was provided by Professor Raymond P. Scheindlin of the Jewish Theological Seminary, author of *Wine, Women, and Death* (Philadelphia: Jewish Publication Society, 1986).

3. Kalonymus ben Kalonymus (1286–after 1328), *Even Bohan* (Lemberg: 1865), 14–18.

4. BT Shabbat 62b–63a.

5. The custom is found in the work of David ben Joseph Abudarham, the fourteenth-century liturgical commentator in Spain. He comments that women who cannot say "who has not made me a woman" should replace that blessing with "who has made me according to his will"—"like one who justifies an evil decree that has come on him." David ben Joseph Abudarham, *Sefer Abudarham HaShalem* (Jerusalem: Usha Publishing, 1963), 11–47.

6. See Prov. 17:5, "He who mocks the poor affronts his Maker; he who rejoices over another's misfortune will not go unpunished." BT Berakhot 18a; *Shulhan Arukh, Orah Hayyim* 23:1,3.

8. The Legal Literature

1. Jacobovitz, "Homosexuality," 8:961–62.

2. *Shulhan Arukh, Even HaEzer* 24:1.

3. Moses Cordovero established such a pious brotherhood with thirty-six rules of membership. The rules encouraged an uncommon emotional intimacy between men. An associate was to choose a partner with whom he would commune every day for the purpose of conversing about devotional matters. Cordovero also suggested that each member of the brotherhood discuss with the same associate every Sabbath eve what he had done each day of the past week. From there he should go forth to welcome the Sabbath Queen.

4. *Bayit Hadash, Even HaEzer* 24:1.

5. *Yam Shel Shlomo,* Kiddushin, 4:24.

6. *Rav Pe'alim,* vol. 1, *Yoreh De'ah,* chap. 44.

7. Rambam, *Hilkhot Issurei Biah* 21:8.

8. Foucault, *History of Sexuality,* vol. 1; Halperin, "One Hundred Years of Homosexuality"; Boswell, "Revolutions, Universals, Categories"; Dynes, *Homosexuality;* Whitam and Mathy, *Male Homosexuality in Four Societies.*

9. *Leket Yosher,* vol. 2, *Yoreh De'ah* 39:2.

10. *Mayim Amukim* 2:42.

11. *Maharashdam, Even HaEzer* 40.

12. *Mishpat Yesharim* 1:111.

13. *Sho'el u-Meshiv* 1:1.185.

14. *Torah LeShma* 378.

9. Rav Moshe and the Problem of Why

1. Rabbi Yehudah ben Samuel HeHasid of Regensberg (c. 1150–1217) was the main teacher in the German pietist movement, whose influence spread over most of Germany in the twelfth and thirteenth centuries.

2. Langa, *Perushei Rav Yehudah HeHasid*, 147–48. The comment that most disturbed Rav Moshe was the gloss on Lev. 20:13.

3. *Iggerot Moshe, Yoreh De'ah* 3:115.

4. *Iggerot Moshe, Orah Hayyim*, 4:115. See Nahimanides' Torah Commentary on Deut. 29:18, where he describes the movement of sexual desire from those objects naturally desired (women) to those objects for which a man had no desire in the beginning, but by a process of increasing indulgence comes to desire, such as sex with men and animals.

5. The idea of the disenchantment of contemporary society was articulated by Max Weber and then expanded on by Peter Berger. By disenchantment they meant that contemporary society has lost its sacredness and mystique. The forces of rationalization and intellectualization in contemporary society have led directly to a disenchantment of the world. Religion provided a "sacred canopy," an overarching comprehensive interpretation of reality that related human life to the cosmos as a whole. Now, instead of greeting the world with mystery and awe, we master it by calculation and reason. When things become rationalized, they loose their sacredness. See Max Weber, "Science and the Disenchantment of the World," in *Readings in Introductory Sociology*, ed. Dennis Wrong and H. Gracey (London: Macmillan, 1967); Peter Berger, *The Sacred Canopy* (New York: Doubleday Anchor, 1969).

6. Mishnah Avot 3:18.

7. However, while we can suggest reasons for biblical laws, and while we might be forced to apply a rule on the basis of an assumed "intent," it must be admitted that no human rationalizing can claim to have exhausted the meaning of a divine commandment. The question of "rationalizing the commandments" was addressed by the sages of the Talmud and subsequent medieval commentators. The most famous medieval advocate of rationalizing the laws of the Torah was Maimonides.

8. This depiction of a multigenerational preserver-innovator debate is based on the work of Menahem Fisch. The central question on which this debate split was the very nature of the authority of the received oral tradition. According to *preservers* (called the *traditionalists* by Fisch) the enterprise of Torah study itself is conceived as a matter of meticulous reception, memorization, and transmission from one generation to the next of a binding legal interpretation of the written Torah. This being the task, the mark of a great scholar is the accuracy of his transmission from his teacher. Preservers are rigidly committed to the teachings that have been passed on

by former generations because these traditions are taken as given whole at Sinai as an addendum to the written Torah. Thus, the claim of having heard a ruling from one's teacher would trump all other claims. No past ruling can ever be overturned, and no later teacher can disagree with a former. The only truly open question in this sort of learning is in regard to the authenticity, reputation, and credibility of the transmitter. The only context that might allow a *preserver* to introduce new legislation is a lacuna in the system for which no received tradition exists. The *innovators* (the anti-traditionalists, according to Fisch) are those sages who address the received tradition as a framework for their discussions, but not as a limit to possibilities. Consequently, the gathering of scholars was important for preservers primarily in the pooling of students who together would have a better chance of remembering, that is, re-membering or making whole an oral law that would otherwise degenerate with time. For the innovators, gathering to study is what creates new Torah, invigorating and developing the Oral law (Fisch, *Rational Rabbis*).

9. BT Bava Metsi'a 59a–b.

10. Ibid.

11. Fisch, *Rational Rabbis*, 84.

12. Boyarim, *Intertextuality*, 34.

10. The Rationale of Reproduction

1. Langa, *Perushei Rav Yehudah HeHasid*, 147–48.

2. The first reference in Genesis is understood as a blessing, while the repeat of the same phrase, "be fruitful and multiply" in Gen. 9:1 and 7 is understood as a commandment. See Rashi to Ketubbot 5a and Gen. 9:7; Nahmanides to Gen. 9:7; *tosafot* to Yevamot 65b, s.v. *v'lo;* and Maharsha to Sanhedrin 59b, s.v. *vaharei.*

3. Tosefta Yevamot 8. The schools of Shammai and Hillel differed on whether the duty was two sons (Shammai) or a son and a daughter (Hillel). The Halakhah follows Hillel. In JT Yevamot 6:6, a similar texts suggests Hillel was not differing with Shammai but adding the option of a son and a daughter. In BT Yevamot 62a, the dispute between the houses of Hillel and Shammai is recorded in two other versions. Either Shammai requires two males and two females and Hillel only one of each, or Shammai requires a male and a female and Hillel either a male or a female. The support for this last and most lenient view of one child is justified by the verse in Isa. 45:18.

4. Isa. 45:18; Mishnah Eduyyot 1:13; BT Yevamot 62a. The verse in Isaiah could be understood to be limiting the duty or expanding it. Even one child contributes to "settling the world" and so might be sufficient. Conversely, since replacement with two does not add to the population, it is not settling the world. And since children do not always survive to adulthood,

the verse could suggest a duty to have more than two. The expansive meaning was the one adopted by the Halakhah. (See Feldman, *Birth Control in Jewish Law*, 48, cf. 12.)

5. Rabbi Joshua based his ruling on Eccles. 11:6, "In the morning, sow thy seed, and in the evening do not withhold thy hand from continuing to sow, for you know not which will succeed, this or that, or whether they shall both alike be good" (BT Yevamot 62b).

6. Because Gen. 1:28 ends with "and subdue it," the rabbis held that only men, who subdue the earth, are duty bound to multiply.

7. *Genesis Rabbah* 8:12. "Rabbi Eleazar in the name of Rabbi Yose ben Zimra [says: Be fruitful and multiply and fill the earth and] 'you [plural] subdue it' *(kivshuha)* is read, but 'subdue her' *(kivshah)* is written. [This means that] the man is commanded to 'be fruitful and multiply' and not the woman. Rabbi Yohanan ben Beroka says both the man and the woman are meant [since it is written]: 'And God blessed them (both) saying "Be fruitful and multiply . . ."' [The reason that there is a difference between the read and written forms of] *kivshuha* and *kivshah* is because the man subdues his wife so that she does not go seeking in the marketplace."

8. *Shulhan Arukh, Even HaEzer* 1:2 and 1:4.

9. The *nazir* is a person who took a vow to live for a period of time as a holy ascetic, denying for spiritual purposes the enjoyment of wine. At the end of the time period when his vow terminates, he must bring a sin offering to the temple for the sin of his temporary rejection of worldly pleasure. See BT Ta'anit 11a.

10. JT Kiddushin 4:12, 66d.

11. BT Sanhedrin 36b; *Yad, Hilkhot Sanhedrin* 2:3.

12. R. Yose said: "The Son of David will not come before all the souls of the *guf* will have been embodied" (BT Niddah 13b).

13. *Tosafot* to Yevamot 12b is permissive, despite BT Yevamot 64a. See Rabbi Moshe Isserles on *Shulhan Arukh, Even HaEzer* 1:3; Responsa *Naharei Afarsimon, Even HaEzer* 18; *Arukh ha-Shulhan, Even HaEzer* 154:25; and Responsa *Tzitz Eliezer* 8:48.1.

14. *Song of Songs Rabbah* 1:2; and *Pesikta d'Rav Kahana* 22:2.

15. Rashi, commenting on Gen. 2:22, suggests that women are indeed a "building for eternity." Women are "built" to contain the growing fetus, wide below and narrow above, like a granary that is wide below and narrow above so that its contents do not bear too forcefully on its walls.

16. BT Ketubbot 8a.

17. Kimelman, "Homosexuality and Family-Centered Judaism," 53–57.

18. Sometimes referred to as well as *hash-hatat zera levatalah,* purposeless destruction of seed. Generally these two terms are used interchangeably. See Feldman, *Birth Control in Jewish Law,* 109.

19. Satlow, *Tasting the Dish,* 246–60.

20. The stoics associated masturbation with a lack of self-control and believed that self-arousal incited "evil desire." Perhaps this is why the Palestinian rabbis under the sway of Greco-Roman culture seem to have been more extreme in regard to self-arousal than were the Babylonians. Ibid., 261–63.

21. Ibid., 246–60.

22. *Zohar,* Vayeshev 188a, Vayehi 219b.

23. See *Bet Shmuel* on *Even HaEzer* 23:1. The *Bet Shmuel* rejects the *Zohar's* extreme position cited in the *Shulhan Arukh*. For skeptical views of the *Zohar's* description of masturbation, see Rabbi Jacob Emden in *Mitpahat Sefarim* 1:20; and *Avnei HaEfod* (Sofia, 1912), Commentary to *Even HaEzer 23 (hetev harah lo)* and *Tzitz Eliezer* 9:51. For the codified statement, see *Shulhan Arukh, Even ha-Ezer* 23:1.

24. Rabbi Aaron HaLevi of Barcelona, *Sefer HaHinnukh,* commandment no. 209. The obligation to sexually pleasure one's wife is one of the three duties of a husband to his wife. He must provide clothing, food, and conjugal pleasure. See *Mekhilta* to Exod. 21:10. The Talmud discusses how often a man is duty bound to have intercourse with his wife and makes the determination dependent on the profession of the husband. It is also important to note that the *Hinnukh* adds to the quoted rationale an aesthetic judgment on male sexual relations: "Moreover, it is a crazy, disgusting, and ugly act in the extreme in the eyes of the Everpresent and all intelligent people." The *Hinnukh* likely infers this aesthetic judgment of male sexual intercourse from the word *toevah,* which means "hateful" or "disgusting." God's disgust, however, is not a rationale, but a mere repetition of the verse. Rationales must provide an answer as to why God so detests the behavior.

25. See BT Niddah 13b, where Rabbi Ami cites Onan but claims his sin was lustful thoughts, not improper seminal emission.

26. *Tosafot* to Sanhedrin 59b, s.v. *v'ah; Mishnah Rabbi Eliezer* 18:338.

27. "When you lay siege to a city for many days to do battle against it to capture it, do not destroy its trees, hewing them with an ax, for from them you eat. You shall not destroy it, for is a tree like a man that can flee before you in a siege?" From this text about the destruction of fruit trees the sages derived a general prohibition of wanton destruction of any kind (*Kitzur Shulhan Arukh* 190:3).

28. *Binyan Tziyyon* 137, Rabbi Jacob Ettlinger, nineteenth-century halakhist.

29. Maimonides, *Mishnah Commentary, Sanhedrin* 7:4. It is important to note that while the argument of whether the rule is biblical or rabbinic seems technical, it is not. What is at the center of debate is the very meaning of sexuality and its relationship to procreation. If the rule is biblical, then semen is marked as the vital fluid that gives humans godlike power, and ejaculation is, depending on the circumstances, either creation or destruction.

Seminal discharge in the vagina is akin to birth, a miraculous channeling of divine power through a man into a woman to create a human being; outside the vagina the same act becomes a criminal frustration of human life, an act akin to murder. If the law is rabbinic, then the prohibition becomes a spiritual discipline, a social enforcement of early marriage, or a pragmatic way to focus the sexuality of husbands solely on their wives.

30. Indeed, the verse that prohibits anal intercourse between men leads the sages to determine that the same act is permissible between married partners of the opposite sex. The term for anal intercourse between heterosexuals is *biah shelo kedarka,* meaning "intercourse not in its usual fashion" (BT Sanhedrin 54a).

31. This early rabbinic ruling nonetheless seemed beyond comprehension to some later scholars. The most dramatic rejection of the talmudic leniency in regard to anal sex with one's wife is found in a work by Rabbi Eleazar Azikri, a mystic of Safed in the late sixteenth century. "There is no sanction at all for unnatural intercourse. And woe to him who is lenient, for the author of the *Zohar* has written that there is no remedy for this sin except great and constant repentance. The following happened right here in Safed in the year 1548 in the presence of Rabbi Joseph Caro, Rabbi Isaac Masoud, Rabbi Abraham Shalom, my teacher Rabbi Joseph Sagis, and several others; a wife appeared before them and reported that her husband had been indulging in such a practice. The rabbis thereupon excommunicated him and wanted 'to burn him with fire.' In the end, they 'ran him out' of Palestine. May God protect the remnant of Israel from sin and guilt" (*Sefer Haredim* 3:2).

32. *Tosafot Rid* to BT Yevamot 12b.

33. Responsa *Mahane Hayyim* 53 (Pressburg, 1862).

34. However, where the threat to life is real, Orthodox rabbis have supported the use of condoms. "While Jewish law generally frowns upon the use of condoms as a contraceptive, it would permit their use as a means to prevent the spread of a life-threatening illness. The Torah would not require an AIDS patient to practice lifetime abstinence. . . . If adolescents are going to be sexually active, they should be aware of precautionary steps" (from Webzine post: *Jewish Law Articles: Examining Halacha, Jewish Issues and Secular Law*, "AIDS: A Jewish Perspective," Rabbi Yitzchok Breitowitz (available online at www.jlaw.com/Articles/aids.html).

35. BT Megillah 13a.

36. Chaim Rapoport, "Judaism and Homosexuality," *Jewish Chronicle (London),* March 2000.

37. Ibid.

38. BT Avodah Zarah 3a.

39. *Tosafot* to Yevamot 12b, s.v. *shalosh nashim.* The context of the opinion is in regard to whether a woman is prohibited from destroying her

husband's seed after intercourse. Since a woman is not obligated in regard to the commandment of procreation, she is not prohibited from destroying the male seed in her body.

40. Novak, "Religious Communities, Secular Society, and Sexuality," 15.

41. These purposes are identical to the specific aims offered by ethicist Timothy Sedgewick in an article written in 1989, "Christian Ethics and Human Sexuality; Mapping the Conversation" (unpublished manuscript).

42. The notion of a universal natural law commanding principles of justice and morality and deriving from reason in accord with nature had an enormous influence on Christian thought. The idea is found in the New Testament. Natural law, in the words of Rom. 2:14, is "written on the hearts" of those who, unlike the Jews, do not have the Mosaic Law. For Paul conscience reveals the law. For Thomas Aquinas the law derives directly from reason. It is what comes naturally to people to think and to do when they are not perverted by passion, an evil habit, or a corrupt nature. Such a law is both given over to the individual to discover and universal in its application. See *Summa Theologica* 2a2ae.154, 11.

43. Fox, *Interpreting Maimonides*, 124.

44. Kirkpatrick, "Evolution of Human Homosexual Behavior," 11.

45. Bagemihl, *Biological Exuberance*, 12.

46. Novak, "Religious Communities, Secular Society, and Sexuality," 25.

47. BT Kiddushin 29b.

48. One text suggests that perhaps he did betroth R. Akiva's daughter; however, it was assumed that the wedding never actually took place. See *tosafot*, s.v. *bartei d'Rabbi Akiva*, on BT Ketubbot 63a.

49. BT Yevamot 63b.

50. "For thus said the Lord, the Creator of heaven who alone is God, who formed the earth and made it, who alone established it, he did not create it a wasteland, but formed it for habitation" (Isa. 45:18).

51. *Arukh ha-Shulhan, Even HaEzer, Hilkhot Pirya v'Rivya* 1:1.

11. The Rationale of Social Disruption

1. BT Nedarim 50b.

2. Isa. 19:14; 21:4; 28:7.

3. As in Ezek. 14:11 and 44:10, for example.

4. There are other stories of Bar Kappara humiliating the wealthy and unlearned Ben Elasah by giving him a poetic riddle to say to his father-in-law as if it were a genuine problem. The riddle was actually a jesting criticism of Rabbi's household and the fear that he inspired. Bar Kappara's behavior in this instance so angered his teacher that Rabbi told him he would never be given rabbinic ordination. See JT Moed Katan 3:1.

5. It is not uncommon for men in the ultra-Orthodox world to be married by or before the age of twenty-two. Women are most often married and have their first child by this age.

6. Rabbi Ronen Luvitz is one of the rabbis who discourage gay people from marriage. He has written a groundbreaking article in Hebrew on the topic of homosexuality; see his "Selidah Sovlanut o Matiranut: Yakhas haYahadut le-Homoseksualiyut" (Revulsion, tolerance or permissiveness: The Jewish response to homosexuality). Rabbi Shlomo Aviner is one of the rabbis who maintain that after marriage everything will work out. He has begun an Israeli organization, Atzat Nefesh (Counsel of the Soul), which is very similar to reparative support groups such as NARTH and Jews Offering New Alternatives to Homosexuality (JONAH) in the United States. Rabbi Aviner published a short correspondence with a desperate young man in the winter of 2002. The following is an excerpt:

Question: I am a young man, but I feel like an old man at the end of his life. For years I have been deeply immersed in sexual lust, in all forms of sin, so terrible and debased that I cannot put them to paper. A thousand times I overcame it only to fall down again. I am hopeless. I wouldn't dare study Torah or to hold a Torah scroll in my impure hands. Nor would I ever dare to marry. I am utterly hopeless. I have seen a thousand psychologists, and they didn't help me at all. In the end a psychologist told me I had come to a level of addiction from which he could not extricate me; I was lost. I think that he is right. I already cannot live without the satisfaction of my desire. I also have no one to talk to about all this; no one understands me. Surely God, too, is disgusted with me and is not interested in me.

Answer: That you are embarrassed is a good sign that your soul is pure. That you are hopeless is wonderful because it testifies that there is within you a spark that is not corrupted, a pure spirit, and with its help it is possible turn the whole situation around a Garden of Eden of wholesomeness. If you are writing me, it is a sign that you have not made peace, a sign that you have not laid down your weapon, and with God's help, you will triumph in the end. Behold, you are a waging a difficult battle against the evil inclination. But know that you are not alone in the struggle. We are all with you. Each man is before his own inclination. [The Ethics of the Fathers asks:] Who is a hero? [It answers:] He who conquers his inclination. . . . It says, "his inclination," and not the inclination of his neighbor. For this reason let no man speak with pride of his conquest over his own inclination. This is not greatness. Perhaps were he in his friend's place, in his situation and with his life circumstances, he would fare much worse than his friend. So, don't judge your friend until you arrive at his place. The evil inclination for sexual sin is one of the strongest in man, perhaps the strongest. It's also a necessary inclination because it helps to unite a man and his wife. Therefore, be strong in your war; you have other fighters at your side with you, each man on his own watch. Surely the master of the universe loves you and understands you . . . fight my friend, fight and in the end you will win. Now it appears that you cannot survive without this . . . but the more that you overcome your inclination, the more you will be in another place, a higher place, and you will see that it is possible to live without it. In the end you will be a complete *baal teshuva* ["master of return," a person restored to existence before a moral or religious decline], clean and pure. In the end you will marry and be happy. *And when you marry, never speak a word of this to your wife. Behold, you have repented, so all is wiped away, as if it never happened, never occurred, consumed and burned.* Regret burns everything up. Learn Torah, learn works of moral edification and faith without stop. From there take strength. This will be a long battle, but look ahead to the light and walk forward, and you will rise in holiness and not diminish. Humble your inclination a little at a time, but with fierceness, moment by moment, day by day. ("Meged Yerahim," *Shevat* 5762 [February–March 2002])

7. Rich, "Compulsory Heterosexuality and Lesbian Existence."

12. The Rationale of Category Confusion

1. It is interesting that three different meanings of "one flesh" appear in the rabbinic literature. According to Rashi the one flesh is the child the sexual union between a man and a woman creates. Ramban disagrees and suggests that the "one flesh" is descriptive of the new kinship that marriage to a woman creates. A man's wife is closer to him, more his "flesh" than his own parents. Ibn Ezra suggests that the "one flesh" is simply the sexual union in intimacy that restores the two to the androgynous one.

2. Ibn Ezra on Lev. 18:22.

3. Boyarin, "Are There Any Jews in 'The History of Sexuality'?"

4. The talmudic discussion in BT Nazir 59a suggests that sexual intent is central to the prohibition, for otherwise why would the verse use the word abomination *(toevah)*, the word so directly associated in Leviticus 18 with sexual violations? However, the rabbinic rulings concerning shaving the genitals and other such practices appear to be motivated by categorical purity.

5. Rashi on Deuteronomy 22:5 thinks this ploy is particularly useful for adulterers, whereas Ramban and Rashbam think the male cross-dresser is not so much plotting a tryst with a particular woman as simply seeking an erotic adventure.

6. As noted in chapter 3, Nissinen describes cross-dressing as a sign of devotion to a foreign goddess (*Homoeroticism in the Biblical World*, 41).

7. One of the running themes of the *Guide for the Perplexed* is that

Judaism came to eradicate the false opinions of idolatry. To this end, many of the prohibitions against mixing, such as seething a kid in its mother's milk, wearing a garment woven of linen and wool, and cross-dressing are designed to keep us far away from heathen practice. In particular, see *Guide* 3:37, where he refers to a pagan ritual that required a male to wear a woman's dyed garment and a woman to wear military gear while standing before the planet Venus.

8. Regarding Maimonides' view, see *Sefer HaMitsvot* 350. For examples of standard modern commentaries, see Hertz, *Pentateuch and the Haftorahs,* 848; and Plaut, *Torah,* 1,497. The association of male homosexual relations with pagan ritual has also been employed thoughtfully by a contemporary rabbi, Rabbi Bradley Artson. He has written a responsum that suggests the Torah prohibited homosexual relations because it knows only of male sexual interaction as either rape or idolatrous practice. According to Artson the Torah simply does not address the contemporary reality of gay coupling. He claims that the form of committed monogamous loving homosexuality is not what the Torah prohibits. See Bradley S. Artson, "Gay and Lesbian Jews: An Innovative Legal Position," *Jewish Spectator.* (winter 1990): 6. I have avoided this rationale for three reasons: 1) It overly historicizes the text. This rationale has been used by the Reform movement to dispense with many traditions, including the separation of milk and meat, which was also associated with pagan ritual; 2) Other sexual prohibitions in Leviticus 18 are not directly associated with paganism; 3) Consent and loving emotional bonds would not seem to permit incest or adultery.

9. Fymer-Kensky, *In the Wake of the Goddesses,* 200–202.

10. Jeffrey Tigay, *The Jewish Publication Society Torah Commentary: Deuteronomy* (New York: Jewish Publication Society, 1996), 480–81.

11. See *Sifrei Devarim* 260; *Mavo LeTalmud* loc. cit.; and S. E. Loewenstramm, "Qadesh," in *Encyclopedia Biblica* 7:35–36.

12. A debate on this issue between Rabbi Akiva and Rabbi Ishmael is found in BT Sanhedrin 54b. R. Ishmael uses the verse in Deuteronomy to prohibit giving oneself over to anal penetration, understanding the verse in Leviticus as prohibiting only the penetrative act. R. Akiva rejects this use of the verse and understands both active and passive partners to be covered by Lev. 18:22.

13. See BT Nazir 59a; Rambam, *Hilkhot Avodat Kohavim* 12:9–10; *Shulhan Arukh, Yoreh De'ah* 182:5.

14. BT Berakhot 43b; Rambam, *Laws of Opinions* 5:9.

15. Daniel Boyarin in "Are There Any Jews in 'The History of Sexuality'?" argues for this rationale as the central one, both in biblical and in rabbinic traditions.

16. Mary Douglas explains that sexual dangers are always related to the body politic. Sexual prohibitions accordingly are explicit exaggerations of difference designed to make an implicit social chaos manageable. "I suggest that many ideas about sexual dangers are better interpreted as symbols of the relation between parts of society, as mirroring designs of hierarchy or symmetry which apply in the larger social system. . . . For I believe that ideas about separating, purifying, demarcating and punishing transgressions have as their main function to impose a system on an inherently untidy experience. It is only by exaggerating the difference between within and without, above and below, male and female, with and against, that a semblance of order is created" (*Purity and Danger,* 4).

17. BT Sanhedrin 108a.

18. *Genesis Rabbah* 26:5.

19. Ibid.

20. Buber, *Midrash Tehillim* 104.

21. BT Hullin 92a.

22. Rabbi Judah Loew, *Sifrei Maharal Hiddushei Aggadot,* 4:113.

23. Stout, *Ethics after Babel,* 145–62.

24. Stout suggests that Douglas's work *Purity and Danger* inspired his theory of moral abomination.

25. Stout, *Ethics after Babel,* 158.

26. Lev. 19:19 does not make this clear, but Deut. 22:9 does.

27. I am grateful to Rabbi Dr. Milgrom for our many conversations on chapters 18–20 of Leviticus.

28. The cherubim are winged creatures with the faces of babies, and they were thought of in Israel as the throne of God (Exod. 25:17–22). Ezekiel's vision of four heavenly beings begins the book. Each being had four faces—that of a human, a lion, an ox, and an eagle—facing different directions (Ezek. 1:4–28).

29. Mishnah Bikkurim 2:8 and 4:1.

30. The difference between wild animals and domesticated animals is significant primarily with regard to the laws of slaughter and to the sacrificial cult.

31. BT Yevamot 83a, Mishna Yevamot 4:5. Here R. Meir holds the opinion ascribed to R. Jose in Yevamot.

32. See Mishnah Bikkurim 4:2, where the *androgynus* must dress like a man and marry a woman.

33. Mishnah Bekhorot 41a; Rashi loc. cit. s.v. *v'hakhamim omrim eino bekhor.*

34. BT Shabbat 53b.

35. BT Berakhot 58b.

36. Meiri on BT Berakhot 58b.

13. The Rationale of Humiliation and Violence

1. In another tradition Nebuchadnezzar used to cast lots to see which of his noblemen he would sexually penetrate that day. When, after the defeat of Israel Nebuchadnezzar did the same to her former king, Zedekiah, his member extended three hundred cubits (roughly four hundred feet!) and wagged in front of the whole company of captive kings (BT Shabbat 149b).

2. *Tanhuma, Parashat Vaera* 8, with interpolations from JT Kiddushin 1:7, 61a. The order in which the kings are mentioned has been rearranged for clarity's sake in the translation.

3. *Genesis Rabbah* 63:10.

4. *Otzar Midrashim* 34.

5. See Cantarella, *Bisexuality in the Ancient World,* 98ff.

6. Foucault, *History of Sexuality,* vol. 2, *Uses of Pleasure,* 215.

7. Boyarin, "Are There Any Jews in 'The History of Sexuality'?" 333.

8. Halperin, *One Hundred Years,* 22–24, 88–112.

9. Ibid., 97.

10. My practice, as I have noted earlier, is not only to refuse to say the blessing of thanks for not being a woman but to say in its place the blessing that women were assigned. I do so for several reasons. First, to the extent that my gender/sexual identity is a divine gift, I wish to receive it in praise and joy. Being gay for me is "according to his will." Second, in doing so I wish to transform a blessing constructed as a submission to painful divine decree, similar in form to the blessing said over the dead, "Blessed be the righteous Judge," to a celebration of difference without hierarchy. Thus it also becomes a prayer that I learn to relinquish my male rights in the service of God, something nearly impossible to do. Also see chapter 4 and the discussion of Kalonymus ben Kalonymus's resigned acceptance of maleness, using the traditional morning blessing.

11. Abudarham, *Sefer Abudarham HaShalem,* 11–47

12. *Exodus Rabbah* (Vilna) 1:14.

13. BT Sanhedrin 54b; Rambam, *Laws of Prohibited Intercourse* 1:14.

14. Kabbalists found equal amounts of male and female divine forces inside the godhead. This reference is not then saying that God is male, but that at this moment in the development of a boy, the maleness below corresponds to that above.

15. Rabbi Joseph Hayyim ben Elijah al-Hakham in *Torah LeShama* 441.

16. Mishnah Sanhedrin 8:7; and Rashi on BT Sanhedrin 73a, s.v. *de-lav orheih.*

17. See Abraham Chill, *The Mitzvot* (New York: Bloch Books, 1974), 455.

18. Gravdal, *Ravishing Maidens,* 1–20, 42–71.

19. Deut. 22:28.

20. Rashi on Gen. 34:1, "Now, Dina, the daughter of Leah." interprets the unnecessary reference to Dina as the daughter of Leah, something already known, to a similarity between daughter and mother. Both were gadabouts. Leah is a deemed so because she ventured out to Jacob, having purchased his company for the night. Genesis 30:16. See also *Midrash Yelammedenu, Yalkut Talmud Torah, Bereishit* 149:95.

21. Bestiality does not easily fit into this paradigm. One could suggest that sex with an animal is violence against the animal. While this might seem a bit farfetched, the tradition did not permit killing an animal that had gored a man to death unless a capital court was convened, witnesses to the event gave their testimony, and the court voted to convict. For an interesting treatment of bestiality see Stout, *Ethics after Babel,* chap. 7.

22. BT Ketubbot 103a.

23. Rambam *Yad, Manrim,* 6:15.nic

24. BT Kiddushin 57a.

25. No doubt such trust is won in part by experiencing the law generally to be just and good, which is itself a form of rationalization.

26. BT Berakhot 33b.

27. *Leviticus Rabbah* 32:8, *Va-Yetze.*

28. BT Kiddushin

14. Admitting Difference

1. I thank Rabbi Doniel Kramer for his alerting me to a tape recording of Rabbi Turk's story about Rabbi Soloveitchik.

2. A popular etymology turns the word *teku* into an acronym for "Elijah will solve all the difficulties and problems."

3. Rabbi Moshe Tendler, following his father-in-law, Rabbi Feinstein, also views gay sex as a "willful, voluntary perversion." See Rabbi Moshe Dovid Tendler, "Treife Sex" (letter to the editor), *The Jewish Week,* June 2, 2000, 6–7.

4. Nathaniel S. Lehrman, "Homosexuality: A Political Mask for Promiscuity: A Psychiatrist Reviews the Data," *Tradition* 34, no. 1 (spring 2000).

5. Rabbi Benjamin Hecht, Untitled article, *Spark of the Week* 5754, no. 27; Boteach, "Reinterpreting Homosexuality as Human Sexuality"; Wolowelsky and Weinstein, "Initial Religious Counseling for a Male Orthodox Adolescent Homosexual." Wolowelsky and Weinstein clarified a few points in a letter to the editor in *Tradition,* 29, no. 4 (summer 1995): 93–94.

6. For some rabbis, like Rabbi Shmuley Boteach, even the comparison to adultery is wrong. Adultery and incest are moral crimes; homosexual relations, says Boteach, are a religious sin. A homosexual is like a lush who insists on eating pork.

7. BT Shabbat 68b. Many halakhists employ the concept as a lenient framework for nonobservant Jews. An interesting example of the use of the legal concept is found in *Seridei Esh* 2:10. In the 1920s Rabbi Jehiel Jacob Weinberg was the head of the Hildesheimer Rabbinical Seminary in Berlin. In a responsum he addressed the issue of the bar mitzvah of a young man who was not circumcised and whose father's business was open on Shabbat. Can the young man read the *haftorah* and can his father be given an aliyah during the synagogue services? The category of *tinok shenishah* provided a framework for lenient rulings on such matters. See as well *Teshuvot Radbaz* 5:64; *Teshuvot Hakam Tzvi* 164; *Hatam Sofer* 5 *(Hoshen Mishpat)*: 22; *Iggerot Moshe, Orah Hayyim* 13.

8. The advice to women is roughly the same except that Torah study is usually left out because it is reserved for men. Lesbians are often told that such extraneous desires will disappear in the context of marriage. While both men and women are promised salvation in marriage, women seem to be more vulnerable to the advice because women in Orthodox society are largely without any constructive role to play outside marriage and family and because no initiative is required of a woman in order to accept a marriage proposal.

9. The American Academy of Pediatrics published a policy statement in 1993 titled "Homosexuality and Adolescence" that was critical of any form of reparative therapy. Some adolescents are uncertain about their sexual orientation; for them a "counseling or psychotherapeutic initiative" aimed at clarification might be useful. "Therapy directed specifically at changing sexual orientation is contraindicated, since it can provoke guilt and anxiety while having little or no potential for achieving changes in orientation." The American Psychiatric Association released a fact sheet in 1994 that stated: "There is no published scientific evidence supporting the efficacy of 'reparative therapy' as a treatment to change ones sexual orientation. It is not described in the scientific literature, nor is it mentioned in the APA's latest comprehensive Task Force Report, 'Treatments of Psychiatric Disorders (1989).' There are a few reports in the literature of efforts to use psychotherapeutic and counseling techniques to treat persons troubled by their homosexuality who desire to become heterosexual; however, results have not been conclusive, nor have they been replicated. There is no evidence that any treatment can change a homosexual person's deep seated sexual feelings for others of the same sex." A 1990 fact sheet produced by the American Psychological Association stated that scientific evidence does not show that conversion therapy works and that it can do more harm than good. Changing one's sexual orientation is not simply a matter of changing one's sexual behavior. It would require altering one's emotional, romantic, and sexual feelings and restructuring one's self-concept and social identity. Although some mental healthcare providers

do attempt sexual orientation conversion, others question the ethics of try-ing to alter through therapy a trait that is not a disorder and that is ex-tremely important to an individual's identity. In 1996 the National Associ-ation of Social Workers (NASW) adopted a policy statement on lesbian, gay, and bisexual issues that was published in *Social Work Speaks,* 4th ed. (City: NASW, 1997). It states, in part: "Social stigmatization of lesbian, gay, and bisexual people is widespread and is a primary motivating factor in leading some people to seek sexual orientation changes. Sexual orienta-tion conversion therapies assume that homosexual orientation is both pathological and freely chosen. No data demonstrate that reparative or conversion therapies are effective, and in fact they may be harmful. In 1998 the American Psychiatric Association rejected reparative therapy as ineffec-tive and potentially destructive. The APA statement said, in part: 'The po-tential risks of "reparative therapy" are great, including depression, anxiety and self-destructive behavior, since therapist alignment with societal preju-dices against homosexuality may reinforce self-hatred already experienced by the patient. . . . Many patients who have undergone "reparative ther-apy" relate that they were inaccurately told that homosexuals are lonely, unhappy individuals who never achieve acceptance or satisfaction. . . . The possibility that the person might achieve happiness and satisfying inter-personal relationships as a gay man or lesbian is not presented, nor are al-ternative approaches to dealing with the effects of societal stigmatization discussed.'"

10. "Much Ado about Changing," *Advocate* (June 19, 2001). See B. A. Robinson, "Analysis of Dr. Spitzer's Study of Reparative Therapy," On-tario Consultants on Religious Tolerance, February 16, 2002 (www.religious tolerance.org/hom_spit.htm). Spitzer only recently published his 2001 study. See Robert L. Spitzer, "Can Some Gay Men and Lesbians Change Their Sexual Orientation? 200 Participants Reporting a Change from Ho-mosexual to Heterosexual Orientation," *Archives of Sexual Behavior* 32, no. 5 (October 2003): 403–17.

11. ABC News interview with Dr. Spitzer about the hazards of change therapy. *Good Morning America,* May 9, 2001.

12. In the early eighties a young man at Yeshiva University, troubled by his homosexual desires, came out to a religious studies teacher and was sent to Aesthetic Realism, the once popular philosophic cult of Eli Siegel, who had a theory for healing homosexuals. The therapy enforced his self-blame and made his situation worse. Six months later the young man attempted suicide and was sent home by the university, never to return.

13. Drescher, "Ethical Concerns Raised When Patients Seek to Change Same-Sex Attractions," 181–210.

14. Rabbi Aharon Feldman, "A Letter to a Homosexual Baal Teshuva," *The Jerusalem Letter,* 1, no. 5 (March 24, 1998).

15. "More with the Rabbis: Rabbi Aharon Feldman," interview, *Trembling before G-d*, DVD.

16. See Katz, *Divine Law in Human Hands;* Berkowits, *Not in Heaven;* and Rackman, *One Man's Judaism.*

17. Exod. 22:24; Lev. 25:36–37; and Deut. 23:20.

18. This process is described in an unpublished article by Rabbi Elisha Ancselovits of Yeshivat Ma'aleh Gilboa.

19. *Piskei HaRosh,* Bava Metsi'a 5:23; Mordechai, Bava Metsi'a 3:19.

20. "Deny the existence of God": JT Bava Metsi'a 5:8; Tosefta Bava Metsi'a 6:17; shedders of blood: BT Bava Metsi'a 61b; no share in the world to come: *Mekhilta Mishpatim* 19.

21. Committee on Jewish Law and Standards, "Travel on the Sabbath: A Statement Unanimously Adopted by the Committee on Jewish Law and Standards," *Conservative Judaism* 14 (1960): 50. The statement was affirmed on February 17, 1960.

22. BT Shabbat 112b.

23. See *tosafot* on Berakhot 39b, s.v. *mevarech al;* Rosh on Bava Metsi'a 3:10.

24. Susan B. Anthony was born in 1820. She met Elizabeth Cady Stanton in 1852 and became an immediate suffragettist. In 1877 she gathered petitions from twenty-six states with ten thousand signatures, but Congress laughed at them. She appeared before every Congress from 1869 to 1906 to ask for passage of a women's suffrage amendment. She fought tirelessly throughout her long life; at the age of eighty she retired from the North American Women's Suffrage Association, which she and Elizabeth Cady Stanton had founded. She died in 1906 at the age of eighty-six, fourteen years before Congress passed the Nineteenth Amendment to the Constitution, giving all adult women the right to vote. The amendment was named the Susan B. Anthony Amendment.

25. Speaking about the decision, Professor Paul Gewirtz of Yale Law School remarked that it is the role of courts "to consolidate cultural developments, legitimatize them and translate them into binding legal principal" (quoted in Linda Greenhouse, "In a Momentous Term, Justices Remake the Law, and the Court," *New York Times,* July 1, 2003, A1).

26. The most notable exception in the United States is *Brown vs. Board of Education,* which fomented enormous social change. In a similar vein the Israeli Supreme Court has enacted legal protection for homosexuals and spousal benefits for same-sex partners much in advance of other democratic legal systems and much in advance of Israeli social mores.

27. In many Orthodox circles the public acceptance of gay and lesbian relationships is seen as a symptom of American society's moral decay.

28. Had Pinhas asked the court, he would have been instructed in due process. Had Zimri separated for just a moment from intercourse, then

Pinhas would have been guilty of murder for stabbing him, and had Zimri in an attempt to protect himself, killed Pinhas, it would have been legitimate self-defense. It was said that Moses was ready to excommunicate Pinhas and would have had not a Divine message intervened. In the Middle Ages, Ibn Ezra is patently uncomfortable with Pinhas. He does not want vigilante justice to be included in the divine praise, so he presumes that Pinhas was indeed acting on the basis of witnesses and warning, i.e., essentially with legal authority.

29. *Mei Shiloah, Parshat Pinhas.*

30. Abraham Isaac Kook, *Arpelei Tohar,* 15. I was informed of this original version of the text by Rabbi Yehuda Gilad. This text was first amended by Rabbi Kook's son, Rabbi Tzvi Yehuda Kook, to read "the matter is fixed by a breaking [of the law] which, of itself, makes us sad, while its end result gives us joy." Then in later editions the entire piece was removed.

31. From a letter written by Don Seeman to "Rabbi Yaakov Levado" in care of *Tikkun* magazine, November 1993. When Don Seeman wrote to me about *satyagraha,* I was still in the closet, and he had no idea that he was writing to a friend. At the end of his letter he wrote that I could not claim to be motivated by the truth force while hiding in the closet, that there was no legitimate way to challenge the halakhic system with *satyagraha* while using the protection of a pseudonym. I thankfully attribute to his heartfelt letter a measure of my decision to come out of the closet and bear the consequences.

32. On the specific matter at hand it should be noted that Rabbi Kook did not advocate any halakhic leniency. To the contrary, he countered emerging scientific opinions of the innate nature of homosexual orientation with the following claim: "The awakening of the new science [of psychology] on the matter of the natural inclination of some people from birth, who for this reason want to uproot the ethical protest to it, [will fail] for the word of the God will stand forever. Bar Kappara already explained this, *"toevah: toeh attah bah"* (abomination: you wander through this). It is a bad inclination that an individual and society must fight. The claim that perhaps you will find an individual for whom it will not be possible to uproot this [inclination] was already anticipated by the sages. Everything that a man wants to do with his wife he may do . . . just like a fish that he brings home from the fisherman. If he wants to eat it roasted, boiled, or baked, so he eats it. [A man may have sex with his wife in any way he wishes, including anal sex.] In this the sages understood the nature of men and even had mercy on the ones damaged from birth." The implication is that anal sex with one's wife is permitted in order to fulfill the desire that a homosexual man may have for anal intercourse with a man. See Rabbi Abraham Isaac Kook, *Orot HaKodesh,* in (Jerusalem: Mosad HaRav Kook), 3:297.

33. Rashi explains the idea of a "decree of the King" well in his comment to Gen. 26:5: "Because Abraham has hearkened to my voice; he has

kept my charge, my commandments, my statutes and my laws." Rashi explains the difference between commandments (mitzvot) commandments and statutes *(hukim):* Commandments are rational duties "that even if they were not written in the Torah would commend themselves to us, such as [the prohibition of] theft and murder." Statutes are "duties that the evil inclination and the nations of the world reject, such as eating pork and wearing a garment of linen and wool mixed together, laws for which there is no reason but which are decrees of the King, commands to his servants."

34. The punishment for violating *niddah* is *karet,* meaning that one is cut off, from the community, from God, from perhaps even future progeny. Without intercourse gay men violate no prohibition of such weight.

35. Given the traditional distinction between moral and religious/ritual ordinances, Rabbi Shmuley Boteach suggests that the prohibition of male homosexual relations should be considered of the religious variety. Just as no one would consider a Jew who eats cheeseburgers to be immoral for doing so, we should not consider homosexuals particularly immoral. For this position he has been sharply criticized in Orthodox circles. Rabbi Yitzchok Adlerstein and Rabbi Ezra Schochet have criticized him on this in the context of his debate with Dr. Laura. (See Boteach, "Dr. Laura Misguided on Homosexuality.")

36. BT Berakhot 19b.

37. Surely some people have claimed as much in regard to *niddah.* In a recent Israeli film, *Tehora,* married Orthodox couples share how *niddah* can be both an enhancing spiritual practice and a terribly burdensome and even painful rigor of detachment.

38. BT Avodah Zara 54a

39. See BT Hagiga 3b, 4a.

40. Lamm, Rabbi Norman, "Judaism and the Modern Attitude to Homosexuality," *Encyclopedia Judaica Year Book* 1974, 194–205. Reprinted in *Contemporary Jewish Ethics,* ed. Menachem Marc Kellner (New York: Sanhedrin Press, 1978), 375–99, and Jewish Bioethics, ed. Fred Rosner and J. David Bleich (Brooklyn: Hebrew Publishing Company, 1979), 197–218.

41. Riskin, Rabbi Shlomo, "Gays Sacrifice Their Future," *Jerusalem Post,* April 30, 1993, 8.

42. The excuses men use to blame their sexual violence on the incitement of women, the "boys will be boys" defense that turns rapists into victims of their own unstoppable sexual compulsions, was anathema to the rabbis. The sages of the Talmud record just such a circumstance: "It happened that a certain man set eyes on a certain woman [and became so enamored of her] that his heart was consumed by his ardent desire [and his life was endangered]. When inquiry was made of physicians, they said, "There is no remedy other than she submit to him." The sages said, "Let

him die, rather than she submit." Not only do the sages deny the dying man the right to demand sexual favors, they refuse to let his "illness" compel her to even talk to him from behind a screen. "Let him die rather than she be forced to talk to him from behind a screen" (BT Sanhedrin 75a). Clearly, lust is not a blanket excuse for the violation of sexual mores.

43. BT Ketubot 51b.

44. Entertaining the transformation of a woman's consent in the midst of a rape is disquieting, to say the least, dangerously participating in typically violent male fantasies by which women can be forced into wild sexual passion by rape. As pointed out later, the rabbis entertain a parallel circumstance by which a male might be deemed a victim of a woman in a similar forced sexual encounter.

45. BT Yevamot 53b.

46. Rabad and Maggid Mishne on Mishne Torah Issurei Bi'ah 1:9. Of course, what is missing in this Talmudic analysis of force, agency and overwhelming pleasure is male-male sex. What might the law say about a man, who, being anally raped by another man, becomes enflamed with passion and desire and finds his "no" transformed to "yes!"? That a man might experience receptive sexual intercourse as pleasurable, let alone passionately so, was obviously not in the cultural lexicon of the rabbis.

47. Rabbi J. David Bleich, "Homosexuality" *Judaism and Healing: Halakhic Perspectives,* 69–73. Rabbi Michael Samuel. "What Can Traditional Judaism Say to the Religious Homosexual?" *Ask a Rabbi,* www.jewish .com/askarabbi/askarabbi/askr731.htm (1999), accessed 24 June 2004.

48. Pirkei Avot 2:5.

49. Rapoport, *Judaism and Homosexuality: An Authentic Orthodox View,* 76–81.

50. Rambam, Hilchot Mamrim 3:3

51. Chajes, *Minchat Kena'ot,* published in *Kol Kitvei Maratz Chayes,* 2:1013.

52. Schwab, "The Shepherd and His Flock," in *Selected Writings,* 174.

53. Wasserman, *Reb Simcha Speaks,* 45.

54. Rapoport, *Judaism and Homosexuality: An Authentic Orthodox View,* 81.

55. Hatred of sin does not appear in Bible. Hatred of evil, on the other hand, is a common pairing. In Hebrew to sin is to "miss the mark." Ordinary human failing does not deserve hatred whereas human cruelty and malevolence do. "Hate evil and love good," (Amos 5:15). "To fear the Lord is to hate evil," (Proverbs 8:13). "Those who love the Lord hate evil," (Psalms 97:12). However, a similar distinction between sinners and sins does appear in a famous Talmudic controversy between Rabbi Meir and his wife Beruria. Beruria challenges her husband to pray, not for the end of

violent sinners by death, but for the end of sin by repentance. Rabbi Meir prayed that the men threatening him not die, but repent, and they did. (Brachot 10a).

56. The widening or constricting of a law's application is a common legal tool. The sages used it temporally (Is the law in force at all times, or only when the Temple stands?), spatially (Is the law in force everywhere or only in the land of Israel?), and in regard to kinds of persons (Is the law in force for everyone, or only for men?).

57. An Orthodox *dayan* (rabbinic judge) once suggested to me that were one to entertain such a halakhic position, the verse in Leviticus might possibly be parsed: "And a male you shall not sexually penetrate in the manner of penetrating a woman (when) it is abhorrent."

Bibliography

Adlerstein, Rabbi Yitzchok. "Lieberman, Schlessinger, and Boteach." *Cross-Currents* 2, no. 4 (2000) (www.cross-currents.com/Archives.html).

Bagemihl, Bruce. *Biological Exuberance.* New York: St. Martins Press, 1999.

Bailey, Derrick Sherwin. *Homosexuality and the Western Christian Tradition.* London: Longmans, Green, 1955.

Bawer, Bruce, ed. *Beyond Queer: Challenging Gay Left Orthodoxy.* New York: Free Press, 1996.

Berkowits, Eliezer. *Not in Heaven: The Nature and Function of Halakha.* New York: Ktav Publishing House, 1983.

Bleich, Rabbi J. David. *Judaism and Healing: Halakhic Perspectives.* New York: Ktav Publishing House, 1981.

Boswell, John. "Revolutions, Universals, Categories." *Salmagundi* 58–59: 89–113.

Boteach, Shmuley. "Dr. Laura Misguided on Homosexuality." *New York Jewish Week,* May 26, 2000.

———. "Reinterpreting Homosexuality as Human Sexuality." *Oxford-Judaism Mailing List,* June 29, 1993 (www.shamash.org/listarchives/oxford-judaism/homosexuality).

Boyarin, Daniel. "Are There Any Jews in 'The History of Sexuality'?" *Journal of the History of Sexuality* 5, no. 3 (1995): 333–35.

———. *Intertextuality and the Reading of Midrash.* Indiana University Press, 1990.

———. *Unheroic Conduct.* Berkeley: University of California Press, 1997.

Cantarella, Eve. *Bisexuality in the Ancient World.* New Haven, Conn.: Yale University Press, 1992.

Chajes, Tzvi Hirsh. *Kol Kitvei Maratz Chayes.* Volume 2. Jerusalem: N.p., 1958.

Douglas, Mary. *Purity and Danger.* London: Routledge, 1996.

Dover, K. J. *Greek Homosexuality.* New York: Vintage Books, 1978.

Drescher, Jack. "Ethical Concerns Raised When Patients Seek to Change Same-Sex Attractions." In *Sexual Conversion Therapy: Ethical, Clinical and Research Perspectives,* ed. A. Shidlo, M. Schroeder, and J. Drescher. Binghamton, N.Y: Haworth Medical Press, 2002. Originally published in *Journal of Gay & Lesbian Psychotherapy* 5, no. 3/4 (2001): 181–210.

Duberman, Martin Bauml, Martha Vincus, and George Chauncey, eds. *Hidden from History.* New York: NAL, 1989.

Dynes, Wayne. *Homosexuality: A Research Guide*. New York: Garland, 1987.

Eilberg-Schwartz, Howard. *God's Phallus*. Boston: Beacon Press, 1994.

Feldman, Rabbi Aharon. "A Letter to a Homosexual Baal Teshuva." *Jerusalem Letter,* 1, no. 5 (March 24, 1998) (www.jerusalemletter.co.il/archives/March24,1998/index.htm).

Feldman, David. *Birth Control in Jewish Law*. New York: New York University Press, 1968.

Fisch, Menahem. *Rational Rabbis*. Bloomington: Indiana University Press, 1997.

Foucault, Michel. *The History of Sexuality.* Vol. 1, *An Introduction*. New York: Vintage, 1980.

———. *The History of Sexuality.* Vol. 2, *The Uses of Pleasure*. New York: Vintage, 1990.

Fox, Marvin. *Interpreting Maimonides*. Chicago: University of Chicago Press, 1990.

Fymer-Kensky, Tikva. *In the Wake of the Goddesses: Women, Culture, and the Biblical Transformation of Pagan Myth*. New York: Fawcett Book Group, 1993.

Gravdal, Kathryn. *Ravishing Maidens*. Philadelphia: University of Pennsylvania Press, 1991.

Halperin, David M. "One Hundred Years of Homosexuality." *Diacritics* 16 (1986): 34–45.

———. *One Hundred Years of Homosexuality and Other Essays on Greek Love*. New York: Routledge, 1990.

Heelas, Paul, Scott Lash, and Paul Morris eds. *Detraditionalization: Critical Reflections on Authority and Identity*. Cambridge, Mass.: Blackwell, 1996.

Hertz, J. H. *The Pentateuch and the Haftorahs*. London: Soncino, 1936.

Jacobson, Issachar. *Netiv Bina*. Tel Aviv: Sinai, 1981.

Jakobovitz, Immanuel. "Homosexuality." In *The Encyclopedia Judaica*. New York: Macmillan/Keter, 1971.

Katz, Jacob. *Divine Law in Human Hands: Case Studies in Halakhic Flexibility*. Jerusalem: Magnes Press, Hebrew University of Jerusalem, 1998.

Kellner, Menachem Marc, ed. *Contemporary Jewish Ethics*. New York: Sanhedrin Press, 1978.

Kimelman, Reuven. "Homosexuality and Family-Centered Judaism." *Tikkun* (July/August 1994): 53–57.

Kirkpatrick, R. C. "The Evolution of Human Homosexual Behavior." *Current Anthropology* 41, no. 3 (2000): 11.

Knight, Douglas A. "Ancient Israelite Cosmology: Images and Evaluations." In *The Church and Contemporary Cosmology: Proceedings of a Consultation of the Presbyterian Church (U.S.A.),* edited by James B.

Miller and Kenneth E. McCall, 29–46. Pittsburgh: Carnegie Mellon University, 1990.

Lamm, Norman. "Judaism and the Modern Attitude to Homosexuality." In *The Encyclopedia Judaica Year Book*. New York: Macmillan/Keter, 1974. Reprinted in Menachem Marc Kellner, ed. *Contemporary Jewish Ethics* (New York: Sanhedrin Press, 1978) and in Fred Rosner and J. David Bleich, eds. Jewish Bioethics (Brooklyn: Hebrew Publishing Company, 1979).

Langa, Yitzchak Shimshon, ed. *Perushe Rav Yehudah HeHasid.* Jerusalem: Wurtzweiler Foundation, 1975.

Lehrman, Nathaniel S. "Homosexuality: A Political Mask for Promiscuity: A Psychiatrist Reviews the Data." *Tradition* 34, no. 1 (spring 2000): 44–62.

Leibowitz, Yeshayahu. *Emunah, Historiah ve'Arachim.* Jerusalem: Akademon Press, Hebrew University Of Jerusalem, 1982.

Lerner, Michael, ed. *Best Contemporary Jewish Writing.* San Francisco: Josey Bass, 2001.

Levinas, Emmanuel. *Beyond the Verse: Talmudic Readings and Lectures.* Translated by G. Moole. Bloomington: Indiana University Press, 1994.

———. *Nine Talmudic Readings*. Translated by Annette Aronowicz. Bloomington: Indiana University Press, 1990.

Lowenthal, Michael. 1997. *Gay Men at the Millennium: Sex, Spirit, Community (New Consciousness Reader).* Los Angeles: J. P. Tarcher, 1997.

Luvitch, Ronen. 2001. "Selidah Sovlanut o Matiranut: Yachas haYahadut leHomoseksualiyut" (Revulsion, tolerance or permissiveness: The Jewish response to homosexuality). *De'ot* 11 (2001): 9–15.

Marx, Tzvi. "A Blessing over Differences." *Jerusalem Report*, 5, no. 24 (April 6, 1995): 51.

McNeill, John. *The Church and the Homosexual.* Boston: Beacon Press, 1993.

Milgrom, Jacob. "Abomination." In *The Encyclopedia Judaica*, 96–97. New York: Macmillan/Keter, 1971.

Nissnen, Martti. *Homoeroticism in the Biblical World.* Minneapolis: Fortress Press, 1998.

Novak, David. "Religious Communities, Secular Society, and Sexuality: One Jewish Opinion." In *Sexual Orientation and Human Rights in American Religious Discourse,* edited by Saul M. Olyan and Martha C. Nussbaum. New York: Oxford University Press, 1998.

Olyan, Saul. "And with a Male You Shall Not Lie the Lying Down of a Woman." *Journal of the History of Sexuality* 5, no. 2 (1994): 179–206.

Plaut, Gunther. *The Torah: A Modern Commentary.* New York: Union of American Hebrew Congregations, 1981.

Rackman, Emanuel. *One Man's Judaism.* Tel Aviv: Greenfield Publishers, 1970.

Rapoport, Chaim. *Judaism and Homosexuality: An Authentic Orthodox View.* Portland: Valentine Mitchell, 2004.

Rich, Adrienne. "Compulsory Heterosexuality and Lesbian Existence." *Signs* 5:631–60.

Rosner, Fred, and David J. Bleich, eds. *Jewish Bioethics.* Brooklyn, N.Y.: Hebrew Publishing, 1979.

Satlow, Michael L. *Tasting the Dish: Rabbinic Rhetorics of Sexuality.* Atlanta: Scholars Press, 1995.

Schochet, Rabbi Ezra. "The Torah: A Moral Compass." *Jewish Journal of Greater Los Angeles,* July 14, 2000.

Schwab, Shimon. *Selected Writings.* Lakewood, NJ: CIS Publications, 1988.

Stout, Jeffrey. *Ethics after Babel.* Boston: Beacon Press, 1988.

Thompson, Mark, ed. *Gay Soul: Finding the Heart of Gay Spirit and Nature.* New York: Harper Collins, 1994.

Trible, Phyllis. *God and the Rhetoric of Sexuality.* Minneapolis: Fortress Press, 1978.

Wasserman, Simcha. *Reb Simcha Speaks.* New York: Mesora Publications, 1984.

Whitam, Fredrick, and Robin Mathy. *Male Homosexuality in Four Societies: Brazil, Guatemala, the Philippines and the United States.* New York: Praeger, 1985.

Wolowelsky, Joel B., and Bernard L. Weinstein. "Initial Religious Counseling for a Male Orthodox Adolescent Homosexual." *Tradition* 29, no. 2 (winter 1995): 49–55.

Index